# The Psyche and the Social World

## Developments in Group-Analytic Theory

Edited by
Dennis Brown and Louis Zinkin

Jessica Kingsley Publishers
London and Philadelphia

*We had originally dedicated this book to our wives, but following Louis Zinkin's sudden death shortly after its completion, it is rededicated to him in love and gratitude for the richness of his life and legacy.*

---

First published in the United Kingdom in 1994 by Routledge

Published in 2000
by Jessica Kingsley Publishers
116 Pentonville Road
London N1 9JB, UK
and
400 Market Street, Suite 400
Philadelphia, PA 19106, USA

*www.jkp.com*

**Library of Congress Cataloging in Publication Data**
A CIP catalog record for this book is available from the Library of Congress

**British Library Cataloguing in Publication Data**
A CIP catalogue record for this book is available from the British Library

ISBN 978 1 85302 928 8

# Contents

# Contributors

**Harold Behr** is Consultant Child and Family Psychiatrist at the Central Middlesex Hospital, London, and a member of the Institute of Group Analysis.

**Dick Blackwell** is Coordinator of Psychotherapy at the Medical Foundation for the Care of Victims of Torture, and a member of the Institute of Group Analysis.

**Dennis Brown** is an associate member of the British Psycho-Analytical Society, a member of the Institute of Group Analysis, and Treasurer of the European Association for Transcultural Group Analysis, and formerly Consultant Psychotherapist at St Mary's Hospital, London.

**Barbara Elliott** is a member of the Institute of Group Analysis.

**D. Colin James** is Consultant Psychotherapist at Addenbrooke's Hospital, Cambridge, a member of the British Psycho-Analytical Society, and a member of the Institute of Group Analysis.

**Jaak Le Roy** is a member of the Belgian School of Psychoanalysis, a member of the Dutch Association for Group Psychotherapy and of the Group Analytic Society (London), and President of the European Association for Transcultural Group Analysis.

**Patrick B. De Mare** is a founder member of the Institute of Group Analysis, and formerly Consultant Psychotherapist at St George's Hospital, London.

**Mario Marrone** is a member of the London Centre for Psychotherapy, a member of the International Association of Group Psychotherapy, and of the Institute of Group Analysis.

**Morris Nitsun** is a District Psychologist, and a member of the Institute of Group Analysis.

**Malcolm Pines** is a member of the British Psycho-Analytical Society, and of the Institute of Group Analysis, and formerly Consultant Psychotherapist at the Tavistock Clinic, London, and President of the International Association for Group Psychotherapy.

**Andrew Powell** is Consultant Psychotherapist at the Warneford Hospital, Oxford, Clinical Lecturer at the University of Oxford, an associate member of the British Association of Psychotherapists, and a member of the Institute of Group Analysis.

**John Schlapobersky** is a member of the London Centre for Psychotherapy, a member of the Arbours Association, and of the Institute of Group Analysis.

**Louis Zinkin** was Honorary Consultant and Senior Lecturer at St George's Hospital, London, a member of the Society of Analytical Psychology, and of the Institute of Group Analysis.

# Preface

Group analysis is a major approach to the understanding of group processes and to the practice of group psychotherapy in the United Kingdom and in Europe, and, increasingly, world-wide. Its theoretical basis, laid down by its initiator, S. H. Foulkes (1898–1976), involves the recognition of the deeply social nature of the human personality. Groups form the matrix from which the individual develops, and interpersonal and transpersonal processes continue to affect the individual in health and disease. However, while Foulkes' theory has often been criticised as vague, its imprecision has been seen by others as part of its strength. It can be applied to many situations – psychotherapy in small, median-sized and large groups, family therapy, institutional dynamics and con-sultation, and in education. It can absorb and illuminate theory and practice in related fields such as individual analysis (both Freudian and Jungian), systems theory, and transcultural processes and socio-political issues. The present volume aims to illustrate this absorption and illumination.

The theoretical basis of Foulkes' writing changed very little in the course of his major publications (1948–75), though his collaborators and others influenced by him have developed their thinking from his starting points. Some of these are represented in the International Library of Group Psychotherapy and Group Process to which this vol-ume contributes. *The Evolution of Group Analysis*, edited by Malcolm Pines in 1983, had been planned as a Festschrift for Foulkes, who sadly did not live to see it. It had twenty-three contributors who had known him before the Institute of Group Analysis (London) had been estab-lished in 1971. However, we still lack an integrated re-examination of Foulkes' formulations in the light of advances made in developing them since his death nearly eighteen years ago. The present volume attempts to do this. Although not claiming to be comprehensive, it brings

together the thinking of a group of colleagues who were chosen because
the editors believe they have something special to contribute from their
own particular perspectives. All but one of the contributors have trained
and/or have been trainers at the Institute of Group Analysis.

The editors' idea of compiling such a work was enthusiastically
responded to by those group analysts we invited. They recognised both
the need and opportunity it represented. They include senior figures
with world-wide reputations, and more junior group analysts who have
already established reputations for original thinking. We were all stimulated by this process, and hope it will provide a coherent view of some
of the major developments in group-analytic theory to date.

We wish to thank our friend and colleague Malcolm Pines for so
readily agreeing to include the book in the International Library of
Group Psychotherapy and Group Process of which he is the Editor, June
Ansell for her efficiency and guidance in turning the first scraps into a
coherent manuscript, and Edwina Welham for easing the publication of
this book by Routledge. She saw it through from the original idea. We
are very grateful to Foulkes' widow, Elizabeth, for making available to
us his preliminary notes for a proposed book on theory that his death cut
short.

# Chapter 1

# Introduction

*Dennis G. Brown and Louis Zinkin*

Group analysis is a method pioneered by S. H. Foulkes (1898–1976). It represents one of a number of approaches seeking to extend psycho-analysis, in which the focus of attention was the internal world of the single patient, to a very different conception of the individual as being in a dynamic interplay with others in various kinds of social groupings (see Pines, Chapter 4). While continuing to practise as a psychoanalyst, Foulkes put forward in his books and papers a series of ideas derived from his own experimentation with placing patients in carefully con-structed groups, and from directing a military neurosis unit during the Second World War. He compared the functioning of people in these 'stranger groups' with that of people in natural groups, their family, work groups, and so on.

In this volume we have sought to survey the present state of develop-ment of Foulkes' ideas. Foulkes was not only devising a new method of therapy based on psychoanalytic principles, he was also beginning to construct a new theory in which the individual cannot be separated from the social context which defines him or her. This is in contrast to Freud's attempt to regard external reality as a given, while he concen-trated on the internal dynamics of his individual patients – adjusting to what Heinz Hartmann (1958) called 'the average expectable environ-ment'.

Such a shift, which regards neither the individual nor society as a primary datum from which to study the other, but sees them as inextricably interrelated, leads to a highly complex level of theorising. Foulkes cannot be said to have worked out a tightly coherent theory. Rather, he put forward some general principles, some new terminology, and some keen clinical observations. These convinced him that working with the individual in the context of the group was an endless source of insight into the workings of the human mind, supplementing rather than replacing the continued study of the single patient in the classical dyadic psychoanalytic situation.

We thought the time had come to collect into one volume a number of essays by distinguished practitioners of group analysis, exploring their current thinking on various aspects of theory. We hope this will enable the reader to grasp how Foulkes' original ideas have been developed, and to ascertain to what extent a coherent theory of group analysis is possible. Inevitably, there are both divergences and convergences as various authors test out Foulkes' ideas in their own practice, and it is hoped that these can be illuminated by multiple authorship within a single volume. We have accordingly attempted to do more than offer a collection of isolated papers, and have used group principles in compiling the book. As far as possible we have encouraged the contributors to read one another's chapters, and we have had a number of group meetings for the contributors to discuss their ideas with one another. This has led to heated argument as well as to a substantial measure of agreement resulting from a common culture.

As co-editors we have had much discussion about the starting point for this exercise, which is to make a preliminary assessment of the legacy of Foulkes' work. What follows is a very brief summary of his ideas and their history from our necessarily subjective viewpoint today.

Most of Foulkes' ideas on group analysis are contained in his remarkable *Introduction to Group-Analytic Psychotherapy* (1948) written in the afterglow of the so-called Northfield Experiment during the Second World War.[1] In this book he wrote of the *deeply social nature of the human being*, stated that *the individual was an abstraction* and that reality and unconscious phantasies were inseparable. He saw the social aspects of human behaviour as having a central place in their understanding and drew on work of the sociologist Norbert Elias (1938) as well as the psychoanalyst Eric Erikson in viewing the individual as permeated by the social. He also quoted Malinowski's view of myth as 'reality lived' not merely story told.

In the same book he described what he called 'a basic law of group dynamics'. This was his oft-quoted proposition that members of a therapeutic group 'collectively [they] constitute the very norm from which individually they deviate'. This is typical of the way in which Foulkes expressed his thoughts. We find it both illuminating and worrying. In so far as a group does invariably constitute such a norm (which is debatable), it is not certain whether this is a desideratum or a false standard set by the group. It is a characteristic example of a formulation which requires further elaboration before it can be generally accepted as useful.

Foulkes also gave there his first description of *therapeutic factors which were group-specific*; that is, not to be found in individual analysis. These were: socialisation, mirror reaction, activation, exchange, and the group as a forum. He described the essential active participation of members in the therapy, and the central role of communication and making things articulate. He saw observation and self-observation in a social setting as crucial to the group dimension, which, in some respects at least, transcends that of psychoanalysis. These facilitate the revision within the therapy group of the boundaries of both the ego and the superego – or as we might say today, of the self.

In *Group Psychotherapy: The Psycho-analytic Approach* (1957) written with James Anthony, he introduced the idea of there being *four levels of communication* in the therapy group: current, transference, projective, and primordial. He also wrote of networks of relationship (later to be called 'the group matrix'), and of processes which are transpersonal.

In *Therapeutic Group Analysis* (1964) he defined the *matrix* more clearly (p. 292), and in *Group Analytic Psychotherapy* (1975a) the *foundation matrix*, in contrast to the dynamic matrix. In this final volume, he introduced the term 'plexus' or 'complexus' to describe the network in which the individual was placed, whether in the family or in the wider social network of friends or colleagues. Although *Therapeutic Group Analysis* is the most comprehensive of Foulkes' works, in our view it is somewhat disparate and uneven in its presentation. This may be because thirteen of the twenty chapters had previously been published in various journals, at least in part, and of the remaining seven, one was written by his second wife, Kilmeny.

Foulkes' final book, *Group Analytic Psychotherapy* (1975a), was subtitled *Method and Principles*, and in it he said that he proposed to write a companion volume on theory. This was left uncompleted on his death, but we are extremely fortunate in having some of his preliminary notes for the first five chapters, which are here summarised:

## CHAPTER ONE – TWO STEPS AND THEIR CONSEQUENCE

He describes the origin of the work in 1939–40, getting families and strangers together (adumbrating family therapy and group analysis). At first he combined group with individual therapy, but this gave way to group analysis as he began to see that what was communicated individually could also be communicated in the group. It was important to encourage a free-floating discussion which could resemble free-association.

There is a growing recognition of conflicts as arising in multi-personal fields, and of the distinction between group and individual as being an abstraction. He uses the Gestalt notion of figure and ground to illustrate the way in which the relationship between group and individual could be viewed. Each can be the figure to the ground of the other, and this depends on the observer. The total field is compared to a three-dimensional jigsaw puzzle, and the individual to one piece of the jigsaw.

## CHAPTER TWO – A NEW LOOK: PSYCHONEUROSIS AS MULTIPERSONAL SYNDROME

Taking the concept of neurosis in its widest sense, Foulkes draws attention to it as being the product of a multipersonal field rather than as arising within the single individual. He sees relationships within the family as being influenced by every member of the family. He takes issue with Melanie Klein's reductive explanations of psychopathology, based on her descriptions of processes occurring simply within the individual infant's mind. He sees regression as involving the whole family, and particularly emphasises the importance of this happening at the birth of a new infant.

> The infant thus grows instinctively in an atmosphere containing these values and reactions. In my view this would also answer the difficult question of why, in different cultures and even in different classes, people shape according to very different shared values. I believe altogether that the basic human problems with which psycho-analysis is so much concerned, as for instance the Oedipus complex, are to a far greater degree, psychologically transmitted than inherited, though the two can never be kept watertight apart.

The *plexus* is a social network which often replaces, but also includes, the family. Foulkes here stresses what he believes to be a fundamental difference from traditional psychoanalysis, that later developments are of equal importance to what the individual carries within as a precipitation of infantile experience inside the family. He also makes the intriguing suggestion that the current situation is influenced by future development. This is reminiscent of Jung's conception of the unconscious as prospective as well as being derived from the past, though unfortunately Foulkes does not elaborate on this idea in his notes.

## CHAPTER THREE – SOCIAL INHERITANCE

Here Foulkes develops his idea that patterns of behaviour, particularly those based on powerful affects, are transmitted psychologically through social interaction rather than genetically. He quotes a little-read book published in 1918 by Benjamin Kidd, which reports experiments in which a variety of young animals, known to be the prey of snakes, are placed in the presence of snakes and show no fear whatever. He describes how young ducks also show no fear of man, until they learn from the alarm shown by the mother. These and other observations (which, of course, were very early experiments in ethology) lead to an emphasis on the importance of learned rather than built-in patterns and give support to the general idea of 'social inheritance'. Such social learning is then said to be of great importance in the development of the ego and the superego, which vary according to culture, though, of course, what is inherited and what is acquired can never be artificially separated. While psychoanalysis 'rightly' stresses the importance of unconscious processes for human life, group analysis takes in sociology, anthropology, psychology, and the *social operation of unconscious processes*.

## CHAPTER FOUR – BEYOND OEDIPUS

Foulkes here enlarges on his modification of the Oedipus complex, again stressing its cultural determination within the family rather than its biological inheritance. The birth of the new infant leads to regression by the whole family. 'Both sides, parents and children revert to their own infantile sexuality', so that both parents and children instigate the Oedipal conflict which is seen as a family conflict, rather than as one existing simply within the child.

Several clinical examples are given of how Oedipal problems manifest themselves in the group. He refers to 'resonance' and shows how the individuals in the group, with their various early experiences, can act in the different roles in the Oedipus drama. Again Foulkes stresses the importance of context, that what something looks like is dependent on the field in which it is studied.

## CHAPTER FIVE – NATURAL GROUPS: FAMILY AND WORK

Here Foulkes divides groups into three broad categories: the family; the infinite variety of natural groups occurring in society, such as work and recreational groups; and the artificially constructed therapy group. In each he uses the notion of plexus. The prime influence in early development is the family environment, later added to by the current situation in the life groups of the individual. Family therapy, then in its infancy, is strongly encouraged but with caution. He does not seem too happy with the activity of some therapists in their interventions and characteristically favours a 'leading from behind' approach. He notes that sometimes a couple, not just a marital couple, but also (for example) mother and daughter or father and son, should be seen together, but again cautiously recommends that the initiative for doing this should come from the patient rather than from the therapist. Seeing the whole plexus can throw light on blocks and resistances from people who can prevent progress.

In secondary living groups, such as work groups, the therapist approaches the group-as-a-whole, but interventions are not necessarily directed to the group-as-a-whole. 'Individual members of the group may change favourably, due to their own inner coherence. Interpretations must be kept within the bounds of intimacy tolerable within these circumstances.' It is important to respect the boundary of the therapeutic system, but Foulkes would not necessarily discourage individuals from bringing up their own personal problems, as would most modern organisational consultants.

It is, of course, in the area of group-analytic psychotherapy that Foulkes felt most at home and where his ideas have mostly been applied, though it should be noted that the general principles hold good for all three types of group. In each case he sees the task as primarily a *therapeutic* one.

Here Foulkes' notes break off. By the time he reaches his notes for the fifth chapter, Foulkes can be seen to be running out of theoretical steam and to be advising more on method. Indeed, it is perhaps for the way he taught a method, a style, an attitude to the group process, that Foulkes is mostly remembered. This is what he passed on to those who worked with him. It was a way of trusting the group process to develop in a therapeutic way once the group no longer requires authority to be placed on the conductor as leader. Though he could at times be confrontative and actively intervene when the process was blocked, his attitude was a patient and relatively non-interfering one.

In this respect, Foulkes reflected a growing tendency to promote the healing role of the setting, by the care with which the group is constituted and the way it is handled, with perhaps correspondingly less emphasis on the power of interpretations by the conductor. Though aware of the transference of the individuals to the conductor, he saw also that transferences existing between the members need to be understood. Foulkes was impressed by the therapeutic potential that patients had in their relationship with one another, and this enabled him to develop a model in which the conductor played a relatively modest and non-active part. This has given rise in his followers to a certain tradition, a way of working with therapy groups which is noticeably different from other forms of group therapy.

We have spoken of Foulkes' 'ideas' rather than of his theory. It might be said that theory was not his strong point, that he was an empirical clinician rather than a theoretician. Nevertheless, his pioneering experimentation with method was always based on the general principle of the essentially social nature of man. We believe that the richness of his viewpoint, obvious to those of us who have incorporated it into our own work, requires closer understanding and explanation of its compelling power – indeed a theory. His ideas do have an inner coherence, but they are only some of the building blocks for a theory of group analysis if it is to be more than psychoanalytic theory adapted for group use.

The general procedure of building up a theory of group analysis has been to follow practice rather than to impose a practice on the basis of theory, much in the way that Bourdieu (1977) has suggested for anthropology in *Outline of a Theory of Practice*. Having fashioned a particular way of working with groups, based on the general principles outlined above, group analysts are establishing a tradition in which further observations can be made, further principles can be abstracted and gradually incorporated into a more and more coherent body of theory. We know a great deal more about the way groups function, how they can be therapeutic and how to conduct them than we can easily explain on the basis of existing theory. We need to pool our ideas to take theory further, as we do in this book.

We hope that the reader of the volume will conclude that we have come quite a long way since 1975. But the very breadth of scope which Foulkes brought to the subject has given rise to difficulties. There is now a rapid spread of training in group analysis from its roots in London, and trainees are attracted to it from many different disciplines. This has meant a diversification of interest, which some may see as a watering-down and others as an enrichment of the group-analytic model. On the whole, as editors, we take the latter view.

In current thinking, there is a welcome tendency to differentiate the human from the natural sciences. The social world constitutes living reality for the individual, unrestricted by overvaluation of narrowly conceived 'objective', 'scientific' procedures. This new view is one which has permeated all the allied disciplines: sociology, anthropology, history and political science. In the growing field of psychotherapy, we need to venture into other disciplines but we need also to find a common language in order to communicate with one another. This is not always easy. For example, psychoanalysts have always found it hard to convince those who have had no direct experience of it, and sociology too often seems a woolly pseudo-science to the medical practitioner. Part of the problem, too, is that other theoretical approaches have not stood still, and in particular, there have been advances in psychoanalysis, analytical psychology and family therapy with its use of systems theory.

We believe it is important in developing group analytic theory not only to talk among ourselves, particularly with group analysts whose interests and experiences diverge from the shared therapeutic base, to consolidate what we have found or speculated about, but also to keep ourselves alert to other influences. For this reason some of the contributors to this volume are Freudian or Jungian analysts, some are not, others are active or have been active in family and marital therapy, organisational consultancy, psychodrama, and the study of large and median-sized groups. Jaak Le Roy, the only contributor who has not been trained or been a trainer with the Institute of Group Analysis (London), has had a Lacanian analysis, and is deeply interested in cultural issues: he has been involved in anthropological fieldwork in Africa, and is currently President of the European Association for Transcultural Group Analysis.

We also believe that we must see group analysis in the context of other analytic approaches to group psychotherapy and dynamics, such as that influenced by W. R. Bion, often referred to in this volume. In Britain the group-analytic approach is often seen as opposite to that inspired by Bion (1961) and formerly predominant at the Tavistock Clinic, from which a gloomy assessment study of its efficacy was made (Malan *et al.* 1976). Bion also had a major influence on the study of group dynamics in organisational workshops and consultancy, pioneered by the Tavistock Institute of Human Relations (Rice 1965).

Foulkes' assertion that the individual is an abstraction at first sight contrasts with the view of Bion and others, such as Anzieu (1984) in France, that the group represents an illusion. Rather than consider the group as an illusion, we could say that the group harnesses and creates imagination, shared and largely unconscious. It seems to us that the group-analytic view that individual without group and group without individuals are equally abstractions is more in tune with poststructuralism and postmodernism (Sarup 1988) as well as newer views of science (Capra 1982). These are completing the undermining of the Cartesian split between the thinking subject and a fixed objective world, of observer and observed.

Foulkes' belief that a group conductor should trust the group might at first seem naïve when one considers how badly groups can behave. What group analysis attempts to do is provide a setting – a small, median, or large group – where mistrust and destructiveness can be contained, understood and transcended, and trust and mutual respect arrived at, however painfully and fitfully. To achieve this, the conductor above all has to remember that, given the right setting and atmosphere, a capacity for honesty and goodwill is at least a potential part of human beings.

In that sense group analysis can be said to be based on an optimistic view of individuals and groups, despite their destructive potential. It implies that ultimately there is no substitute for trust in a world where others are needed as allies in self-development – as in an empathically responsive nursing couple, a mutually respectful and enjoyable family, or a society which respects and welcomes differences rather than demanding totalitarian uniformity. The group-analytic approach explores and promotes connectedness.

In the course of compiling this volume, we have considered novel forms of presentation, such as a series of linked dialogues between therapists from different backgrounds, but we have decided that it is best for each contributor to have the chance to explicate one particular aspect of theory in his/her own way, but not to do this in isolation, and each has read the contributions of the others. There has thus been the opportunity for each to see their own work in the context of the others, a project which we feel Foulkes would have found congenial.

In the final chapter, we shall try to evaluate to what extent these varied contributions carry forward Foulkes' legacy, how they connect, and to assess what contradictions between them still need to be resolved.

## NOTE

1 For a description of the work done at the Military Neurosis Unit at Northfield, Birmingham, which inspired the Therapeutic Community Movement, see Main (1946, 1977), de Mare (1985), Bridger (1985), as well as Foulkes (1948, 1964).

# Chapter 2

# Towards a unifying concept of the group matrix

*Andrew Powell*

## I FOULKES' CLINICAL CONCEPT

The concept of the matrix is of central importance to group analysis, a lingua franca uniting practitioners across continents and cultures. It is a concept so fundamental to us that we make use of it as naturally, and as necessarily, as drawing the next breath. Yet the discovery made by S. H. Foulkes, that *the group-analytic group behaves and functions like a living organism*, has eluded any systematic formulation which could be encompassed by existing depth psychology. Blackwell's contribution on systems theory in this volume points to why this should be so.

We know that Foulkes chose the word 'matrix' deliberately because of its derivation from the Latin word 'mater', meaning mother (1975a). This gives the matrix a human frame of reference, a metaphor of nurture and growth which reflects the practice both of group analysis and its forebear, psychoanalysis. Later, Foulkes was to write:

> The matrix is the hypothetical web of communication and relation-ship in a given group. It is the common shared ground which ultimately determines the meaning and significance of all events and upon which all communications and interpretations, verbal and non-verbal rest.
>
> (Foulkes 1964: 292)

> The network of all individual mental processes, the psychological medium in which they meet, communicate and interact, can be called the matrix.
>
> (Foulkes and Anthony 1965: 26)

> Inside this network, the individual is conceived as a nodal point.
>
> (Foulkes 1964: 118)

In further formulations of our observations we have come to conceive these processes not merely as interpersonal but as transpersonal.

(Foulkes and Anthony 1965: 26)

The mind is not a thing which exists but a series of events, moving
and proceeding all the time.

(Foulkes 1973: 212)

These wise and provocative insights have encouraged a number of
group analysts over recent years to grapple conceptually with the matrix
(Blake 1980; Roberts 1982; Muroff 1982; Van Der Kleij 1982, 1985;
Lintott 1983; Ahlin 1985, 1988), as well as others whose work will be
described later, but no coherent theoretical framework has emerged. It is
not yet clear if this is because a construct such as 'the group mind' is
simply not susceptible to structural analysis in the way that Freud
approached the individual psyche or because science has come of age
since the birth of psychoanalysis and our conception of what comprises
consciousness has changed.

After S. H. Foulkes qualified in medicine, he joined Kurt Goldstein's
department in the Frankfurt Institute of Neurology for two years, and
later, when he was director of the Psychoanalytical Clinic there, became
involved in the activities of the adjacent Institute for Social Research
(Pines 1978). In 1933 Foulkes came to England as a refugee from Nazi
Germany; like Melanie Klein who had arrived seven years previously,
he soon established himself in practice as a psychoanalyst. But seeds
had been sown which were to bear fruit a few years later when Foulkes
began to ask himself what would happen if his patients, whom he knew
individually so well, were to start meeting together. The decisive step he
took was informed by a deeply held conviction which he summarised as
follows:

Each individual – itself an artificial, though plausible abstraction – is
centrally and basically determined, inevitably, by the world in which
he lives, by the community, the group of which he forms a part.

(Foulkes 1948: 10)

In bringing together his individual patients to form an analytic group,
Foulkes found himself irretrievably estranged from many of his
psychoanalytic colleagues. Perhaps the problem was that within the
frame of reference of psychoanalysis, Foulkes' actions could only be
conceptualised as acting out in the countertransference. But Foulkes
could not turn back. He went on to state:

The old juxtaposition of an inside and outside world, constitution and environment, individual and society, phantasy and reality, body and mind and so on, are untenable. They can at no stage be separated from each other, except by artificial isolation.

(1948: 10)

Foulkes writes descriptively but keeps theory to a minimum, perhaps with good reason, for it is hard to honour the concept of 'the group' without using terms which, because of the reductionistic nature of meta-psychology, at once split the group into parts. Yet the notion of the 'matrix', which embodies the principle of connectedness within the group, so fascinated Foulkes that he was anxious to find a concept which could do it justice.

Freud wrote in 1895: 'Let us picture the ego as a network of cathected neurones well facilitated in relation to one another' (p. 323). Seventy years later, Foulkes and Anthony were to write: 'The social matrix can be thought of as a network in quite the same way as the brain is a network of fibres and cells which together form a complex unit' (Foulkes and Anthony 1965: 258).

The problem of definition is not so much what the matrix is, as what it is not. Foulkes conceived of it as within us and outside us, extending from the microcosm of the individual psyche to the macrocosm of the social world and beyond. To the workings of the individual mind, Foulkes gave the name *the personal matrix* (1975b). Foulkes went on to describe within the group what he called *the dynamic matrix*, 'the theatre of operation of ongoing change'. This can be taken as metaphor, or as a pointer to the existence of interpersonal and transpersonal processes which acquire a reality and continuity of their own throughout the life of the group. I have suggested elsewhere (Powell 1989) that the therapy group, while physically existing as a mere, intermittent artefact, comes to have a *continuity of psychic reality* transcending its punctuation in space and time; this is an assumption we make every time we address the group-as-a-whole and, as I shall investigate later, turns out, I believe, to be more than a metaphorical truth.

Last and not least, Foulkes grandly gestured towards *the foundation matrix*, which he claimed was 'based on the biological properties of the species, but also on the culturally firmly embedded values and reactions' (1975b). The concept of the foundation matrix has been further developed in this volume by Le Roy (Chapter 12).

Taken together, what Foulkes implied was that the fundamental principle of connectedness can be apprehended by the human participant-observer in a variety of situations, from soliloquy to the small group and beyond to the world stage. Whether in relation to the inner world of internal objects or the external group of lived human relationships, there exists a reticulum of mental processes which both join the members of the group, however constituted, and pass through them to compromise the 'group mind'. Foulkes saw this product of the interaction of individuals not as a static structure but as a flowing, dynamic pulse, analogous to the relationship of mind to matter in the individual psyche.

Foulkes is reaching after 'the whole', which is why the ideas of Goldstein attract him so powerfully. In his first book he was to write:

> The healthy organism functions as a whole and can be described as a system in a dynamic equilibrium. . .[it] has constantly to adjust. . . there is always a creative element present. . .[it] acts as if it knew its aim and had a choice as to the means to achieve this aim. . . . To take into account all these factors. . .we speak of the *'total situation'*.
>
> (1948: 1; my italics)

Intuitively, Foulkes went on to take the short step from the Gestalt of the whole organism to the Gestalt of *the group-as-a-whole* and now found himself possessed of a vision of the group which could not be reconciled with psychoanalytic theory. His insight, like Kekule's vision of the benzene ring, may have been born of reverie, in Foulkes' case begotten of a psychoanalytic training; but the content of the vision was no longer one of *reductionism* but of *synthesis* (Powell 1991a).

Let us look more closely at what this implies for Foulkes' four levels of group process (Foulkes 1964: 114). The first level describes the world of physical and social reality. It does not much relate to analytic group work, so Foulkes has little more to say about it. But it certainly does have a bearing on 'the total situation' in which the group is embedded; to this we shall return later, when considering the psychophysics of the matrix.

Level two refers to whole-object transference relationships in which the matrix is displayed through the workings of the dynamics of the family of origin. While comparing with classical analytic work, there is additionally in the analytic group a forum for a rich dramatisation of father, mother and sibling transferences, tending either towards the re-enactment of what once went before or, equally importantly, to a search for what was missing in the matrix of that family of origin.

Foulkes' third (or projective) level illuminates how aspects of the self are projected for defensive reasons into other group members. This is the level of part-object relationships, where the mechanisms of splitting and denial operate and where extremes of idealisation and denigration hold sway. The therapeutic task within the matrix at this level is for group members to be helped to take back and own split-off parts of the self.

Levels two and three derive from Foulkes' earlier psychoanalytic training and method of enquiry; the meaning of the whole is to be discovered by means of its dissection into constituent parts. This has been above all the domain of the 'personal matrix', given over to the expression of highly prized individuality (in the western hemisphere at least). But the 'dynamic matrix' has also proved amenable to psychoanalytic investigation. The works of D. W. Winnicott, John Bowlby and Melanie Klein are of particular relevance; it is no coincidence that all three writers are concerned with the essential object-relatedness of the human infant, for the analytic group provides an ideal milieu for the working out of the internal object world, dramatised through emergent transferences to other group members and to the group-as-a-whole.

Winnicott (1951) was the first to describe how the infant creates a special kind of illusion in the space which exists between infant and mother. Within this space, the infant takes ownership of a series of transitional phenomena, over which it can maintain omnipotent control until it is ready to relinquish them in favour of external reality. Similarly, the group matrix can serve well this function of the transitional object (James 1980; see also Chapter 5 in the present volume). The matrix belongs to nobody and yet to everybody, a space into which phantasy can be projected at will and which can then be carried around as needed by the group member between groups, a prized possession not unlike the toddler's bit of blanket.

At an earlier level of developmental need, we can regard the group-as-a-whole as standing for the primary 'care-giving other', according to the ideas of Bowlby (1969), whose work forms a unique bridge between object-relations theory and ethology. The quality of attachment we make to the group, be it anxious or secure, and how we accomplish our eventual separation from it, are highly revealing of the nature of earlier, unresolved transferences (Glenn 1987). The individual is 'born into' the group with as little choice about who comprises this mother, father and family as in his or her family of origin. In this sense, the group is *not* under the omnipotent control of any one person, which is just what makes it a secure place from which to take new developmental steps.

Still within the ambit of psychoanalysis, and exploring the part played by the primitive mechanisms of splitting and projection as described by Klein (1946), R. D. Hinshelwood (1989) has put forward a model of the matrix in which fragments of experience, especially painful affects, can be disavowed by discharging them into the network. Initially these fragments flow into other group members; the end-point is to find the group (or institution) projecting the unwanted affect into the matrix itself. This process leads to increasing depersonalisation of the individual and a sense of alienation from the institution (the 'faceless bureaucracy'). But the individual becomes at the same time deeply fused to the group or institution since the matrix, to a degree, *is* now the individual.

This is a reminder to us that the matrix has no inherent moral disposition. Using it as a waste-bin will have one consequence; using it for creative containment will have quite another. For instance, W. R. Bion (1970) holds that the pre-thought elements of the baby's mind (beta-elements) are projected on to the mother's breast, which acts as a container in which they can be transformed into primitive elements of thought (alpha-elements). These are duly returned to the baby, who can then utilise them in the construction of its own thoughts.

Louis Zinkin turns to this concept of Bion's in drawing a developmental parallel between mother and group. He argues that the group as container/breast likewise brings about a transformation of its psychic contents from a lower to higher level, adding: 'we cannot conceive of any evolutionary change, that is, any progressive change from a lower to a higher level of organization as taking place except in some kind of container' (1989a: 227).

We have here a concept which begins to take leave of psychoanalysis, because the thrust is away from the restructuring of defences and towards transformation, a theme which Foulkes adumbrated in his reference to the fourth and final level of group process.

About this, the deepest level, Foulkes writes: 'This. . .is the one in which primordial images appear, according to Freud's concepts and those particularly formulated by Jung concerning the collective unconscious' (1964: 114).

The reference to Freud may have been wishful thinking because nowhere, in the Standard Edition at least, does Freud discuss primordial imagery. In contrast, the work of Carl Jung abounds with such images, for they are no less than a royal road to the archetypes of the collective unconscious; this bedrock of our cultural, collective existence may prove to be the closest we can come to a psychological realisation of the 'foundation matrix'.

## II   THE CONTRIBUTION OF CARL JUNG

In 1942, Jung wrote: 'for analysis is always followed by synthesis, and what was divided on a lower level will reappear, united, on a higher one' (p. 189). Freud's theories are tailored to the unassailable individuality of the human being, so that the psyche is treated much like a personal possession. Emotions such as humility and awe, which transcend our immediate, proprietary concerns, find no mention in Freud's work. But Jung sets our individuality against a backdrop of archetypal configurations which shape our behaviour and of which we are largely unaware.

Jung says of the archetypes that they

> represent the life and essence of a non-individual psyche. Although this psyche is innate in every individual, it can neither be modified nor possessed by him personally. . . . It is the precondition of each individual psyche, just as the sea is the carrier of the individual wave.
>
> (1946: 169)

Archetypes which become manifest in human form include the animus and anima, the persona and the shadow. Of the abstract forms, the one we meet as group analysts every time we conduct a group is the 'mandala' (Sanskrit for 'circle'); it has most likely been the archetype for wholeness since early man first sat round a fire, safe from wild animals and able to relax and reflect (Powell 1989).

Analytic groups are, of course, highly sensitive to the arrangement of chairs, and whether the circle is complete or broken through absences. This has a profound impact on the unconscious life of the group to which the conductor, if necessary, will draw attention.

Within the mandala is found a motif, usually based on the squaring of the circle, often in the form of a cross, or quaternio. The quaternio itself signifies an image of wholeness, arising out of a *conjunction of opposites*; for instance, in the physical realm the elements of air, earth, fire and water and in the realm of emotions, love and hate, despair and joy. Jung writes:

> [The mandala's] basic motif is the premonition of a centre of personality, a kind of central point within the psyche. . . . The energy of the central point is manifested in the almost irresistible compulsion to become what one is.
>
> (1950: 357; author's italics)

Jung calls this process 'individuation', a search for what in each of us is indivisible, or whole. It is expressed above all in Jung's concept of the self as *the totality of the psyche*, comprising, he says: 'consciousness first of all, then the personal unconscious, and finally an indefinitely large segment of the collective unconscious whose archetypes are common to all mankind' (1950: 357). While it is to the ego that Jung gives the task of biological growth, survival and reproduction, the self is the locus of the life task of individuation.

How might the process of individuation be realised within the therapeutic group, not only in relation to the 'personal' and 'dynamic' matrices of Foulkes, but, most importantly, to the 'foundation matrix'? Romano Fiumara, arguing that Foulkes' concept of the matrix gives us a clue, writes as follows:

> [it] enables us to outline, theoretically, a 'surprising discovery': what we are used to considering as intrapsychic...is in fact a property shared by the group...the intrapsychic is not distinguished from the interpersonal nor from the transpersonal since what belongs to the individual is shared by the group, and 'society' shows itself to be inside the individual just as it is outside of him or her.
>
> (Fiumara 1983: 117)

The archetypal configuration of the mandala which comprises the very structure of the analytic group acts as a powerful stimulus for us to *undertake together the task of becoming more who we are*, a new frame of reference which encourages us to refer to the 'group self'. About this, Zinkin writes:

> the group-self, in turn, provides the group members with some notion of a larger transcendent self, ultimately a sense of 'all there is', or in gnostic language 'the All' or the pleroma, as being undivided, and that this is a religious experience.
>
> (1989b: 213)

It would be a mistake to equate this 'religious' experience with the notion of worship readily leading to some kind of collective mystical illumination. On the contrary, the 'higher union' to which Jung refers is only to be discovered by the hard-won integration of powerfully conflicting opposites (the *coniunctio oppositorum*). Zinkin emphasises that good and evil are opposites to be combined and are thus given equal status, that the shadow has to be integrated rather than disowned. For example, with reference to archetypes in human form, the wise and nurturing mother invoked by Foulkes must be integrated with the archetype of the witch mother, or goddess Kali (Prodgers 1990).

Jung's recognition of the need to bring together opposites in order to realise the whole has its time-honoured equivalence in the Chinese concept of yin and yang (Wilhelm 1951) and in the law of Karma (Hanson and Stewart 1981). Each affirms the universal principle that existence, and in the human case, personal destiny is characterised by a balance of equal and opposite forces, be it in the domain of matter or psyche. It should hardly surprise us, therefore, to find that the matrix as a structure has been illuminated by opposing psychological theories, based respectively on analysis and synthesis. For the former, we are indebted to the psychoanalytic frame of reference. For the latter, Foulkes as group analyst inclines more to Jung than Freud. The disjunction here, which Foulkes never confronted in theory, *does, however, find expression in the analogue of figure-on-ground*, in which the part (via analysis) is set against the whole (via synthesis). More recently, with advances in the 'new physics' of wave/particle duality, we can see the figure–ground constellation is a remarkable 'higher level' mirror to a fundamental discovery in quantum field theory, that it is not the case of 'either/or' but one of 'both/and', a subject to which we shall be returning.

## III   A REVISED TOPOGRAPHY

Whatever the substance and ultimate structure of the matrix, it may help to clarify what we are talking about if we provide a simple topography, one which for obvious reasons would not have occurred to Freud. This is to delineate the matrix as either inside us (the embodied matrix, as I have called it), or outside us as the unembodied matrix (Powell 1991b). The justification for making this 'artificial isolation', to use Foulkes' phrase, rests with the notion of duality we have already introduced. There *is* an inside and an outside, just as there is *also* a continuum along which the matrix extends unbroken (for a discussion of the mathematics of continuous versus discontinuous transformations, see Barrow 1990: 34). We need to consider both aspects of the matrix; at the same time we should not narrowly equate 'inside' and 'outside' with the human body, for the words 'embodied' and 'unembodied' are intended as spatial metaphors which refer to a relational interface. (I have suggested elsewhere – Powell 1990 – that it may be a mistake to situate the mind within the physical brain.)

Taking first the discontinuous aspect of the matrix, that part separable and which we can identify with the individual human psyche, Fiumara (1991a) has argued that just as the brain is a Darwinian machine, so is the mind its functional, psychobiological equivalent. He suggests that from the outset, mind is that which gives meaning to our bodily experience of pre-natal physiology; mind and body are co-terminous. Birth forces a differentiation between mind and body, for there is no longer the same 'fit'. But the human psyche retains for ever a kind of nostalgia for that first imprint of somatopsychic undifferentiation, a psychophysiological 'trace memory' providing us with a measure against which to set post-natal experience and so to find meaning in states of differentiation.

Barbara Elliott, in her description of 'womb phenomena' in this volume (Chapter 8), suggests that 'The impression which occurs in the womb becomes a memory without any mind–body interaction. . .a mental image without any wishes or impulses linked to it.' This surely points to the same phenomenon about which Fiumara is writing. Elliott extends her argument by proposing that while pre-natal life excludes object relations, 'by working backwards in time', the womb can none the less come to acquire the meaning of an internal object.

According to Fiumara, mind and matrix are synonymous, since each individual mind connects with all other minds. This renders the (embodied) matrix susceptible to psychobiological investigation. He further points out (Fiumara 1991b) that Foulkes himself talked of a 'body level' of group process (Foulkes 1968) which would lie between the third (projective) and fourth (primordial) levels. This body level represents a union of psyche and soma in which an individual's unique genetic character interleaves with the principle of universal connectedness. Fiumara's focus on the psychobiology of the matrix thus gives substance to the 'nodal point' to which Foulkes had earlier referred (1964:118).

We need next to turn our attention to what the nature of the network might be, for there can no more be a network without nodal points than there can be nodal points without a network. Both are logically required, being parts of one and the same.

In doing so, we pass from psychobiology to psycho-physics; there is, after all, no good reason to limit ourselves to the narrow compass of biological systems when considering the nature of transpersonal mind (the social unconscious of S. H. Foulkes, or the collective unconscious of C. G. Jung).

It is no coincidence that Rutherford's model of the atom as a nuclear mass surrounded by orbiting electrons mirrored the Newtonian concept of a heliocentric solar system with the planets held in their orbits by the gravitational field of the sun. In the year in which Freud wrote 'Three

Essays in Sexuality' (1905), Albert Einstein put forward the special theory of relativity, in which the notion of absolute time was abolished. While Freud was publishing his 'Papers on Metapsychology' (1915a), Einstein proposed his general theory of relativity, showing among other things that space-time is curved. Just as Freud was completing the first draft of the paper 'Group Psychology and the Analysis of the Ego' (1921), Heisenberg, Schrödinger and Dirac formulated a new theory called quantum mechanics, based on the uncertainty principle. From the 'micro-universe' of sub-atomic events on the one hand to the 'macro-universe' of unimaginable distances and cosmic time scales on the other, the world of physical sciences had been stood on its head.

A few examples of such discoveries may help throw some light on the nature of the unembodied matrix. Until Einstein formulated the general theory of relativity, the universe was thought to be composed simply of matter and empty space. Ernst Mach broke this mould by showing that the inertia of a material body existed not as its intrinsic property but as a result of that body's interaction with all other matter in the universe. Einstein extended Mach's principle to demonstrate that no physical entity can be separated from the environment in which it exists. *The observer cannot escape participation and reality cannot be divorced from experience.*

For a time, there did seem to be one absolute limitation imposed by Einstein's special theory of relativity, that events in the universe happen at a speed not greater than the speed of light. This last certainty was demolished by advances in quantum theory. In 1972 Clauser validated a theoretical prediction made eight years before by John Bell, when he demonstrated experimentally that *a change in the spin of one particle in a two-particle system affects its twin simultaneously, even if the two have been widely separated in the meantime* (Dossey 1982), something which Einstein had declared impossible.

The implications of such universal connectedness are spelled out by the physicist David Bohm, who writes:

Ultimately, the entire universe (with all its particles, including those constituting human beings, their laboratories, observing instruments, etc.) has to be understood as a single, undivided whole, in which analysis into separately and independently existent parts has no fundamental status.

(1980: 174)

and:

What is crucial. . .is that, according to the theory of relativity, a sharp distinction between space and time cannot be maintained. . . .Thus, since quantum theory implies that elements that are separated in space are generally non-causally and non-locally related projections of a higher-dimensional reality, it follows that moments separated in time are also such projections of this reality.

(1980: 211)

This 'holoverse' subsumes the collective unconscious (Jung 1963). It encompasses all life forms and material substances, organic and in-organic, and comprises the matrix of all known space and time.

We now know that not only is our universe getting bigger, it is getting cooler (the thermodynamic arrow of time) and this increase in entropy (disorder) has brought with it increasing differentiation; for instance, the formation of the ninety-two elements which comprise the periodic table. According to Newtonian physics, it was thought that this increase in entropy would simply lead to 'the clock running down'. However, there was considered to be no immediate cause for alarm since the universe, being eternal, was regarded as a perpetual-motion machine. Time sooner or later would go into reverse, like the swing of a pendulum, and so everything would go on. But when the implications of the second law of thermodynamics finally sank in, there was con-sternation, for, within our universe at least, time was now shown to be unidirectional; the clock could not wind itself up nor, within a mechan-istic philosophy, was there any place for Divine intervention. Reas-surance had to be sought in the (then) recent findings of nineteenth-century geology, which indicated that the clock had some billions of years still to run.

With hindsight, it is extraordinary that Charles Darwin (1859) dis-cerned an evolutionary biology while envisaging a universe that was not even static but thought to be steadily running down. Now, over a hundred years later, strong evidence has emerged that the universe is itself in evolution. Entropy no longer heralds a gradual slide into chaos but, as Ilya Prigogine and others have shown (1984), when systems become sufficiently disorganised (what is called the 'far-from-equilibrium condition'), sudden and unforeseen transformations occur; *a new order materialises, with properties which could not have been accounted for by the earlier system.* Further, this same principle of spontaneous reorganisation would also seem to be operating at the level of particle physics, in which electrons make unpredictable quantum leaps from one energy state to another. Micro- and macro-molecular systems turn out to have this property in common; fortunate indeed, for the great divide in modern physics has lain between quantum field theory, dealing with the smallest imaginable events, and the theory of relativity, concerned with the largest. We can now begin to envisage a unifying principle at work both in the case of the biology of evolving species and in the parent universe.

At this point it is worth remembering that all theories about the structure and function of the unembodied matrix, just as with the embodied matrix, must necessarily be formed through the activity of the human psyche. All therefore share the same status of being at one remove from ultimate reality. This is as true for theories of relativity, quantum mechanics and the 'holoverse' as it is for the work of Freud. But we need not be discouraged by this fact, since all such interpretations are valid in so far as we are ourselves made of what we measure.

## IV   MIND AND MATTER AS TWIN FACETS OF THE MATRIX

> Its lines of force may be conceived of as passing right through the individual members and may therefore be called a transpersonal network, comparable to a magnetic field.
>
> (Foulkes and Anthony 1965: 258)

What the philosopher Gilbert Ryle (1949) showed forty years ago to be logically a fallacy, that of the Cartesian divide between mind and matter (the myth of the 'ghost in the machine'), has long since been substantiated in the domain of particle physics. We know that there is no such 'thing' as an atom. What comprises the nucleus consists of an ever-lengthening list of smaller particles (such as mesons, in turn composed of quarks and anti-quarks, and so on), many of which exist for only a short time (millionths of a second), and others (protons) which have endured unchanged throughout the time span of the universe.

Quantum field theory has shown that even when the object of study is a single photon, 'matter' exists both as particle and wave, depending on the experimental instrument (and which perforce includes the observer). Energy in wave form is without limit or boundary. The distinction between solid form and 'space' is no more than a product of our special sense organs, functioning at a given level of magnification and in a related time frame.

It would seem that we are all participants in a psycho-physical and limitless matrix which is no less physical for being largely invisible. It has, indeed, been proposed that the human aura which some people claim to see, and which possibly Kirlian photography also reveals, may be none other than the direct visual perception of a vibrant electromagnetic field (Brennan 1987). Such radiation without doubt exists and extends some considerable distance, so that far from being physically separated, we are thoroughly immersed in each other's electromagnetic fields. This proximity lends a new meaning to the term 'projection'.

Not only are solid matter and space confluent, so too are mind and body. Just as particle and wave represent two sides of the same coin, so do mind and matter ineluctably coexist (Zohar 1990). This astonishing fact, of physical and mental interpenetration, calls to mind Foulkes' statement: 'it is always the transpersonal network which is sensitised and gives utterance or responds. In this sense we can postulate the existence of a group mind'(Foulkes 1964: 118).

We now have a basis on which to argue the case for the group mind *not only as metaphysical but physical*. Further, we no longer have to maintain that the principle of mental functioning to which it must adhere is the Newtonian one of causal determinism; there is room for a new psychology which allows, for instance, for *synchronicity* and in which 'flexibility and spontaneity are the key notes', as Foulkes reminded us long ago (1948: 69). For instance, group analysts have reported from time to time experiencing events within the group which appear to fly in the face of Newtonian physics. Within a single session, the pattern of all which has still to unfold in the life of a group may be strangely adumbrated. Or a group member may 'know' what happened in the group when he was physically absent (Usandivaras 1991). At other times, when the unforeseeable happens, such as a death, sudden and profound changes may sweep through a group, lifting it to an unpredicted and unpredictable new plane of experience (Dick 1981). It is reasonable, if not yet quite respectable, to report such clinical events; these phenomena may prove to have far-reaching consequences for both the theory and practice of group analysis.

Is there anything we can say about the relationship of the embodied to the unembodied matrix? At present we cannot do much more than note that the matrix seems to be expressed along a continuum, psycho-biological at one end and psycho-physical at the other, twin facets of a great and mysterious evolutionary process. On the theoretical front, we will have to wait for advances in the new physics towards 'a grand unified theory' before learning how these fields combine. The astrophysicist Stephen Hawking (1988) suggests that what is now being called 'the theory of everything' will be 'the ultimate triumph of human reason – for then we would know the mind of God'. This speculation brings us, by way of conclusion, once more to consider the 'total situation' to which Foulkes alluded.

To the extent that the matrix can be realised as a psychological construct, it would seem to be most readily grasped through the concept of wholeness; here, Jung's concept of the archetypes, in particular the mandala, is invaluable. But Jung fought shy of the notion of the principle of a real transpersonal connectedness; the collective unconscious is, according to Jung, something handed down from one generation to the next, a genotypic inheritance.

If we are prepared to give a psychological significance to the findings of the new physics, we must revise this formulation. We do not need to discount Jung's theory of the archetypes. But a literal-mindedness now enters in, a concreteness of which we are understandably suspicious, given that our therapeutic practice is founded on metaphor (Powell 1982). We are faced with the possibility of a transpersonal reality over which we have no control (except in so far as we care to admit it to ourselves). This is, of course, the bread and butter of theological discourse. Has the matrix been an invention of the human mind, or have we, in a small way, stumbled on something that was long there?

My view (Powell 1992) is that the 'total situation' of which Foulkes speaks is yet again an attempt to capture in words what we instinctively sense, that the whole is profoundly more than the sum of its parts. We have to find a word for this totality of meaning, and the name we give to it is, of course, God. Through a glass darkly, we can just make out the unfolding of a tapestry of cosmic proportions. This is the evolutionary significance of mind; we are impelled towards a view of ourselves as part of the greater whole.

How much the human race is able to respond to, and be guided by, this burgeoning awareness will most likely determine the eventual outcome of the species. On a global scale, we deny the principle of connectedness at our peril. The Gaia hypothesis of James Lovelock (Russell 1982) forewarns us that, far from mankind bending nature to his will, it is ultimately the earth which has us in her palm. Our species will be short-lived unless we honour and respect the infinitely rich variety of life forms which comprise the eco-system to which we belong. The same principle of mutual respect applies every bit as much to our group-analytic work, where the key to growth and understanding lies in recognising our human interdependence; our membership of the therapeutic group depends not only on our unique personal attributes but also on becoming a valued part of the greater whole. Nor, in our work as group analysts, do we have to play God, for we know that the group has it in it to be wiser than any one of us. This should correct any tendency towards grandiosity on our part. Rather, we are privileged to take our place in that circle which is, ultimately, without circumference and whose centre is everywhere.

# Chapter 3

# The psyche and the system

*Dick Blackwell*

---

Group analysis, so Foulkes hoped, would provide not only an effective means of psychotherapy, but also an approach to social phenomena, a way of understanding the individual and her society and the relationship between them. It could, he believed, provide a meeting point for psychoanalysis and sociology, for social psychology and anthropology. I do not think he expected group analysis to integrate entirely or to supersede these other disciplines, but he did wish to locate it in relation to them. Thus, in considering systems theory I shall try to address not only its relevance to group psychotherapy but its more general significance and relation to group analysis within the wider social content.

## THE SOCIAL CONTEXT

Let me begin with a position statement – or perhaps a meta-position statement is more accurate. I believe there is no position within the social sciences or humanities that is not a political position; no theory nor form of knowledge devoid of political implications. Knowledge, as Foucault (1980) has argued, embodies and reflects the power relationships of the society within which it is conceived.

Politics concerns the organisation of the relationships between people as they engage in the production and consumption of goods and services: food, shelter and necessities of life as well as luxuries. It concerns the allocation of wealth and power and the processes of decision making. Social science involves the generation of forms of knowledge and its application. This generation and application takes place within the overall organisation of relationships within particular societies. The organisation of the society, the political context, is thus the meta-context for any other activity. Even though social science strives to detach itself from this context in order to study it, it can never fully escape from it.

This, if you like, is the systemic paradox of social science. It is always a part, a product even, of the system it describes. This is a most important beginning because the first major problem for systems theory has been its relationship to politics. Indeed, it is illuminating to understand much of the development of systems theory as an attempt to find models of human behaviour devoid of political implications; models rooted in something more neutral and universal, the 'pure' sciences of biology, engineering and physics. But as Collingwood (1961) points out, science is not the simple drawing of conclusions from available facts. A scientific enquiry involves the posing of a question and an attempt to answer it. Questions arise because particular people at a particular time want to know the answer to those questions. The questions represent a problem facing a particular group at a particular time.

This brings us to the second major problem for systems theory, which is its relationship with history. The principle of equifinality asserts that a system may reach its current state in a variety of ways. Furthermore, these ways are not important in understanding how the system works, nor in attempting to change it. The system is as it is and can be understood in its own terms (how each part functions in relation to others to maintain the whole), without any understanding of how it came to be that way.

Thus systems theory can be viewed as a theory which has attempted to divest itself of political and historical dimensions and to locate itself outside the political and historical context. It may well be that this gave the theory and its practitioners a sort of freedom to think and to manoeuvre which would have been lost in a more direct engagement with history and politics. So it may not have been, necessarily, a bad thing. However, in order fully to understand its development, its implications and its potential, it is necessary to reconnect it to its own wider system: its historical political context.

Two more points need to be made in this connection. The first is that the idea of the universe as a system with each part contributing to the unity of the whole can be traced back at least to Hegel. It may be traceable to other philosophers too, but what is significant about Hegel is that his was a dialectical system, based on the synthesis of conflicting opposites. Both Freud and Foulkes were heirs to this tradition in German philosophy. Psychoanalysis can also be read as a dialectical theory. The biological drives and needs providing one moment, the requirements of society, mediated particularly through the family, for conforming to particular patterns of social behaviour providing the other. The ego then becomes identifiable as a synthesising process. No longer a structure, nor a concrete entity, the ego can be understood as a system of rules for processing and synthesising information from both the biological and social levels. I shall return to this below. My point at this stage is to note the extent to which Freud sought to distance himself from the dialectical tradition and produce a universal theory rooted in biology. He also distanced himself from the social and political turmoil of his own historical era. Thus the 'ego' in much psychoanalytic theory reconciles the conflicts of a *universal* biological predisposition with the *universal* requirements of a civilised society. Relatively little attention is paid to the differing requirements of different societies at different times.

Freud's response to the First World War was not an application of his theory to the political and historical intricacies of that event. Instead, he sought to address what he saw as the horrific folly of it all, through his postulation of a universal death instinct. Of the 1917 revolution in Russia he seems to have had little to say.

Thus the inclination to explain the particularities of human history in terms of timeless universals and to ignore those particularities not readily explained is a characteristic of both psychoanalysis and systems theory. It may seem unfair to observe that a theory ignores what it cannot explain. Indeed it would be, were it not for the fact that both psychoanalysis and systems theory have generally shunned the idea that theories are specific instruments to explain specific phenomena, and have set themselves the more ambitious project of explaining the basis and the totality of human existence.

Group analysis, while being a more modest enterprise, has similar contextual characteristics. First, there is an inherently dialectical relationship between the individual and the group. Although he never uses the term, Foulkes' writing grapples constantly with this dialectical tension in a way that theories of the group-as-a-whole or single entity, such as those of Bion and his followers, and theories of individual analysis in the group such as those of Wolf and Schwartz, do not.

Secondly, Foulkes at one time had close links with the Frankfurt Institute for Social Research which shared a building with the Frankfurt Psychoanalytic Institute, of which Foulkes was a member. He was therefore close to some of the major exponents of the dialectical tradition and its application to the analysis of society in all its historical complexity. The Frankfurt School, as it became known, sought to integrate a psychoanalytic understanding of the individual with a Marxist understanding of political history. Its members continued this project after they were forced to leave Germany in the 1930s. After the Second

World War Adorno, Horkheimer and others sought to shed light on fascism and Nazism through their study of the authoritatian personality. Marcuse and Fromm became known for their analysis of the American society to which they had moved. In contrast, Foulkes came to England and developed a theory of group psychotherapy. It was a theory which embodied much of the tradition to which he never explicitly referred. It was a theory which could be applied to the analysis of wider social processes, but Foulkes himself never aimed it beyond the therapeutic community of the hospital. And when it came to providing a model for his understanding of the individual as a nodal point in a social network, it was not to Marxist sociologists that Foulkes turned, but to the biologist Kurt Goldstein and his model of the brain as a network.

Foulkes here had moved beyond Freud in the conception of biological causality. He had moved to a view of social process as the cause and the remedy of psychological problems. Yet it was still in terms of biology that he presented his model.

The foregoing is not intended as adverse comment on Freud, or Foulkes, nor on the various developers of systems theory. I am simply trying to establish the extent to which these writers wrote for a specific audience at a specific time within a specific social context, and within specific professional and intellectual traditions. Some of these dimensions are explicit in their work and the way it was received, some are not. It is within this framework that I propose to discuss systems theory, in its various forms.

## VARIATIONS OF SYSTEMS THEORY

To talk of systems theory is no longer to talk of something specific and identifiable. It is to talk of a sprawling field of ideas with much in common but also with many significant differences. These ideas have been applied in a variety of ways by a great number of practitioners. Because they have been applied at different times in different places to solve pragmatic problems, they have often been mixed in an extraordinarily eclectic way. A family therapist may, for example, be quite clear on one page that 'system' is a concept to be applied in making a hypothesis about a family, only to write a few pages later as if the family system were something quite concrete and the sole determinant of family life. However, from this complex, interwoven field, it is possible to identify four distinct versions of systems theory. Although these versions tend to be mixed together in practice, there is some heuristic value in distinguishing them so as to recognise different aspects and threads of systems theory and their different implications and potentialities.

## The systems hierarchy

This model derives from von Bertalanffy's general systems theory, often referred to as GST (1966). It proposes a hierarchy from cell, the smallest biological system, to society, the largest system. It provides a three-tier formulation (for addressing any system) of subsystem, system and supra-system. Thus a group is a system in which each member is a subsystem, and the larger organisation within which it exists is its supra-system. When a nuclear family is the system being analysed, it can be divided into a sibling subsystem and a parental subsystem. Either the community, or the extended family, might be regarded as the supra-system within which the family functioned.

Central to this version of systems theory is the concept of a boundary, which may be open or closed. This boundary defines the integrity of the system, separating it from other systems at the same level, and from its subsystems and supra-systems. The relationship between systems is defined by the transactions that take place across the boundary between them. These boundaries also encapsulate the separate functions of subsystems which in their co-ordinated activities constitute the larger system.

Much use has been made of this approach in structural family therapy. Family structure is defined by the nature of the boundaries between individuals and between generations; that is, between the parental and sibling subsystems. Boundaries that are too rigid (too closed in GST terms) lead to lack of communication and isolation between individuals and between parents and children, while boundaries that are too weak, or non-existent (too 'open' in GST) lead to lack of clear identity and clear roles. Pathology is understood in terms of boundary problems, and the therapist's task is to help the family restructure itself through renegotiating its boundaries.

This model can also be applied to larger organisations, and a good deal of use has been made of it to clarify roles, functions, responsibilities and lines of authority within institutions. In group psychotherapy it can be applied to conceptualise the boundaries and integrity of a group and the relationships between the members. The group conductor's role can be understood in terms of managing the boundary between the group and the institution or outside world within which it functions, and facilitating the negotiations between group members across their personal boundaries.

There are a number of theoretical problems within this model. First, there is the nature of the boundary. At the biological level boundaries are semi-permeable membranes; actual physical entities through which energy and information are supposed to pass. At the social level this is clearly not the case. Within a family there is not, in the same way, a physical boundary between parental and sibling subsystems. Whatever may be said about the 'door to the parents' bedroom', it is only a part of the way in which relationships between generations are organised. Boundaries in families take the form of rules or agreed codes of conduct. There are certain things parents do not do, or discuss, in the presence of the children. There are certain sorts of behaviour and conversation that do not take place between a child and a parent. These are not prevented by a physical barrier but by conformity to a set of rules or conventions. In a psychotherapy group there is no physical barrier to preserve confidentiality. Like a boundary in families, it hinges on an agreement to observe a rule.

The time boundary of a therapy group provides a further complication. There is no membrane between 8.29 and 8.31 but the group ends at 8.30. What stops it? Another rule? We might say, borrowing from communication theory, that 8.30 is a context marker. But we cannot avoid the fact that the boundary of a social context is quite different from the boundary between one biological cell and another or between a biological organism and its environment. And it has to be said that it is arguable whether the two sorts of boundary really have anything in common at all.

James Durkin has adopted the practice of placing a rope round a therapy group. Members step outside it to comment *on* the group process, and inside it to engage emotionally *in* the process. But this use of a rope on the floor, which physically restricts no one, merely serves to highlight the symbolic nature of the boundary that serves only to distinguish one sort of group contribution from another.

In a large organisation the problems can become more complex. In biology, energy and information pass through the membrane. In a factory, there are raw materials, half-finished products, finished products, money, requests, negotiations, commands. Can all these be reduced to energy and information? The answer to this question at a pragmatic level may well be yes, sometimes they can. Sometimes the only way to deal with a very complex situation is to focus on one dimension. If one looks closely at the sense of unity or integrity of a particular group in an organisation and sees how that is defined, what its boundaries are, one may then see ways in which that integrity is preserved or undermined, and this may well help to answer a particular problem. As long as one remembers the limitations of a particular idea it may at times prove useful. At other times it may cause as many difficulties as it solves.

This problem with boundaries is a particular example of the difficulties which beset the shift from a biological or pure science model to a social science model. Bateson (1972) stressed the importance of separating 'energy', a physical property given by the equation $E=MC^2$, from 'information', which was something quite different. Hutten (1983), a physicist, argued that information was given by the form which energy took. But Bateson claimed there could be information in the absence of energy. It takes no energy not to send in a tax return. But the absence of that return will be treated as information by the tax system which will be triggered into a particular course of action as a result of not receiving it. It is a fascinating debate which is not resolvable here. But it highlights the complexity which is obscured by talking simply about the passage of 'information' and 'energy' across something called a 'boundary'.

This problem concerning the nature of a boundary is illustrative of a more general problem of epistemology concerning the relationship of the description to the thing described. This version of systems theory tends to say that organisations or families *are* systems. This is crucially different from regarding systems theory as a model which may be applied to certain aspects of organisational family or group life.

A further area of this sort of systems theory which is both useful and problematic is the relationship between the different levels of the system. One version of the different levels holds that a higher level of system is of a higher logical type, such that all systems at the lower level are members of the higher level. Thus group is a higher level than individual, community is a higher level than family, and the 'organisation' (such as a business) is a higher level than its departments (production, advertising, marketing, and so on).

Another version regards levels of hierarchy as higher and lower levels of system. Thus 'management' can be conceptualised as a higher level than 'workers', parents as a higher level than children.

A third version is the meta-level version, which holds that anyone outside a system has an overview of the whole system, not available to anyone inside it. This view often develops into a 'meta is better' simplification, and a hierarchy in which the further one stands outside a system the more clearly one is able to understand it. This view belongs more properly in the first-order cybernetic version of systems theory, but it is included here because it is another aspect of the way in which differential amounts of power and authority may be attributed to different levels of systems and thereby legitimated.

The first version is useful in seeing how something that is a problem at one level of a system – for example, symptoms of one family or group member (that is, a disorder in the individual system) – may be functional in stabilising the larger or higher-level systems of group or family.

The second version may similarly be applied to understand how conflicts can be pushed down through an organisational hierarchy, in such a way that unresolved and even unacknowledged conflicts between those at higher managerial levels – directors, consultant psychiatrists, and others – can be 'acted out' by those at lower levels, junior executives or junior doctors or nursing staff. Similarly, a child's distress or symptoms may be seen as a manifestation of unresolved conflicts between parents.

Difficulties concerning the conceptualisation of levels occur, first, where the way in which the term is used is not made clear; secondly, where it is used (to obscure or justify certain uses of power) in such a way that hierarchy is presumed always to be a good thing and the enforcement of hierarchical authority is presumed to be usually, if not invariably, in the best interests of the system. This easily leads to the obscuring or justifying of abuses of power, whether in families, organisations, or nation states.

This indeed leads to what is perhaps the major criticism of this form of systems theory; that it fails to deal adequately with conflicts of interest within the system. It tends to assume that health and well-being are homogeneous to all parts of the system, so that if everything is in order all will be well, and that disorders at whatever level can be corrected by clarifying boundaries, roles, functions, and hierarchies. The potential for totalitarianism in such a line of thinking is rather obvious, though not acknowledged by many avid systems theorists.

**The first-order circularity model**

This is the model which, more than any other, has underpinned the development of family therapy. It has been the joy and the fascination of a whole generation of family therapists to observe that families interact in *patterns* of behaviour, including speech. These patterns recur, and thereby there emerge role relationships which constitute the 'structure' of the family. The patterns have no one cause and cannot legitimately be attributed to the instigation, attitude or behaviour of one person. Everyone plays their part and each behaviour is a response to the one before and a stimulus to the one after. Most importantly, no one is to blame. Members of families or other groups interact like actors in a play, each with her own script. Except that it is not called a play. It is called a system. If one member forgets her lines or tries to ad lib a few new ones, she is corrected by another, or the others simply continue with their own parts, ignoring the aberration until the deviant member returns to her role. This is called 'homeostasis': the capacity of the system to correct errors and stabilise itself. If one player gives up her part entirely – for example, a depressed mother becomes an angry wife – another will take up the significant bits of her part; for instance, her erstwhile assertive and competent husband will become depressed. This is called 'first-order change' and is a variation of homeostasis. The parts have changed a bit but the plot is essentially the same. The essential rules of the system have been preserved. Only if these essential rules can be changed will the actors be free to assume genuinely new parts and create a new play. Observers of such a system can discern the rules in the way that an uninitiated observer might learn the rules of chess, simply by watching the games for long enough.

In its most dogmatic form, this theory tends to assume that the players themselves are powerless to change the system. They may also be powerless to understand it, but even if they do understand it they are unable to change it. Hence an outsider is needed to intervene actively to restructure the system through direct intervention or to create a crisis through which it will change itself, by (paradoxically) prescribing the very rules which keep the system going.

The interactional behaviour is not just behaviour, because all behaviour is communicative. These systems not only interact but they also generate meaning. The way in which behaviour is decoded as communication is influenced by the way it is 'framed'. If the same piece of behaviour is given a different meaning it is 'reframed'. Thus a father's behaviour in restricting the leisure activities of his children, which is framed by other family members as autocratic and repressive, may be reframed by a therapist as an expression of anxiety and concern. If other family members accept the redefinition, then the communicative import of the behaviour is changed; the response of others will alter and the system may be set off on a new course.

This model owes much of its genesis to the brilliant pioneering research of Gregory Bateson and his team in Palo Alto, California. Like a group-analytic conductor, Bateson held together and inspired a disparate team including Don Jackson, Jay Haley and John Weakland who, over a ten-year period, produced some of the most imaginative and innovative work since Freud. Bateson's particular genius was to pose questions which undermined existing preconceptions to generate new avenues of enquiry.

The research project began with the hypothesis that the patterns of speech, behaviour and experience which led to a person being labelled 'schizophrenic' could be rendered intelligible by first assuming that they were appropriate to the social context in which they occurred, and then investigating that social context – the family of the person labelled 'schizophrenic'.

This research on families generated much of the thinking outlined above. Jackson (1957 and 1965) wrote about rules and homeostasis to describe the way families seemingly resisted the therapist's best proposals for change. There was also much theorising about the cybernetic concepts of positive and negative feedback, one to correct a deviation and one to exacerbate it. There was even some confusion as to which was which, the terms being used in different ways as innovators struggled to find a conceptual framework to articulate their experience with families. Lynn Hoffman's paper on deviancy amplification remains a classic of this era (1971).

Central to all this became the famous 'double bind' hypothesis: one of the most researched, disputed, maligned and misunderstood concepts in the history of psychology. Essentially, it was an attempt to describe a context of communication of a specific sort of paradoxical nature. This context, it was argued, could produce translogical thought; poetry, art, schizophrenia. The 'double bind' hypothesis sought to spell out the rules of the context. But in the subsequent rush of numerous other researchers to test this hypothesis it became distorted beyond recognition. Even Bateson's own group started to believe they could identify double binds as behavioural sequences and count them as they occurred in observed families. This, as he subsequently remarked (1969), was nonsense.

But it was infectious nonsense. In 1980 Paul Dell noted that a vast quantity of research that had accumulated, purporting to test the double bind, was an exercise in epistemological confusion. Dell pointed out that what the double bind embodied was a different conception of knowledge and learning from that embodied in contemporary psychology research and psychiatric theory and practice. It was concerned not with the measurement of behaviour or the experimental reproduction of social contexts (a natural group like the family is, in any case, arguably not reproducible under experimental conditions), but with the recognition of pattern, the understanding of communication and the construction of meaning.

But Dell was too late. By 1980 careers had been launched, Ph.Ds written, articles published, and the psychiatric establishment had organised itself to contain the subversion. A theory as radical as the double bind has to be either disproven or modified in order to be incorporated. Double bind suffered these two fates in reverse order. First it was modified in order to be conventionally researched. Then it was declared disproven. Out it went as a respectable academic theory and out went most of anti-psychiatry, the movement of the sixties built on R. D. Laing's own development of the hypothesis as part of a philosophical and political critique of conventional psychiatry.

All that was left as a major movement was family therapy. Family therapy, like a good political strategist consolidating the work of a pioneer (like St Paul after Jesus), hedged its bets. It produced its radical theorists and speculators working in non-statutory settings: the Milan Group, the Mental Research Institute at Palo Alto, the Family Institute in Cardiff, and innovators such as Professor Salvador Minuchin who seemed able to innovate within the establishment. All continued to keep alive the 'new epistemology' of the double bind, and to develop innovative ways of engaging with families. At the same time family therapy became a 'treatment' – not so much an innovative view of life, but a way of fixing up the people labelled as 'sick' or 'deviant' by psychiatry and social work. Technique became the order of the day as individual family members became slowly but progressively objectified as components in a system. This division in a way sums up the value and the shortcomings of this particular version of systems theory: on the one hand, a fascinatingly innovative way of conceptualising individual behaviour and experience in relation to others; on the other hand, an approach which disconnects the observer from the observed. (See the next version, second order cybernetic model, which reifies the observed system and provides a ready tool for the manipulation of families, a model in which the outside observer always knows better than the inside participant.)

What it bequeathed to group analysis was, first, a different way of conceptualising the individuals who made up the group. They were not just personalities formed by early object relations, Oedipal conflicts and other inner world phenomena, but were historically and concurrently members of and participants in interactional contexts. Foulkes' idea of individuals having scripts could be elaborated in the language of interactional systems. Secondly, it enabled the group to be conceptualised as a developing system with its own rules and homeostatic tendencies (Skynner 1986; Garland 1982; Blackwell 1984).

## The second-order circularity model

Part of the misunderstanding of Bateson rests on the question of the subjectivity or objectivity of the observer. For Bateson, reality was always shaped by the way it was viewed. The observer was always part of a system with the object of observation. In many ways his approach echoed that of Kuhn (1962) who saw all scientific findings as products of a particular paradigm – a model of how to conduct scientific investigation which embodied a whole set of values and assumptions about what questions were important, what experimental procedures were acceptable, what could already be regarded as knowledge.

This position has been developed both clinically and theoretically. Therapists in Milan and Palo Alto were among the first to insist that explanations of family dynamics were provisional hypotheses, which could not be tested as right or wrong, but only evaluated as more or less useful formulations.

Theoretically, Maturana introduced the idea of an 'observer position'. What is observed depends on the position of the observer. 'Reality' must therefore be placed in parentheses. 'Reality' is brought forth by the performance of an 'operation of distinction'. Such operations of distinction require a language in which the distinction can be made. 'Reality' is therefore brought forth through language. Since language is social, a community of observers is implied, who agree on a particular version of 'reality'. Scientific explanations, according to Maturana, are 'pacifiers'. They satisfactorily answer certain questions under certain conditions. But they 'bring forth' rather than reveal 'reality'.

A similar line is the constructivist position pursued by von Glaserfeld (1983), who distinguishes between 'match' and 'fit'. A key may fit a lock but it does not match the lock. It matches an identical key. Explanations of reality, according to von Glaserfeld, fit reality, they do not match it. Theories are simply tools that enable us to do certain things such as putting satellites into orbit or conducting therapy. But they do not reveal reality.

Von Foerster (1983) takes a related position in claiming that knowledge is the capacity to do something, 'if you can do it, you know it'.

Maturana (1988) distances himself from the constructivists because he says their view implies a *reality* which can be 'fitted' if not 'matched'. His view, by contrast, included no *reality*, but only the 'reality' in parentheses agreed upon by a community of observers which brings it forth through language.

These formulations have major implications at both the therapeutic and the political level. Most importantly, they problematise all procedures of assessment and diagnosis. All formulations about the problems, pathology and personality of individuals are rendered provisional. Furthermore, they are open to interrogation and criticism according to their usefulness. This means we can question not only the diagnosis or theoretical formulation but also the direction of therapy which follows from it, and the goals it sets. Interpretation is similarly problematised. It is no longer a question of whether an interpretation is right or wrong, but what happens as a result of it. Therapy becomes much less the exploration of one mind by another, but rather a conversation in which a particular reality is constructed through the language and communication of the  participants.

Crucially, this formulation opens the door for ideology to be placed firmly on the therapeutic agenda. If theories are provisional, more or less useful, and to be judged by the direction in which they lead, then the next step is surely to ask whose personal, social, economic, and political interests are served by a particular direction. Significantly, the theorists of this school of systemic thought do not take that step. Largely they retain a political neutrality based on individual responsibility.

This reflects some of the problems with this particular formulation. Essentially it is a modern existentialist model. Its focus is primarily on the struggle of the individual to make sense of her own experience, to bring forth a reality, to tell a story that gives her life meaning and direction. But because reality is made up, there is nowhere to search for morality. Although constructivists such as Watzlawick (1983) may argue that it is not an amoral position, but a tolerant, benevolent and responsible position, it is hard to find any basis for these virtues within the theoretical formulation itself.

When one comes to ask questions about whether child abuse, or marital violence, has occurred, whether the Vietnam war or the Gulf war really happened, or how much the CIA supported Saddam Hussein's rise to power, then the placing of reality in parentheses raises serious concerns. As Bertrand Russell pointed out, it is impossible to refute the proposition that the world was created ten minutes ago by an omnipotent being who put us all here with fictitious memories, historical documents, buildings, technology, and so on. But it is rather unlikely; and the reality of history has rather more credibility.

This second-order cybernetic model has similar problems. Theoretically it is internally consistent, but there is a point at which it becomes both improbable and problematic. Its neutrality and problematising of reality mean that it lends little help for any group that insist their reality is more real than another. It is in this sense a genuinely libertarian and non-coercive theory. It undermines the idea that 'meta is better', since a meta-position is no more than another observer position, one more view to be taken into account. On the other hand, it provides no real basis for social or political criticism or action.

It might thus be seen as reflecting the interests of a professional elite, concerned to distance themselves from prevailing political trends: not providing support for the New World Order, but not coming into conflict with it either.

### The aesthetic systems model

Bateson himself had no doubt that the Vietnam war was wrong, and so was the development of nuclear weapons. Perhaps the reason he often located himself within the systems hierarchy model was a desire to cling to some sense of a natural order which might provide a basis for moral choice. He also proclaimed himself to be primarily concerned with *truth*. Here, therefore, he struggled with the apparent relativism of the cybernetic model, which included the observer in the system with the observed, against a sense that this itself might be part of some wider context in which truth and meaning could be discovered.

Frequently throughout his work he returned to poets and artists for a glimpse of some aesthetic truth that transcended the logic of science. And persistently he tried to extend the logic of science to incorporate it. He returned often to Pascal's observation that the heart had its reasons that reason could not at all perceive. Then he argued that the reasons of the heart had precise algorithms which could be mapped out if only he could find the right analogy or the right language. Eventually he found himself at the borders of science, Eastern philosophy and humanistic psychology – arguably a long way from systems theory, but in his view still very close to it.

His final effort (Bateson 1979) was to try to describe the 'pattern that connects' – a sort of patterning of mind of all living creatures, which enables us to recognise pattern in the world we inhabit, and to recognise other living creatures. Much of this was a conventional eco-systemic model which emphasised the place of humans in a natural ecology which they could either live with harmoniously or destroy through their attempts to dominate it. But beyond this was his conception of mind, not as something possessed by an individual, but as something people were part of; something of which individuals possessed properties and characteristics, but something that transcended individual persons and connected them with others; something which carried implicitly a basis for value and morality; something which resonated in the aesthetic of art, poetry, and music.

Keeney (1982) tried to give this line of thought therapeutic form, and found himself in conflict with second-order cybernetic theorists defending a more pragmatic and instrumental approach. Much of their concern seemed to be that therapy was becoming mystical, if not mystifying, instead of a craft and a skill that could be learned. Keeney struggled because he had no social or political framework within which to root his concerns. Like Bateson himself, he had moved so far away from any tradition of critical social theory that it was difficult to anchor his position in the real world. It was not until critiques rooted in the feminist challenge to patriarchal values by Hoffman and Goldner appeared that the instrumentalist position began to be superseded. But still Bateson's aesthetic remained elusive. Still it remains elusive.

## Speculations on the future

All of this poses vast areas of questioning for psychotherapy and for the relationship of the psyche to the social world. I would like to sketch out these areas briefly, in three subsections: (1) intellectual development, postmodernism and the subject; (2) individual development; (3) therapeutic practice.

### Intellectual development, postmodernism and the subject

In its struggle with epistemology and the nature of reality, and in its struggle to understand the individual as a component of a social context, a shifting dynamic of cultural values and interpersonal relations, systems theory has come close to the postmodernist social theorists. It is curious that, while Lacan provides a point of engagement for psychoanalysis with postmodernism, systems theory somehow fails to make this sort of connection. I want to suggest that there are two principal reasons for this. The first concerns the external world of politics and power; the second concerns the interiority of individual experience.

Systems theory is comfortable in understanding the individual within the family system, and with extending that view to understanding individual behaviour as something brought forth by specific contexts, such as work organisations. However, to engage itself fully with the postmodernist debate it would have to consider the cultural and political dimensions of family and organisational life, and the ways in which the individual is politically and historically constructed. This would plunge it straight into the political arena which it has heretofore so successfully stayed clear of.

Furthermore, it would then be engaged in a debate about the structure of individual experience – the subjectivity of individual people – an area which, since the early contretemps between psychoanalysis and family therapy, it has tended to avoid, often referring to individuals as 'black boxes' whose input and output could be observed, but about whose interior processes it was best not to speculate.

That systems theory stays disengaged from the postmodernist debate is regrettable. The microanalysis of the interactional and communicational dimensions and determinations of subjectivity provided by the cybernetic models could contribute much to understanding how cultural and political values are developed and regulated in everyday life. The political and cultural dimensions and the struggle to understand subjective experience which postmodernism addresses could generate more politically conscious, culturally sensitive, and less individually alienating models of systemic therapy. Particularly an engagement with Foucault's conception of knowledge in both form and content as an embodiment of power relations could give the systems theory understanding of the relativist and constructivist nature of reality the political dimensions it currently lacks. And were it to engage with Lacan's sense of the gap between reality and language it could restore the two as a dialectic, rather than reducing one to the other, and generate a creative space between them.

Without such developments it is hard to see how Bateson's aesthetic can become more than a problematic question mark against the development of systemic theory.

*Individual development*

It is with these possibilities in mind that we can assess more fully the contributions of systems theory to understanding individual development. What it has done, most significantly, is to provide a framework for understanding what actually happens in families: for connecting the internal world of the individual to the interactions of the social context, for relating the *internal* object to the *external* object. It thus becomes possible in a new way to question the extent to which both conscious and unconscious phantasy are the product of individual mental activity, and to what extent they reflect the reality of a social context, not necessarily consciously perceived or remembered. Some of this is already anticipated in Bollas's (1987) conception of the ego as the embodiment of rules for relating to the primary object, the mother. What needs elaboration is that the infant–mother relationship exists in the interactional context of the mother–father relationship, and the relations with other family members; within what might be called a family culture or matrix with its specific interactional and communicational rules.

Similarly, the Oedipal conflict can be reassessed as a real struggle of loyalties and allegiances, within which the developing child's physical and emotional desires must be negotiated. Furthermore, it seems likely that the real seductiveness of one parent and the real resentment of the other may be more significant determinants of the nature of Oedipal resolutions than the strength of libidinal drives or phantasies of punishment.

This emphasis on a social context as an arena of communication enables us to reconceptualise not only family relationships, but also the way in which peer relationships and the contexts of education, recreation and work contribute to the development of a repertoire of individual behaviour and experience which we are accustomed to calling 'personality'. Behaviour in these contexts is no longer seen as simply a reflection or projection of individual personality. Instead, these contexts are dialectically constitutive in a process of becoming.

*Therapeutic practice*

In the context of group psychotherapy we can see that the individuals bring not only their past, but also their present. De Mare (1991) has introduced the term 'transposition' to describe the way in which the group and its members can be experienced, not only as a reproduction of past relationships, as in transference, but as a reproduction of a whole contemporary social context. Hopper (1982) makes a similar point in his discussion of the emergence of politico-economic values in the dialogue of a therapy group.

Seen as an evolving system, a context in which new communications and experiences become possible, the group becomes much more than a place in which individual pathology is revealed. Its process and culture become much more than the projection of individual feelings and internal object constellations. As Hopper (1991) has noted, individual psychopathology is only a part of a group's context; it is not solely constitutive of the group. Lacan (1966) describes progress in analysis as taking place through the projection of the past into a discourse in the process of becoming. It is a discourse that he seems to regard as a dialectical discourse. We could therefore talk of the projection of the past into the dialectic of becoming. It is this dialectic that Foulkes sought to articulate as the group-analytic process. Transposition can be similarly understood as the projection of the contemporary relationship patterns and experiences into this same dialectic of becoming. What systems theory provides in its conceptualisation of the communicational intricacies of these patterns and experiences is, if it can be integrated with postmodernist political analysis, ways in which we can understand the emergence of the political in the personal. In group analysis, we can begin to analyse issues of gender, class, race, and other areas of culture, politics, and oppression, in ways which have not previously been part of our analytic practice.

Second-order systems theory can finally give the group conductor her full place in the dialectic of becoming – not as an interpreter, nor as a facilitator, catalyst, or observer, but as a full participant in an evolving process. The conductor's theory is no longer a privileged access to the reality of the group unconscious, nor an accurate map of what really happens in groups. It is instead a story told in a language through which the conductor enters a discourse with other members of the group. Her analytic detachment is an observer position; but it is *her* observer position, her unique place in relation to her group, not some universal view from 'on high' about what is really going on in the group.

Bateson's struggle to extend systems and communication theory to capture the moral aesthetic expressed in art and literature adds another level of understanding to the group-analytic discourse. Murray Cox (1987) has laid special emphasis on something of which most psychotherapists have some awareness: the impact of metaphor. We can conceptualise the group as characters from different novels, met together to constitute a new story. To this process they bring metaphors from their previous stories, but they also need to create new ones in the story of the group. When the group becomes a discourse of struggle to generate metaphors which speak, integrate and constitute the individual and collective experience of the members, then it has begun to leave the realm of logical scientific discourse, and to seek, through the language of everyday life, to enter a realm of political transcendence.

What Bateson crucially grasped was that the 'unconscious' (Pascal's 'reasons of the heart') was constituted not by objects but by patterns. Thus a pattern could be transferred from one object to another (transference) and the unconscious did not know the difference. Metaphor is the process through which unconscious pattern becomes conscious experience. This is why it is necessary to speak of internal objects or to use the myth of Oedipus. The language of speech, of consciousness, of rationality is essentially a language of objects located in time and space. The unconscious is formed in a different language: a language of pattern, of analogue, of picture. A metaphor can express in the language of consciousness; that is, the language of the conscious struggle to make sense of the world, the analogic patterning of the unconscious. It can thus synthesise conscious and unconscious processes.

## CONCLUSION

To write now about systems theory is to be beset by a paradox. Systems theory is no longer about systems. Writers in the family therapy tradition are now increasingly concerned with the processes of constructing, dissolving, and reconstructing realities. This in a way represents the progress and transformation of the second-order cybernetic stream of systems theory. However, at the heart of the paradox lies the fact that systems theory was hardly ever a single coherent theory, though it was often referred to as if it were. Nor is it entirely satisfactory to regard it as a collection or assortment of ideas and theories about systems. From the start concepts about systems have been mixed with ideas from communication theory, from hypnosis and from Eastern philosophies such as Zen Buddhism. This was all part of a movement within psychiatry, social work and psychotherapy to advance our understanding of and work with the relationships between people. Systems theory gave its name to this movement. Through the development of family therapy it formed a sort of antithesis to the way in which conventional psychiatry, psychoanalysis, and analytic psychotherapy located their definitions and explanations of symptoms and problems *within* individuals.

Group analysis, while it had always sought conceptualisations beyond the intrapsychic, had retained psychoanalysis as a base, beyond which it was generally reluctant to move too far. It was therefore unable to constitute itself in dialectical opposition to this tradition in the way that the family systems movement did. However, group analysis is now well placed to pursue the synthesis of these two movements, and to develop an understanding of psychotherapy as an intersubjective dialectical process. The systems movement is focused on the observation and understanding of interactional behaviour and the construction of reality through language. The psychoanalytic tradition is concerned with the exploration and understanding of the individual lived experience and the articulation of that experience through language. It is a dialectic between the explanation of the observer and the experience of the participant. In an analytic group each member is an observer, an explainer, and commenter on the participation of others. At the same time she or he is also a participant observed by others. The group analyst, too, is both observer and participant.

The relevance of systems theory is not in the rigorous conceptualisation of the group as 'a system' nor of individual members as members of 'a system'. It is, rather, in the use of ideas and concepts from the systems theory (communication theory/family therapy) movement to inform the observer position within this dialectic.

The recognition of each group member as holding a specific observer position which may correspond to or differ from that of others while retaining its validity promotes the acceptance and development of diversity and individuality within the group. Where Foulkes saw members of a group as collectively embodying the norm from which they each deviated, we can now see them also as embodying the diversity of which they are all, including perhaps the therapist, afraid.

# Chapter 4

# The group-as-a-whole

*Malcolm Pines*

The distinctive feature that marks group analysis out from other schools of group psychotherapy – and from psychoanalysis – is the firmly held basic assumption that the distinctions that are usually made between 'individual' and 'group' are unnecessary and artificial. The precious notion that we all cling to our own individuality and ownership of our own minds – 'I am master of my body and captain of my soul'(N. Pines, 1925 onwards!) as the nineteenth century attempted to proclaim – is indeed but a notion or theory. Foulkes asserted that the real nature of what we call 'mind' arises from each individual's need for communication and for reception. Language goes on in the mind of the individual and is experienced as one's own thoughts, but language is a shared property of the group and originates in our needs for communication, for survival and adaptation (Foulkes and Anthony 1957: 244). This means that the individual is penetrated to the very core by culture and grows into 'normality' quite unconscious of those colossal social forces that have shaped and moulded him or her. The full nature of an individual's psychic reality can only be seen by situating the person in context, on the ground from which they originate. Here we see Foulkes' indebtedness to Kurt Goldstein, the psychologist and neurologist, with whom he had worked and who so strongly emphasised the figure–ground concept for the functioning of the organism. Beyond the infantile amnesia and defences which protect this unconscious repression, above and beyond this, we are unaware, ignorant of much of our psychic make-up, of our cultural attitudes, not because they are repressed but because we are convinced that they are right and proper and need not be examined. The restricted range of what we term 'normality' is made clear to us when we are in contact with other cultures, looking-glasses to some of the most basic of human physical and mental functions. We take for granted how we eat, excrete, exchange, and fashion the business of our daily lives. Thrown into other contexts than our own, other sounds, languages, positions, affiliations, we discover that our sense of safety and wholeness is to a large part based on being part of a socio-psychological network.

## NETWORK

This concept of 'network' is at the basis of group-analytic theory. Foulkes defined an individual as a person occupying a nodal place in the social network, again deriving this concept from the Gestalt psychology of Kurt Goldstein (Goldstein 1939; Foulkes 1990: 39–56). Goldstein, a profound philosopher of biology, had studied the response of the injured, brain-damaged person and had demonstrated that it is the whole person who actively responds to and attempts to adapt to injury of the central nervous system. In disease, the equilibrium of the central nervous system cannot be maintained, and the damaged part, instead of functioning as a nodal point in the network, now represents a focal point for disequilibrium to which the whole organism now has to adapt. By analogy, there is a social network, which forms and in many ways 'is' the person, and in illness we can trace processes of disturbance in the network, which then manifest through one person, the presenting patient, as 'illness'. These processes are very clear in infant and child psychiatry and can be revealed in the world of adults, provided that we are prepared to examine and to understand the socio-psychological background. This approach is well supported by research; for instance, the studies of the relationship of depression in women to particular social processes (Brown and Harris 1978).

Some assert that the group-analytic approach is mainly socio-psychological, which replaces the psychoanalytic depth of study of the individual by a more superficial study of group life, but this is an inaccurate attribution and categorisation. Foulkes repeatedly stated that the 'social' is deeply inside each one of us, and what seems to be 'outside' or 'inside' is itself a construct by ourselves and by our cultures. Individual and social, intra- and interpersonal, are like the Moebius strip, eternally unfolding and infolding. This is what the group-analytic situation enables each one of us to recognise and experience. It is in this group-analytical experience that we can begin to appreciate the degree to which we are bound together through unconscious forces. As Foulkes wrote, 'The very fact that we can easily understand each other and that this understanding can extend to such depth, is a token of our membership of a shared culture' to which he gave the name of 'foundation matrix' (Foulkes 1990: 223–33).

## The group-as-a-whole

The concept of 'group-as-a-whole' is intrinsic to group analysis; it was there from the start. Foulkes wrote in his first book:

> While having an eye on each individual member and on the effects they and their utterances have on each other, the conductor is always observing and treating the group-as-a-whole. The group-as-a-whole is not a phrase, it is a living organism, as distinct from the individuals composing it. It has moods and reactions, a spirit, an atmosphere, a climate. . . .One can judge the prevailing climate by asking oneself: 'What sort of thing could or could not possibly happen in this group? What could be voiced?'
>
> (1948: 140)

> The conductor can gauge his own distance to the group by asking himself, 'What sort of thing could I say within this situation, and what could not be said?' In fact, it is the group-as-a-whole with which the conductor is primarily in touch and he experiences its individuals inside the setting. You should sense what this group needs at any given moment, be it encouragement, reassurance, or stimulation, steadying or excitation.
>
> (Foulkes 1948: 140)

Foulkes' capacity to grasp this notion and to base both theory and practice on it arose from his recognition of the depth and strength of social forces in the human psyche. For him society is not 'outside' the person: it is internal and penetrates to the innermost being of the individual. Thus within a given culture persons are rooted together in a foundation matrix, sharing not only a common language but also unconsciously holding common assumptions regarding the most basic of life processes – feeding, excreting, and sleeping, and assumptions as to the nature of their world. Undoubtedly he had understood this from the seminal work of the sociologist colleague whom he had met in Frankfurt, Norbert Elias, whose book on *The Civilizing Process* Foulkes had introduced to the psychoanalytic world in 1936 (Foulkes 1948; Mennell 1989).

Thus Foulkes' concept of working with a small group did not represent an individualistic psychoanalytic position, whereby a therapist can observe and treat numbers of patients instead of one at a time, an economy of time. From the start he regarded the group as an entity in itself, a 'common matrix within which all relationships develop' and 'axiomatic that everything happening in a group involves the group-as-a-whole as well as each individual member' (Foulkes 1948: 49).

By firmly holding on to this concept the group analyst can consider the ways in which individuals take part in the therapeutic process, which also enables the therapist to intervene at an individual level when this seems appropriate. This gives the therapist a degree of freedom of action that may not be allowed to one who needs to confine his or her actions solely to the group-as-a-whole level.

At this point I shall briefly consider how other persons have used the group-as-a-whole concept, as there is much confusion on this issue that I hope to clarify.

### W.R. Bion (Pines 1985)

The approach initiated by Bion is well known to predicate unconscious modes of functioning of the group in relation to its leader and to its work task. Powerful and primitive forces acting as resistances to the work of therapy hold the group in thrall. These patterns that Bion termed 'basic assumptions' are those of dependency, fight–flight, and pairing. His assumption was that interpretation of these patterns could release the blocked work capacity and that this was the major, indeed the prime, task of the group therapist. Though Bion recognised that man is a group creature who is at war with his social nature, he did not elaborate on the rootedness of humans in their social structure, in contrast to Foulkes. This leads to a considerable limitation in applying his ideas to group life in general.

The same argument applies to Henry Ezriel (Ezriel 1973), who based his work on a schema of how object relations would reappear in the group setting. His work represents the strict application of one version of psychoanalytic theory to the group setting and fails to take into account the intrinsic dynamics of group life or indeed the fundamental sociality of human life.

### Dorothy Stock Whitaker (Whitaker 1985)

A far more flexible and illuminating scheme is set out by this author. Her work was considerably influenced by Bion through his concept of group mentality but, since then, has gone on independently and with

originality. Less influenced by psychoanalytic theory, though acknowledging the work of Thomas French on 'focal conflict', she has integrated many aspects of social psychology and group dynamics in her
important writings. On the whole, her work is more concerned with
'non-clinical' settings, studying how group dynamics appear in all
group situations. She studies how group themes emerge through the
flow of associations, how norms and belief systems develop in the
course of group life and what solutions they offer to the inevitable
dilemmas of individuals interacting in groups. She writes that the 'group
as a whole can be described in terms of mood or atmosphere, shared
schemes, norms and belief systems, structure, boundaries, roles and role
distinctions, conflict, consensus and developmental stages', and writes
that 'whole group phenomena are generated by the interaction of group
members but they are not merely the sum of individual contributions.
They can properly be said to "belong" to the group as a whole.'

Dorothy Whitaker's comprehensive and well-argued theory is a
powerful and useful tool for therapists. Where Foulkes differs is again
in his insistence on the power of those social and cultural forces within
the individual that go into the formation of both normal personality and
of its disorders. His concepts of network, matrix, and group-specific
forces are distinctive. But the group analyst can learn much from
Dorothy Whitaker's technique, but needs also to retain the more psychoanalytic nature of observing without intervening until she or he feels
the need to do so. This need may lead to interaction with individuals as
well as with the group-as-a-whole and will not necessarily deal with the
developmental conflicts of group life that Dorothy Whitaker has so well
illuminated.

*Yvonne Agazarian*

In Agazarian's group-as-a-whole theories and also possibly in her
practice there are considerable resemblances to Dorothy Whitaker. This
is not surprising, as they both declare an allegiance to Lewin's social
psychology and to the group dynamic researches which were stimulated
by him from the 1950s onwards. But Agazarian has pioneered a group-
as-a-whole approach that applies systems theory systematically, and
most definitely gives the group prime place for the observations and
actions of the group conductor.

Her theory of the 'invisible group' (Agazarian and Peters 1981)
'presents group concepts that are distinct and discrete from individual
psychology. It is an integrational system theory which spells out the

structure and functions of individual and group dynamics as two discrete but related systems'. The conductor observes from two perspectives – individual and group systems – that coexist simultaneously in
space and time. The individual dynamics are characteristically expressed in member-role behaviour, modified by interaction in the group;
unconscious group-as-a-whole dynamics are expressed in characteristic
group-as-a-whole role behaviour which affect the development of the
group-as-a-whole and which in turn affects individual group members.
Agazarian keenly observes processes of group development and differentiation and takes sub-groups as the basic unit of observation, not
any one individual. Sub-groups make visible the boundaries that are
developing, boundaries that contain differences which need to be made
visible for the group to pursue the group's developing problem-solving
skills (Agazarian 1989).

Agazarian is constantly further developing her work within the systems framework, and the contribution of psychoanalytic theory plays a
lesser part. The conductor's role in Agazarian's work is clearly observable and definable in monitoring and aiding the development of the
group as a problem-solving situation. In contrast, the group-analytic
therapist's role is not so well defined or described, which allows for the
development of individual styles that reflect both the personality and
beliefs of the conductor but which, despite many apparent differences,
all rest on the same group-analytic theory base.

My own understanding of the group-as-a-whole concept has been
developing over a number of years. Working with groups which meet
over a very long period of time, either once or twice a week, I have had
the opportunity to observe and indeed to wonder at the capacity of
group members to create a working unity, a body of persons who share
a psychic life within the group boundary of space and time. Even if only
meeting once a week they can develop a depth of experience and of
understanding of that experience that remarkably changes some aspects
of each individual's psychic life. It is clear that this must arise from the
transformational potential of the group situation and the fact that the
burden of the work is carried by the group members themselves. They
engage in exploration and understanding both one another's individual
mentalities and, increasingly, the way in which each functions within
the group and what is carried for the other as well as for themselves.
Gradually, psychic boundaries seem to become more permeable, the
boundaries which define each one person as distinct from another – the
'self boundary', in a sense – and those boundaries which define the
inner structure of each individual. These are the boundaries between

conscious and unconscious, internal boundaries of self- and other-representations, of the psychic structures of ego, superego, and id, the boundary between reality and fantasy and so on. For many persons, such changes in self-definition make possible the useful interpenetration of one person's mind by another's; for other persons, what is needed is a strengthening of those boundaries so that the person becomes less open to what is experienced as invasion or intrusion.

Thus over time there seems to be an increasing sense of 'fitting in' of the group members, creating what to myself as participant observer, and I believe to the group members also, is an increasing sense of coherency. I shall address this issue of coherency later but for now confine the meaning of the word to a sense of understanding what is going on, that it makes sense and becomes increasingly meaningful.

At the start Foulkes borrowed the term 'psyche group' from Moreno's colleague Helen Jennings. He gave depth and strength to this concept by introducing his own concept of the group matrix. As this is discussed elsewhere in this volume I will restrict my own comments to the matrix as an evolutionary concept that refers to the developmental history of a group which is based upon the communicational network laid down by its participants over time. On the basis of this communicational network a form of psychological organisation develops in a group based upon mutual experiences, relationships, and understandings. The shared history of interpersonal relationships in the group and of the shared work in deriving meaning from their work together lays down this dynamic group matrix. It is this process which establishes a deeper sense of coherency, both conscious and unconscious, that I believe is intrinsic to the concept of the group-as-a-whole.

**The two meanings of the word 'group': cohesion and coherency (Pines 1986)**

I have always been struck by the wisdom of words, and I want to consider our basic word 'group' in this respect. According to the Shorter *Oxford English Dictionary* there are two roots for the word 'group'; one is Germanic and the other Latin. The more ancient Germanic origin of the word 'group' is derived from the word for 'crop'; that is, the gizzard of a bird. For within the crop of an animal is to be found an agglomeration of substances that have been swallowed and which have lost their discrete nature and are now clumped together to form a fibrous mass. Thus in individual elements partly digested, glued together to form a bolus, we can see the image of a primitive group. This is a group where elements stick together, now partly changed by being mixed together in this agglomeration which has an external boundary, being shaped now into a sort of ball but which lacks any internal structure. The force that holds this mass together can be termed 'cohesion'. The dictionary defines cohesion as 'unity of material things held together by a physical substance such as cement, mortar, glue or by a physical force such as attraction or affinity.' This well describes the sticky mass of the organic bolus but also can be used as a metaphor to describe some aspects of group life. A group which sticks together displays a force that will resist being pulled apart, will resist invasion. In group psychology there has been a great deal of attention paid to this concept of cohesion, and it has been put forward as a cardinal principle for group psychotherapy. Groups which do not hold together, which do not exert a force of attraction or affinity for its members do not develop the capacity for psychological work, for experiencing and dealing with the psychic work that is involved in facing painful issues. It has also been recognised that the forces of cohesion can act as resistances to differentiation and development, and it is possible to see Bion's basic assumptions, for instance, as instances of powerful group cohesive forces.

The other origin for the word 'group' comes from the Latin, and is connected with a concept of 'grouping' as an active process. No longer the *passive* agglomeration of only partly differentiated substances, grouping refers to objects which are actively grouped together in order to display an organisational principle. The dictionary defines coherence as

> unity, firstly of immaterial, of intangible things, such as the points of an argument, the details of a picture, the incidents, characters and setting of a story; or secondly of material and of objective things that are bound into a unity by a spiritual, intellectual or aesthetic relationship, as through their clear sequence or their harmony with one another; it therefore commonly connotes an integrity which makes the whole and the relationship of its parts clear and manifest.

So here we have the dictionary describing 'an integrity which makes the whole and the relationship of its parts clear and manifest.'

It is this concept of *coherency* which I wish to put forward as perhaps the prime factor in the evolution of 'the group-as-a-whole' (Pines 1986).

The group-analytic group meets under conditions set down and maintained by the group analyst as 'dynamic administrator'. Thus the basic issues of time, space, reliability, confidentiality, the privilege of verbal communication over action, the understanding that people meet together in order to increase their understanding of themselves and thereby to gain greater mastery over their inner lives is the basis of the work. These organisational principles are part of the group analyst's own mentality, derived from his or her training and position in the training matrix of the group-analytic community. It is this basic structure which will be tested again and again through the life of the group and which gradually becomes internalised by the group members themselves, so that in the long run they themselves become the organisers of the group (Pines 1985). Thus each member of the group occupies the position of a 'double agent', both member and recipient of the group processes but also supporter and vital link in the group structure. Thereby the group members gradually come to work at 'higher' levels of psychic organisation, maturing over time as the life of the group develops; this double process plays an increasing part in holding the group together and yet at the same time allows members to experience deeper, more regressive, more loosely organised aspects of self through their own inner explorations and through participation in the psychic lives of the other group members.

To return to the developmental aspects of the group matrix, I find it helpful to think about the group in terms of an increasing coherence that makes the whole and the relationship of its parts more clear and manifest. The achievement of coherence in the group process enables its members to retrace the developmental path of coherence in childhood (Pines 1985). The path of childhood development can be seen as the organism's gradual attainment of a state of coherency; concepts of self and of identity all imply development of a form of coherency, the parts fitting together to make a whole. Now that studies of child development increasingly centre on the observation of the mother–infant pair, the concept of coherency again comes to the fore. How do any particular infant–mother or caregiver pair fit together? How much intuitive or intelligent understanding is displayed by the caregiver towards any one particular child, and what are the capacities of any particular child to respond 'understandingly' to the actions of the caregiver? We know that there is a whole range of possibilities between the harmonious interplay of a skilled intuitive caregiver with a responsive and receptive infant, and the painfully destructive incapacity of the pair to relate to each other. Modern observational techniques allow for the recognition of the most subtle example of successful and unsuccessful translation of impulses and needs by the infant and successful or unsuccessful response of the caregiver.

All this can be subsumed under the concept of 'dialogue', a process which begins as an interplay of gestures which gradually lead on to the precursors of conversations, finally arriving at the stage of verbalisations (Leal 1982). All the time the infant is being drawn into communication with the social world, internalising the gestures of the social world which are offered to it and which are also offered as responses to the infant's own gestures. Thus, as Foulkes so clearly saw, the social is laid down deeply within the individual from the very start. For this is a language of gestures that belongs both to the most intensely personal, to the unique mother–caregiver dyad, but also to that set of responses communicated through culture to the caregivers as the appropriate gestures to make to infants.

Within the realm of developmental psychology it is to Vygotsky that we have to turn for a satisfactory model to explain this form of development. Vygotsky spoke of the 'law of proximal development' (Weitsch 1985). By this he meant that the social world, the caregivers, are always drawing the infant onto the next possible stage of development. They are offering gestures to the infant for the infant to grasp, initially by chance but then to build into the infant's own behavioural repertoire, that show an understandable and intelligible response.

## Coherence and narrative

The persons sharing the therapy group under group-analytic conditions (free group discussion, slow/open group with consistent membership over lengthy periods, conductor maintaining a mostly interpretative stance) are basically constructing narratives of current and past life experiences. These narratives will be reshaped through the reception given by their fellow group members. This reshaping virtually gives expression to a new coherency for the persons; a life story that gives fuller weight to development in the context of family, as that context is to some extent replayed in the here and now of the group (see Chapter 6, by Dennis Brown). Thus, for each person, there are two personal narratives, the here and now in the group and there and then, in the past, and it is the dynamic juxtaposition of these stories that gradually fits the two together. Robin Skynner has addressed this in terms of the 'templates' that the group members gradually fit together (Skynner 1986).

Group members mostly enter therapy in the hope of finding relief from suffering without radical change, the search for self-understanding gradually becomes the prime mover, as persons discover that this is predominantly what the situation offers, aid to self-understanding through work with others engaged in the same enterprise. Self-understanding is the search for what unifies our diverse experiences with our phantasies, our dreams, our relations with others.

## Coherence and metaphor

The philosophers Lakoff and Johnson (Lakoff and Johnson 1980) argue that metaphors are not merely a matter of words, for human thought processes are largely metaphorical. Metaphors bind elements into coherent systems, and if you look at the structure of our language, we express a multitude of experiences through metaphors, many of which are related to the body image. From birth onwards, our body image, with the dimensions of vertical, horizontal, and depth, becomes a way of expressing experience. Up-ness is connected with happiness, health, consciousness, awakeness; down-ness with illness, sadness, grossness, the hidden aspects of the self, with the unconscious. Western society privileges the vertical, and psychoanalysis gives persons the opportunity to plunge into the depths of the self. Eastern cultures privilege the horizontal, and emphasise balance and harmony. In a group-analytic situation, the horizontal dimension, the self in relationship to others, has to be acknowledged and worked at, at the same time as each individual can also come into contact with their own vertical depth. Thus, the bringing together of the vertical and the horizontal, the in-between and the within, is part of the coherency that may be achieved by group members.

## THE GROUP SETTING

Metaphors of holding and containment are increasingly applied to analytic groups. They usefully express the reality of a situation, where persons allow themselves to relate to others at depth. Deeply significant relationships develop which involve powerful affects, and were there not a sense of reliability and strength of the group setting these developments could not take place. As developed by Winnicott and Bion, containing and holding refer to very early relationship experiences (see Chapter 5, by Colin James). Holding is a metaphor based on the physical experience, the holding that caregivers give to infants, but is a metaphor which coherently brings together a great variety of parental, predominantly maternal, acts and attitudes. Containment relates to the maternal capacity to take in, to understand, and appropriately respond to an infant's needs, which are predominantly expressed through distress.

By an understanding that leads to an appropriate response, the caregiver creates a coherent pattern out of the infant's initially inchoate actions. The infant seems to begin to understand hunger as part of a relationship in which hunger will be communicated, understood and responded to by food and by loving care, so that the infant's emotional needs will be fed at the same time as the physiological needs are satisfied. In group analysis, the group-as-a-whole, formed by the members and the conductor together, take on these functions of holding and containment, so that individual needs are fairly reliably understood and responded to appropriately (Kosseff 1991).

Within psychoanalytic theory, Hans Loewald addressed this notion of coherency as a major therapeutic process. Freud had described the ego as 'a coherent organisation of mental processes', many of which are functioning at an unconscious level. Thus, there is a distinction between the coherent unconscious and the repressed unconscious phantasies, which are not organised under this principle of coherency. Regarding the therapeutic process as one in which the patient internalises aspects of the interaction process between patient and therapist, what is internalised becomes an inherent part of the coherent ego. Thus, there is an exchange between the more primitive, chaotic, and incoherent parts of the unconscious self, largely expressed through responses to the therapeutic situation manifested through the transference. There is an exchange process whereby the primitive is understood and responded to by the therapist, who acts at a higher, more organised level both of consciousness and unconsciousness. The therapist's intuition and countertransference responses arise from the unconscious coherent ego and thus, through internalisation processes, the therapist's responses become part of a new organisation of the patient's unconscious mental life. Loewald writes:

> It is of the utmost importance, theoretically and clinically, to distinguish more clearly and consistently than Freud ever did between processes of repression and processes of internalisation. The latter are involved in creating an increasingly coherent integration and organisation of the psyche *as a whole*, [my italics] whereas repression works against such coherent psychic organisation, by maintaining a *share* of psychic processes in a less organised, more primitive state.
>
> (Loewald 1980: 76)

As I have written elsewhere:

> There is an essential paradox in the group situation. The basic func-

tions of holding and containment co-exist with a culture that is based on analysis and translation, which are sophisticated levels of higher functioning. Thus, there are inherent contradictions in the group situation, a delicate, stable, yet unstable balance that has constantly to be monitored and managed. Early developmental processes re-enacted in the group can be held, contained, and tolerated as the group can function at a higher level and is available to the individuals, often more adequately and appropriately than were the containers and holders for patients' early experiences. Thus, members develop their capacity to think in the face of pain and to tolerate and to know the unthinkable.

(Pines, unpublished)

So, finally, I come to an attempt to define the group-as-a-whole in group-analytic terms: it is the basic concept underlying the approach to a group that meets in a standard group-analytic situation, which privileges communication and in which the therapeutic aim is to enable both individual and group coherency to emerge over time at both conscious and unconscious levels. Increased unconscious coherency represents the establishment and enrichment of the group matrix.

## NOTE

The special issue of the journal *Group* (13: 3-4) is devoted to 'The-group-as-a-whole'. Edited by Yvonne Agazarian, it contains a comprehensive overview of contemporary approaches to the topic.

# Chapter 5

# 'Holding' and 'containing' in the group and society

*D. Colin James*

'Holding' and 'containing' are commonly used and even more commonly misused concepts from different theoretical psychoanalytical traditions. Their importance within psychoanalysis cannot be doubted as they are an integral part of the fabric of what is known as 'object relations theory'.

They have achieved a major place in psychoanalytic theory and clinical practice as applied to the development of the individual. Here, echoing the discipline of group analysis, an attempt is made to apply these two concepts in order to understand the development of the person in relation to a group.

A second theme of this chapter is a natural and inevitable consequence of looking at group phenomena through these two concepts. It concerns the relationship of the individual's experience in the small group, to the larger group, and to the outside world; to areas of experience and behaviour of people in large groups and in society.

It is assumed as a starting point that the phenomena which these two concepts deal with are vital to the well-being of the mature individual and are also important to the development of citizenship. It is implied that in looking at the theory of group analysis or of any other theoretical model dealing with this area, we have to be able to take in other people's points of view, however different they might seem from those to which we have become accustomed. This in some way resonates with the task of the mature adult having achieved an ability to integrate the value of the 'other', and yet to maintain his individuality (Winnicott 1958, 1969).

Becoming a whole person is one aim: becoming a useful citizen is another. The two concepts studied in this chapter, 'holding' and 'containing', should help us to understand more of the development of the individual, and from there to be able to come to terms with the value of the 'other', and from there, to that of 'others'. In a nutshell, people need healthy societies in order to be able to develop their full potential as human beings; healthy societies are made up of healthy people.

On the other hand, in order to be able to conceptualise holding and containing, one must have a rudimentary acceptance of the idea of object relations theory. Freud certainly implied an object relations theory and the work of Klein elaborated his ideas. The basic tenets of object relations theory have been most clearly depicted by Winnicott (1960), Fairbairn (1951), Balint (1952) and Sutherland (1963). A very full exposition of this theory has been presented by Greenberg and Mitchell (1985), and Kernberg (1976) has written extensively and creatively on this topic.

The theory, especially as emphasised by Winnicott and Fairbairn, essentially implies that the human subject is object-seeking for its survival, development, and maturation.

The acceptance and utilisation of object relations theory and these two concepts within group analysis are relatively recent, and we can find historical and theoretical reasons for this.

Foulkes was sceptical of the validity of object relations theory, and yet he was the man who insisted on the social kernel of mankind's existence, the social focus which was able to make sense of man's relationship with his fellow beings, and brought from psychoanalysis a different view of group process, and evolved and founded the groundwork of group analysis. In a communication to the business meetings of the Controversial Discussions on technique, of the British Psycho-Analytical Society, Foulkes (1942) contributed a long written contribution to the discussions. While, from his experience of working with psychotic patients, acknowledging many of the phenomena which he had described, he was at pains not to give a primacy to phantasies and the concepts of objects. He pleaded that words, although originating as expressions of something emotional, when they come to have meaning they are quite concrete, and become concrete things in the mind. Yet at the same time he stated that 'the whole of mental life, conscious or unconscious is suspended between the two material realities of body and mind, and always directed towards the outside world, to which in a certain sense the body itself belongs.' He agreed that phantasies were important, but not that they were 'primary motors'. He considered that regarding inner objects and phantasies as of primary importance was a mistake, and that one's primary concern was to analyse these phenomena, and achieve rational and scientific thinking in understanding them (Foulkes [1943: 362], in *The Freud–Klein Controversies 1941–45*, P. King and R. Steiner (eds) [1991] p. 362).

I feel that these two aspects of Foulkes' position, being sceptical of the primacy of the inner world on the one hand, and yet being very concerned about relatedness to people in one's outer world on the other, were arrived at as much from the intense political pressure engendered at the time of the controversial discussions, and that the bifocal nature of his thinking was the result of a social environment that was rather frightened. (That is not to say that I believe that the whole of the controversies were about that point but, in my understanding, Foulkes' theory of group analysis *and* his stance about object relations theory imply a duplicity of thinking not entirely due to himself.)

Later (Foulkes 1957), in a discussion of a paper by Fairbairn on the critical evaluation of some basic psychoanalytical concepts, agrees that the focusing of Freud's theory and concepts of the individual makes it difficult to study man within a purely one-person psychology, and agrees that man is a social animal, and best studied in a group setting. Fairbairn's emphasis was that man was object seeking rather than pleasure seeking and that his behaviour is determined more by the reality principle than the pleasure principle.

Despite Foulkes' concern about the social context of man's experience, he does not, it seems to me, answer the essential question of the internal representation of these relationships, and does not link up the possibility of studying those social relationships in terms of transference. I believe that this is partly a stance against the emphasis of other analysts that all psychoanalytic phenomena are best understood from within the transference relationship. The very fact of man's social nature must have an impact on the internal representations of experience from early life, and if one accepts any internalisation of the social world, there must be a sense of 'internal' relationships, which would need some understanding in terms of object representations. Again, I feel that Foulkes did not answer the problem of how those social relationships are internalised, and again I think that this was a 'sign of the times'. I believe that we can match up these two focuses, and integrate the internal and the social by using the concepts of 'holding' and 'containing', but in order to do that, we have to examine the nature of the internal mechanisms in terms of object relations theory: a multi-object concept, resonating with a social focus. I have previously contended that they are important components of the methodology and utility of group analysis (James 1984).

The concepts of 'holding' and 'containing' are very specific within the psychoanalytic corpus of knowledge of intrapsychic functioning, and owe this specificity to their origins: the first to Winnicott's theory of the relationship between infant and mother and its repercussions for future development; and the second to Bion's theory of containing, and its emphasis on intrapsychic experience and functioning, emanating from the work of Melanie Klein, elaborated by Bion (1962), and by Meltzer (1978).

Kernberg (1980), who has for some time, alongside Sutherland (1963), studied and expounded Fairbairn's work, maintains that object relations theory is the crossroads where psychoanalysis and social theory meet.

Most people working with groups use ideas borrowed from this theory, and certainly there has been a tendency in the last decade or so within group-analytic circles to begin to use and explore object relations theory and its relevance to group processes. Let it be noted that this parallels another, paradoxical, tendency to move away from psycho-analytic theories and formulations as a whole, but I believe this is due to a generalisation of psychoanalytic concepts without attribution to their source.

There is, however, a dichotomy. This chapter is not meant to be a contribution to that debate, and yet by the very nature of the concepts dealt with here it may be seen as one, and a position statement would seem to be appropriate.

In the application of the concepts of 'holding' and 'containing' in individual analysis, the task is to use the associations and experience of the patient in the context of the relationship with the analyst, and these two concepts are best understood in that setting within the transference relationship. Likewise in a group setting, the conductor has to attend to the details of the moment, and the setting, and not actively attempt or even behave as if he or she is 'holding' or 'containing' the group, or the individual in the group. He certainly might bring that with him as his contribution to the work, but it is a position, a stance, an attitude rather than a magical quality that can cure all ills. The moment-by-moment task remains in the context of what he brings to the group to examine and think in the presence of the events in the group; to maintain a view of the group-as-a-whole, and to see the individuals in the context of that view.

My main aim is to use these two concepts to help us to understand the experience and development of an individual in relation to a group.

A second theme, which I believe is an inevitable result of the attempt to explore the experience of an individual in a small group, takes us to the implication of that experience for the person in relation to larger groups and to society and to the external world at large. The more we understand the experience of a person in relation to a small group, the more, I think, we are led to question the nature of the individual's experience in relation to the large group, the very nature of the behaviour of larger groups, and the individual's part in forging that behaviour. Along with Trist (1987), I believe that it is increasingly necessary for us to examine and to be familiar with the processes in large groups for our social survival in our rapidly shrinking social world; shrinking, that is, in terms of the immediacy to our experience of events and phenomena far away. We are becoming increasingly familiar with them because of increased communication.

In parallel with this, Isobel Menzies-Lyth (1981), writing about Wilfred R. Bion, refers to the group as the 'natural extension' of psychoanalysis. She adumbrates the serious study of group phenomena, and sees this as important as is the understanding of the individual.

Within group analysis there is a tendency – some might say a regrettable and increasing tendency – to see group analysis as separate rather than as an extension of psychoanalysis and thereby to miss the contribution which both schools have to offer.

Instead of redirecting, or redescribing the theories differently, and seeming to regard the individual as split in two parts, one part as an individual, a unique but isolated individual, and the other part as a group-orientated social animal, we should, I think, view the person as having a continuum of experience which is constantly evolving and being influenced by internal object relationships, close relationships, group relationships, and large group relationships.

I wish to share what I see as a definite synthesis of the two concepts, which historically have been regarded as quite separate, and which in my view give deeper depth and meaning to the underlying phenomena when taken together as different aspects of the same view.

There are in this discussion several focuses which we have to keep in mind:

1 Foulkes' description of the matrix within group-analytic theory;
2 Winnicott's ideas concerning the relationship between mother and infant, and the importance of that experience for later development of the personality, and further, for the very perception and integration of social phenomena which are vital for the social functioning of the individual.

3 Bion's concern for a clear understanding of psychic functioning that leads to a capacity to think about the psyche and its relationship to the external world, especially in regard to people in one's external world.

As a student of group analysis, I was subjected to the then current view that, on the one hand, there was Foulkes' theory of groups, and on the other there was Bion's theory; they were seen as very different, and to be kept separate.

At the same time, as a student of psychoanalysis, there was a theory of development in infancy, which laid great importance on the early interaction between infant and mother, and which was emphasised as being Winnicott's concept of 'holding', while there was also a concept of 'containing' which was attributed to Bion, and to projective identification and 'thinking'.

It was with a great sense of excitement that I discovered a link between Bion's paper 'A theory of thinking' (1962), in which he clearly depicts the infant's need of the mother's capacity to 'contain', and Winnicott's paper, 'The theory of the parent–infant relationship' (1960) in which he asserts that the infant, in his utterly resourceless state, depends on the mother's 'holding' capacity. These two papers, although published quite separately, had been given at the same conference, the International Congress of Psycho-Analysis in Edinburgh in 1962. I think that it was partly my awareness that these two papers had at least been given at the same congress that led me to explore links further. I must have had in the midst of my confusion some idea that there were links since I could not discern in my own behaviour nor in that of the people around me, especially in my patients, that profound a difference between what I regarded as personal and internal mental experience, and what I witnessed as social behaviour in therapy groups and more generally in other social contexts. Whereas I could acknowledge the separateness of 'holding' and 'containing' within their respective theories of origin, and whereas I could recognise and respect other different emphases and implications of those larger theories, I could not differentiate their importance for the infant's relationship to the mother at a crucial point in development. It is vital to grasp that there is an essential difference in the focus used in these two concepts.

'Containing' refers essentially to the mother's capacity to receive, through projective identification, primitive elements of experience (not of whole persons), and to make the 'contained' available for the infant to take them back in a modified form into its awareness, in order for it, the child, to be able the more to understand its experience – modified, that is, by the mother's functioning. It is something of an anomaly, therefore, to think of the group as a container.

Whilst I appreciate that the group can be seen as the container as clearly described by Zinkin (1989a), I wish to distinguish that usage from the one implied here, since this process demands a more active commitment to the task of understanding than Zinkin implies. There are certainly resistances to this process in all of us, but if these can be clarified the likelihood of the group-as-a-whole becoming a container is enhanced. This difference of opinion is similar to that which I have with Brown (see below).

Winnicott's 'holding', on the other hand, does imply a notion of 'the total situation', and it is the binocular view of the minutiae on the one hand, and the 'total view' on the other, which makes for a productive result, in using these two concepts together, provided that one gives due respect to the complexity and different emphases of the two concepts.

In relation to groups, Bion's (1961) theory about the phenomena observed in groups is at first sight radically different from that of Foulkes' (1964) work on these phenomena. The technique of each school seems quite different, and of course there are different aims in the techniques. The theories are different, and so different phenomena are emphasised. The methodology of using groups for therapeutic purposes is at first sight radically different. But let us suppose that while a Foulkesian group analyst is looking at the 'matrix', and an observer with Winnicott's concept of 'holding' in mind is attempting to evaluate the reconstruction in the group of previously deficient holding experiences, yet a third observer (and one steeped in Bion's notion of 'containing') is seeing that task for the individual in using the setting to understand his or her own behaviour, and that of others, and is taking a view that the group is able to provide that function. Can we possibly conceptualise that all those things are going on? It would be folly to think that they were not, and many more besides, each with their own descriptive piece of theory somewhere.

I have elsewhere (James 1981) drawn attention on the one hand to the well-recognised differences in emphasis between Bion's views of group phenomena and those of Foulkes, whilst also drawing attention to marked similarities and valuable overlappings. These two theories present the practitioner in group work and the participant in understanding his or her experience in a group setting, with the possibility of something 'new' being discovered.

Bollas (1987) has written on object relations theory and early experiences with the object. Seen as a direct extension of Winnicott's work, it implies that early experiences cast a shadow as a record of early experience on the developing person. We might know something about this experience but might not have thought it. Bollas focuses on evidence for this phenomenon in individual work, but I would extend this to our experiences in groups, but we need the opportunity to learn how to think about that experience.

I hope to demonstrate that from the background of his psychoanalytic work which Bion brings to the group field, we see so many of the very basic elements of human development and experience in the very space of the group. There is something fundamental in being able to see the very earliest phenomena of development, repeated time and again in the group, and it is the difference of approach which makes the exploration of the theories of these three men so fascinating. The consensus suggests that group behaviour is not something that 'just happens' in groups, but is of a primary nature, and implies as Bion (1961) mentions, that the individual, for his or her fuller development, needs groups.

I shall attempt to tease out the elements from these various theories that depict a similarity of concern from quite different theoretical backgrounds and approaches. I shall outline the main hypothesis of Foulkes' theory, of Winnicott's theory, and of Bion's theory respectively, in order to enhance our understanding of a person's experience in a group set up to study such phenomena; but perhaps more importantly to understand the relevance of one's own experience in a group setting in terms of what it can tell us about the individual's experience in the social sphere. It is hoped that this exercise will enable us to get a deeper view of the individual's experience as a citizen of the world with all that that implies for the person concerned, but, as importantly, for what it implies for large-group and societal phenomena.

Both Bion and Winnicott describe the dependency of the baby on its mother, Winnicott emphasising the resourcelessness of the infant, utterly dependent for long periods of time. The interaction with the concerned and attentive mother strengthens the infant towards being able to deal with dependency on her, and her 'containing' and 'holding' capacities further the individual's development.

It might seem fanciful to think of the dependency of the infant as in any way related to the experience of an adult in relation to a group, and yet, if as Foulkes and Bion and many others believed, the essential milieu for the individual is the 'social', then it would seem that just as the baby 'needs' mother in order to survive and develop socially and personally, so adults would 'need' to be able to function and relate in the group in which they find themselves. Here, I believe, there is a close relationship between Bion and Winnicott, and paradoxically between Bion and Foulkes. The ramifications behind each of their formulations to arrive at that point are historic and well known. What is sadly missed so often, is the fact that in recognising that common point, we might be able to understand the differences, not as polarised and in conflict, but very much as different emphases and aspects of a common whole.

To facilitate this I shall look at the central concept of the group matrix according to Foulkes, and then the development of the concept of holding according to Winnicott, and finally the concept of containing or container/contained according to Bion.

Whilst we may make links between these three theories, I wish to share my experience that only when I can view each in the context within which they developed can I see the similarities and respect the differences. I believe that only from that position can we make further progress in understanding group processes from a psychodynamic perspective.

## FOULKES' GROUP MATRIX

The interacting psychological processes taking place in a group involve the individuals in different specific ways and constellations: 'Just as the individual's mind is a complex of interacting processes (Personal Matrix), mental processes interact in the concert of the group (Group Matrix)' (Foulkes 1973).

Foulkes saw the essence of man as being social and not individual. This view has been extensively studied and elaborated by Behr and Hearst (1982), who point out that it is the group which is the basic psychological unit, though the biological unit is the individual organism. The matrix, as seen by Behr and Hearst, is the basis of all relationships and communication, a web of intrapsychic, interpersonal, and transpersonal interrelationships within which the individual is conceptualised as a nodal point. Foulkes thought that in group analysis what is reproduced is the matrix of evolving personality. He saw the group-analytic method as imposing within the group setting the individual's task of sorting out his or her relationship to other people, to the group-as-a-whole and to the leader. The group matrix is the operational basis of all relationships and communications. Foulkes conceptualised the individual as a nodal point in a network of relationships, borrowing an analogy from Goldstein of a neuron being the nodal point in a total network of the nervous system, which always reacts and responds as a whole. An aphorism of Foulkes' was, 'As in the case of the neuron in the nervous system so is the individual suspended in the group matrix'.

From what I have said already in relation to Winnicott's concept of holding and Bion's concept of containing, each with their emphases on the role of the mother at an early phase of development, I find it interesting to note that the Oxford English Dictionary refers to the origin of the word 'matrix' from the Latin for 'womb', and particularly to the definition of a matrix as 'a place or medium in which something is bred, produced, or developed'.

I trust that this brief view of Foulkes' concept of the matrix, which can be compared particularly with Andrew Powell's chapter, will be sufficient for the present time.

## WINNICOTT'S HOLDING

An important aspect of Winnicott's concern about infant development is the emerging of a sense of the social, of the world outside of oneself, of oneself and mother as a pair in relation to other members of the family, but unquestionably also of a sense of a social sphere that is important. Throughout his work he is concerned with the differentiation of 'self', a self in relation to an 'other' and a self in relation to other people in the world. In both his papers 'Psychoses and child care' (1952) and 'Transitional objects and transitional phenomena' (1951), he talks of the need to recognise three areas of experiencing:

> It is generally acknowledged that a statement of human nature in terms of inter-personal relationships is not good enough even when the imaginative elaboration of function and the whole phantasy both conscious and unconscious,...are allowed for....Of every in-dividual who has reached to the stage of being a unit with a limiting membrane and an outside and an inside, it can be said that there is an inner reality to that individual, an inner world that can be rich or poor and can be at peace or in a state of war.
>
> (1951: 230)

Winnicott pointed out that while being able to differentiate between an inner and outer reality, there was also a need to recognise a third area. The third part of the life of a human being is an intermediate area of experiencing, to which inner reality and external life both contribute. Winnicott's concept of the transitional object is the beginning of this exploration about this intermediate or third area of experiencing, and it is this statement that for me forms the link between Winnicott's ideas to those of Foulkes. In a previous paper (James 1982), I attempted to draw similarities between Winnicott's descriptions of the experiencing of this third area and the links which Foulkes makes about the interrelatedness of people in a group, to emphasise the similarities of the extension of Winnicott's concepts of the transitional object and transitional phenomena, and their importance in the gaining of a sense of the 'social', to a recognition of the importance of Foulkes' concept of the matrix as a construct with considerable explanatory power to describe the experience of a person in a group. On the other hand, in making this link between certain aspects of Winnicott's theory and certain aspects of those of Foulkes I was mindful of the impact of development on the social sense on the one hand, and of the repetition of early experiences in group settings as portrayed by Foulkes' theory, on the other. It was also this seemingly similar emphasis with very different backgrounds which led me to attempt to make a further link with Bion's theories.

It is from the concept of a 'shared illusory space' between infant and mother, which Winnicott studied and described, that later (1960) led him to examine in more detail the relationship between parent and infant, and to develop the concept of 'holding'. He accepts that to begin with we have to see the baby not as such, but as part of an infant–environment unit, and goes on to delineate the relationship and the dependency on 'mother' implicit in the infant's condition. His well-known phrase 'there · is no such thing as a baby', comes from his assertion that the inherited potential of the infant cannot become an infant unless linked to maternal care. The concept of 'holding' is used by Winnicott to denote not just the physical holding of the infant, but the total provision of physical and emotional concern which the ordinary mother gives to her infant. He implies a very important phase in de- velopment, subsequently leading to a relationship, in his phrase 'the total environmental provision, prior to a concept of "living with" ' (1960: 43).

In the earliest phases he saw the infant as being maximally dependent on the mother, and he described, in utmost detail, the delicate state of moving from utter dependency to relative dependency, stressing throughout the force in the individual always, normally, moving towards independence.

Winnicott saw that the infant was able eventually to clarify the boundary between inner reality and external reality *from a position of shared reality*; a deficit in the capacity to share from the mother's side or on the infant's part led to a deficit in the later development of independence, and interdependence. The latter term refers to the adult capacity to be able to 'contribute-in' to relationships, as well as to receive from others. This feature of his work is pertinent to the task of an individual in a group relating to other members of the group, and to the group-as-a-whole. Quite often, people have difficulty in this task in group settings, because of earlier difficulties, which is not to say that relating in group settings is ever easy for any adult.

In his paper on transitional objects and transitional phenomena, Winnicott (1951) was concerned with the earliest phases of human development, and maintained that the events in these earliest phases influence profoundly the organisation and development of the personality, referring particularly to the capacity for separation and individuation, and to the ability to develop a true sense of self. Winnicott was particularly concerned with the process involving the development of a sense of self, as opposed to a 'false-sense' of self, which he saw as being present in many disturbed patients. A sense of self would be seen as a requirement for the capacity to relate to other selves, and this aspect of his work is particularly pertinent to our present task of understanding the nature of relationships with others, especially in a group setting.

Winnicott's concern with the intermediate area of experiencing, the shared illusory space, is of particular importance in our understanding of shared group experience.

His emphasis on the importance of the 'carer' – namely, the mother – in the earliest phases of life, resonates into our adult social experience; we need to be part of that shared experience, and the adult 'carer' part of us needs to guard and enhance the value of that shared space.

Another way to conceptualise the link is to say that in the holding phase the infant is maximally dependent, and this varies from absolute to relative dependency, and towards independence. Winnicott's sustained emphasis of the similarity between infant care and psychoanalytic care is a feature of his contribution to our understanding of the importance of environmental factors, from the earliest phases of life, in contributing to and maintaining the possibility of normal mental health.

In his extension of the concept of the transitional object, Winnicott (1971a) wrote of cultural experience as being located in the space between the individual and the environment. This lends itself to be looked at in the context of the group and also implies the importance of experiencing oneself as part of a group in order to be able to experience 'culture'.

## BION'S CONTAINING

Wilfred Bion (1961, 1962a, 1962b, 1963, 1970, 1979) approached this whole area from a different background, and though he had more direct experiences with groups than Winnicott, there are some close links between the two theories. I do not wish to make these theories appear similar to each other. This would be a simplistic view, since the backgrounds from which these concepts originate are complex and quite different from each other. I am not in this presentation going to examine these differences in approach and theories between Foulkes and Bion in relation to phenomena in groups *per se*.

There is much work to be done in this area. Brown (1985) has made a clear contribution to this task but looks at the differences between Foulkes and Bion in terms of approach and technique, whilst I believe that there are similarities and differences between Bion and Foulkes. Here I am trying to look at phenomena that might underlie those differences. Bion (1952) stated his intention to show that the adult in his or her contact with the complexities of life in a group, resorts, in what may be a massive regression, to mechanisms typical of the earliest phases of emotional life, and pointed out that the adult must establish contact with the emotional life of the group in which he or she lives. He saw this task as *appearing as formidable to the adult as the relationship with the breast appears to be with the infant.*

I am going to look at the psychoanalytical background of Bion's theories in order to clarify links with Winnicott's theories about development and with Foulkes' theories about the matrix, in an attempt to extend and deepen our concept of the matrix not merely as something social and external but having profound roots in the inner world of the individual, involved in the matrix and in the earliest phases of development.

Central throughout Bion's work is the concept of projective identification (Klein 1946). This refers to a group of phantasies and accompanying object relations having to do with the ridding of the self of its unwanted aspects and the depositing of those unwanted 'parts' into another person, and, finally, with the 'recovery' of a modified version of what was extruded. In his 'A theory of thinking' (1962a), Bion outlines a scheme that is at first sight complicated partly because of the language he uses, but which, inherited potentialities notwithstanding, implies that the capacity to develop a thinking apparatus depends on the interaction in the earliest phases of life with mother. Here there is a similarity to Winnicott's theory. The outcome, however, of Bion's formulations is radically different.

As a model, Bion uses the hypothesis that the infant has an inborn disposition, a preconception corresponding to an expectation, of the breast. When a preconception such as this is brought into contact with the realisation that approximates to it, the mental outcome is a conception. Bion puts this in another way: the preconception of an inborn expectation of the breast, the prior knowledge of a breast, the empty thought – this preconception mates with an awareness of the realisation when the infant is brought into contact with the breast itself, and this mating is synchronous with the development of a conception.

Bion further uses this model to serve for the hypothesis that every junction of a preconception with its realisation produces a conception, and that, therefore, a conception will be expected to be constantly conjoined with an emotional experience of satisfaction. Bion, however, limits the term 'thought' to a mating of a preconception with a frustration. Thus he proposed that an infant whose expectation of the breast is mated with the realisation of 'no-breast-available-for-satisfaction', experiences a sense of 'no-breast' or 'an absent breast' inside. Then the infant has to make a decision, either to evade the frustration or to modify it, and this step depends on the infant's capacity for toleration of frustration and on the relationship with the mother. If the capacity for toleration of frustration is sufficient, then no-breast-inside becomes a thought, and an apparatus for thinking it develops.

Although this hypothesis seems complicated, if we follow the idea that a personality capable of maturity ultimately recognises a notion of an absence and emptiness inside, or a 'no-breast-inside' as a bad internal object, then this personality ultimately recognises the bad internal no-breast as a thought. A capacity for tolerating frustration thus enables the psyche to develop thoughts as a means by which the frustration that is tolerated is itself made more tolerable.

If, however, the capacity for toleration of frustration is inadequate, the bad internal no-breast confronts the psyche with the need to decide between modification or evasion. The end result of this part of Bion's hypothesis is that all thoughts are treated as though they were indistinguishable from bad internal objects. What should be a 'thought', the product of the juxtaposition of a preconception and a negative realisation, becomes a bad object indistinguishable from a thing in itself and fit only for evacuation. Consequently, the development of an apparatus for thinking is disturbed, and instead a hypertrophic development of the apparatus for projective identification takes place. If frustration can be tolerated, the mating of conception and realisation, whether negative or positive, initiates procedures necessary to learning by experience. Bion relates the development of the capacity to tolerate frustration as being intimately linked with the contact and perception of the relationship and experience of, and with, the mother. If the mother can appear to contain the evacuated elements in this process, they can be re-experienced, re-integrated and a capacity for development of thinking grows. If, however, the mother cannot tolerate the projected elements, the infant is reduced to having to continue projective identification, instead of developing thinking, with increasing force and frequency.

In *Elements of Psychoanalysis* (1963), Bion postulates that the most primitive experience is governed by what he calls 'beta-elements', which are the raw elements of sensuous and emotional experience in which psychical and physical are indistinguishable, and which lend themselves only to projective identification. These elements are experienced in a concrete manner, as if they are lumps of faeces or bad emotions, which are evacuated into a breast that is not there. As the infant does this, the mother, the good object, turns no-breast into a breast and replaces, as far as the infant is concerned, the frightening, anxious experience into a more positive one by virtue of the feeding and holding situation which she provides. The infant experiences, according to Bion's postulate, that the beta-elements, the primitive-experience elements, are transformed by the breast, which is shorthand for the total experience with the mother at that point, into alpha-elements which have psychic meaning and which can be stored, repressed, elaborated further and symbolised. These are the elements of dream-thoughts, and the transformation from beta to alpha gives sense and meaning to the infant's experience, via the mother's response to the infant's projection.

Bion's conception of the container and the contained is a model for an object helping the infant to sort out those aspects of communication that are at first inchoately emotional. In order for projective identification to occur, there must be a conception of a container into which the projection can be sent. In other words (Grotstein 1981), if the maternal response to the infant's need is adequate, the infant can re-introject the breast as a container capable of performing other functions, the function of converting beta-elements into alpha-elements. This model of the conjunction of the container and the contained extends the basic model for the development of thought, to the perception of relationship and to transference and countertransference interplay. It provides the basis for a differentiation between the psychotic and non-psychotic functioning of the personality. The relationship between the container and the contained can be symbiotic, providing a basis of fruitful relationships and learning from experience, or it can be experienced as mutually destructive.

The assumption from Winnicott's concept of holding is that the maternal preoccupation towards the needs of the infant supports and contains the inherited potentialities of the infant, towards the development and strengthening of the ego and towards the development of independence (which, of course, is never complete in any human life).

Bion's theory, on the other hand, focuses on the minutiae of the developments of either the capacity to tolerate frustration and to use benign projective identification to model on the mother's alpha-function towards the development of alpha-function independently, and from there to be able to develop thoughts about one's own experience of frustration; *or*, if the mother's containing function is deficient, then projective identification used by the infant remains or becomes excessive, and there is a distortion in the development of a capacity for containing thoughts.

In Winnicott's (1969) article on 'The use of an object and relating through identification', we arrive at a position very similar to Bion's, in which the development of a capacity to use the mother in order to develop oneself depends on the mother's ability to survive (the infant's hate). The holding function of the mother is very close here to the containing function of the mother, in Bion's terms.

The importance for group analysis of these theories, and the phenomena that they attempt to describe, is that, implied within Foulkes' concept of the social context of the individual's life, are elements of both Winnicott's 'holding' function and Bion's 'containing' function. It is my own contention that the psychoanalytic emphasis of Bion's theory and Winnicott's theory respectively will enable us to understand and utilise more fully our understanding of the individual's experience within the matrix.

The essentially psychoanalytic emphasis of each of these theories rests on the inner psychic experience of the individual in his or her task, within the group, of maintaining a balanced view of both inside and outside.

While these phenomena are universal in small groups, they are also prevalent in larger groups, whose very source and nature prevent initially their being regarded as anything remotely likely to lead to an understanding of these experiences.

It is interesting to learn from De Mare (1991) (and Chapter 13 in this volume) of his hypothesis that it is only in a median group or even perhaps a larger group, that true 'dialogue' can take place. I assume that this is after the individuals have become accustomed to the threat of the more anxious aspects of larger gatherings. Friere (1972) suggests that dialogue can only take place when the person on the receiving end of one's communications is regarded as a human being.

Friere's concern is with the releasing of human capacities which are otherwise repressed by societies, and particularly by a failure to communicate social experience in language. It is a contention of Trist (1987) that for our very survival in the world as it is today, we as human beings learn to communicate in larger and larger groups, and that our citizenship will be enhanced by the experience, and by our increasing capacity to serve as representatives for larger and larger groups. This resonates for me with the 'carer' role of the participant in a small group, and is based on the divergence between being afraid and anxious of the 'group', whilst at the same time being connected, and seeking group experience. Is this not in line with what Bion describes of the infant's experience with the mother (albeit represented initially by the breast), and Winnicott's contention of the infant's and therefore the eventual adult's dependence on the capacity of the mother to help the infant from the stage of being resourceless and dependent, to being able to use the 'object' in order to enhance its sense of self, and to participate in experience with an 'other' and 'others' for its very own development?

But why are larger groups more anxious places, especially if we follow some of the lines of thought developed here? If there is a need for group and social experience, why are people anxious about it? Although the unconscious destructive forces in human beings must be accepted and worked with, is there not a problem in terms of organisation and development of human groupings which might not yet have enabled us to see the value of being able to be comfortable in large-group settings? The study of the large group can be fruitful (see Kreeger 1975). Turquet (1975), wrote about the anxieties in the large group as being worthy of study for what one learns not only about the individual, but on the more positive side, what of value one learns of the large group, for itself, and for the individual's benefit.

In appreciating the impact of Bion's work, not so much on groups as in his prophetic sense of going to the heart of the matter, Lawrence (1985) describes the frustrating work of 'learning' in groups. In describing the learning experience, specifically in relation to working conferences, the emphasis is on the use of groups for learning – learning the dangers of some group phenomena and of the immense value of others, leading to a respect and valuing of the group as a necessary means of challenging the individual to trust the personal–group interaction. There are echoes here, again, of the frustration which the infant experiences in Bion's terms when a satisfaction which is expected is not achieved.

Lawrence continues the theme to the learning about, or forging of, the capacity to overcome the anxieties and see further than one might dare imagine; of the value of the group, not as representing a mother-breast-container-comforter, but as a source of the capacity to strengthen one's resolve to understand immensely complicated issues concerning the interaction. There are a myriad links from this position to other aspects of large-group phenomena, and this links with De Mare's ideas referred to above.

This has been taken a step further in looking at the impact of dreams, not in small groups, but in larger gatherings (Lawrence 1991). In following a theme which he discovered in the relevance of the use of dreams in a study group, his explorations led to investigation of the impact of local and more widespread interpersonal and social issues which impinge *into* one's very dreams. The residues of the day described by Freud might not be 'just' residues; they may be deep manifestations of the impact of the social matrix on the more personal 'manifest' content of a person's dreams. The 'social dream matrix' is a pertinent way of exploring further the interaction of the person with the group, and vice versa.

Foulkes' notion of individuals being connected with a matrix in an ongoing group might be merely the start of our understanding of the importance of our interaction with the 'social' environment, with what Foulkes called the 'foundation matrix'.

Turquet (1975) writes of his work in large-group settings. While he emphasises the difficulties and anxieties which people experience in such settings, his overall view is of the value of the learning experience in such settings. Like Khaleelee and Miller (1985), Turquet reports his experience largely from training settings organised with the specific purpose of studying and learning about the difficulties of how organisations function.

Khaleelee and Miller report on their experience in the Group Relations Training Programme of the Tavistock Institute of Human Relations (the Leicester Conference). There is evidence in their work in studying society and in consulting to organisations, from an organisation-as-a-whole perspective, of the concern which the individual has about society. They say that 'by defining a task boundary it is possible to evoke, experience and observe societal dynamics in a group; society and the group are present in the individual'. This resonates with Armstrong's notion of 'the organisation in one's head'; a notion that we carry in us a view of the organisation in which we find ourselves, which influences our perception of the phenomena (Armstrong 1991a and b, and 1992).

The task of such programmes is to attempt to understand and encourage participants to understand this experience in large settings. The evidence is that the individual's understanding of themselves influences the actual phenomena experienced. Much of the time people are not consciously in touch with these phenomena. The anxiety due to the awesomeness and awareness of our deprivation if we are not in touch with this group element is an essential component of our existence.

## CONCLUDING COMMENTS

I shall finish by tracing, as I see it, the line of development from the most dependent infant to the most mature citizen. I do this in order to understand some of the things societies need in order to function optimally.

The sequence which Bion describes in his paper on the theory of thinking, involves modification of frustration by the individual. This, as I have summarised, depends on mother's containing capacity. The frustration which is tolerated makes way for the development of thoughts. Thoughts have, according to Bion, to be worked on to make them available. For thoughts to be translated into action involves 'publication', which is regarded by Bion to be the making of sense-data available to consciousness. Because the individual is a political animal and, according to Bion, cannot find fulfilment outside a group nor satisfaction of any emotional drive without expression of its social component, so, as the infant can tolerate frustration and begin to 'think' about his or her experience, so the citizen has to be able to understand his or her experience in relation to society. The more that this is achieved, the more effective and valuable society becomes.

Alongside our social needs we have our narcissistic needs and these have to be balanced in our roles as citizens. Whereas the individual depends on the group or society, society functions in proportion to the involvement of the individuals of which it is made up.

We would all agree that the aim of the individual is to develop an identity, a sense of self, and to be able to relate to others with optimum pleasure and responsibility. The parallel between the infant's relationship to its 'container' or its holding environment on the one hand, and that of the individual to the group, on the other, is to my mind self-evident. I believe this analogy can also be applied to larger systems, and see a need for each 'citizen' to be comfortable and responsible in that role.

From much of the work of the authors quoted in this chapter, one gets a sense of the interdependence of the individual, the group, and society. This was stated eloquently by Joan Riviere in 1936:

Another point, which economists realise much better perhaps than other people do, is the degree of dependence of the human organism on its surroundings. In a stable political and economic system there is a great deal of apparent liberty and opportunity to fulfil our own needs, and we do not as a rule feel our dependence on the organisation in which we live – unless, for instance, there is an earthquake or a strike! Then we may realise with reluctance and often with resentment that we are dependent on the forces of nature or on other people to a terrifying extent. Dependence is felt to be dangerous because it involves the possibility of privation. An unrealisable desire for individual self-sufficiency may arise, and an illusion of an independent liberty may under certain conditions of life be indulged in as a pleasure in itself.

(Riviere (1936) in Hughes 1991: 171)

# Chapter 6

# Self development through subjective interaction
## A fresh look at 'ego training in action'

*Dennis Brown*

As a psychoanalyst who came later to group analysis, I shall attempt in the present chapter to describe and explain a process characteristic of well-functioning small stranger groups, and not of individual analysis. It contributes, I believe, an important element to what are experienced as 'good sessions' in group work. It forms the basis for actually becoming more fully oneself in reciprocity with others. Psychoanalysis can be only a preparation for such a move. The most concise term I can find for this process is 'self development through subjective interaction'. It is more specific than Foulkes' expression 'ego training in action', and nearer to the clinical experience I wish to describe. Later in the chapter it will be illustrated with three vignettes: The Man Who Could Not Understand; The Woman Who Would Not Feel Understood; and The Drowsy Group, Including the Conductor.

Exploration of the process requires consideration of the concept of intersubjectivity. While the development of intersubjectivity is indirectly recognised as important in modern psychoanalysis – for example, in the emphasis now given to countertransference and unconscious interaction between the personalities of analysand and analyst – I will argue that in group analysis the achievement of awareness of intersubjectivity with a *range* of other personalities, not restricted to the analyst, and in their presence, powerfully promotes maturity and a capacity to engage in mutually validating relationships.

Others come to be treated as subjects rather than objects, partly because they demand it. The exploration of each individual's private inner world occurs against the background of the inner worlds of others within the developing matrix of the group (see Chapter 2, by Powell). It is augmented by tacit encouragement to discover how internalised relationships, rooted in the past, can distort and limit engagement in new and more satisfactory relationships based on the actuality and potentiality of the experiences of self and others.

## 'EGO TRAINING IN ACTION'

Foulkes characterised psychoanalysis as 'vertical' analysis, conducted in an asymmetrical relationship and emphasising the detailed recon-struction of the past of the individual patient. In contrast, group analysis is 'horizontal' analysis, conducted within a circle of equals, among whom problems rooted in the past can be played out and modified (Foulkes and Anthony 1965: 42). This allows what Foulkes describes as 'ego training in action'.

> 'Action' here does not mean doing or, literally, acting or role play-ing; nor is it the equivalent of 'acting out' in psychoanalysis. The group provides a stage for actions, reactions and interactions within the therapeutic situation, which are denied to the psycho-analytic patient on the couch. However, the ego to which we refer is the ego in the psycho-analytic sense, the inner ego as a metapsychological concept, which is activated and reformed.
>
> (Foulkes 1964: 82)

Foulkes' description of the process of therapy as 'ego training in action' originated in the prominence of Freud's structural theory during his training in Vienna, and in his early professional practice in Germany and Britain. According to this theory, the personality is divided into the instinct-dominated id, the conscience-carrying superego, and the adapt-ive and mediating ego. The ego is the seat of conflict resolution, signal anxiety, defence, and of reality testing: appraising stimuli from within and outside the individual.

Gradually, Freud had moved some way from a purely one-body psychology. He had written of the character of the ego as a 'precipitate of abandoned object-cathexes' (Freud 1923: 29), and realised the im-portance of identification (Freud 1921: 105ff). In the ego defence mechanism of 'identification with the aggressor', Anna Freud (1936: 109ff) pointed to the interchangeability of self and object representa-tions, later to be described in detail by Jacobson (1964). Recently Bollas (1987) has written about the ego embodying rules for relating to the primary object, mother. It 'develops "rules" for processing intrapsychic and intersubjective experience. . .as mother and child negotiate para-digms for processing all of a life's experience' (p. 72). We could also say, however, that it comes to embody rules for relating to various constellations in the family network, and to the social context, to differentiate but also to connect and belong.

Thus, in a review of modern views of the ego, Padel (1985) draws attention to four ego functions, which will be strikingly familiar to a group analyst: (1) scanning of the field; (2) dividing it with alternation of attention between at least two features, and exploration of each from the vantage point of the other; (3) re-uniting it and viewing the field from a third position; and (4) refinding each object by identifying with the other.

This last function is especially interesting, as it involves moving beyond 'asymmetrical' discriminatory functions towards the complementary 'symmetrical' thinking included by Matte-Blanco (1975) in his theory of bi-logic. The latter allows the discernment of analogies and connectedness, and thus the possibility of self–object de-differentiation (Milner 1987). This type of thinking is necessary for empathy, intuition, and the experience of being part of something that includes oneself, whether a dyad, a group, a species, or the cosmos (see chapters by Blackwell and Powell in this volume). It could be considered as playing a part in what Foulkes called 'resonance' in groups.

As a psychoanalyst, Foulkes was ahead of his time with his ideas of the individual as an abstraction, a nodal point in a network, of the interchangeability of figure and ground, of context and what happens in it, of inside and outside, and of disturbance being located between people. However, during the time Foulkes was developing the theory and practice of group analysis, and was not involved in the development of psychoanalytic theory itself, the latter was being radically affected by object relations theory, and to a lesser extent by self psychology. Like group analysis, both of these emphasise relationships, and the interactional and contextual element in individual development and functioning. In that sense they have moved further away from a one-body, purely biologically based theory towards a theory of interacting systems: intrapersonal, interpersonal, and – in the case of group analysis – social; hence the title of this volume, *The Psyche and the Social World*. Both types of analysis – group and individual – are increasingly being seen as occurring in overlapping subjective worlds. Indeed, it is interesting that the psychoanalyst Klauber (1987: 24), recently and quite independently of Foulkes, distinguished between vertical analysis, based on the individual patient's history, and horizontal analysis, based on transactions in the present between patient and analyst.

## 'SELF DEVELOPMENT THROUGH SUBJECTIVE INTERACTION'

I propose that Foulkes' visionary views, laid out in his first book (Foulkes 1948), and the subsequent advances in analytical thinking, call for the idea of 'ego training in action' to be amplified to allow for a circular and spiral movement that includes: (1) discovering how we experience and relate to others in terms of our inner worlds of internal object relationships; (2) discerning how these experiences rooted in the past can be transformed into more flexible new experiences in the shared world of 'here and now'; and (3) learning to attune ourselves to other people, and to make sense of them and their experience as well as our own. Such learning requires the development of a capacity for empathic sensitivity that increases our relatedness to others, through both identification and differentiation. This final achievement is, paradoxically, near to the point from which we all, to varying extents, start; it involves the unfolding of capacities central to the early infant–mother relationship, as Stern (1985) has argued on the basis of developmental research. Mutual responses between the subjective experiences of infant and mother are the building blocks of the baby's sense of self. This three-phase process is what I shall refer to as '*self development through subjective interaction*'. It involves the recognition and development of a sense of intersubjectivity.

## INTERSUBJECTIVITY

Conceptualising the processes of the discovery of inner worlds, discerning new opportunities to transcend blocks rooted in them, and learning to relate to others in empathic mutuality, can draw not only on developmental studies but also on both object relations theory and self psychology. Foulkes acknowledged neither directly. However, as Malcolm Pines noted in his foreword to Foulkes' *Selected Papers* (Foulkes 1990: xv), Foulkes thought not of internal objects – isolated, intrapsychic representations of key figures to whom instinctual drives are directed – but of internal object relationships. Although he never wrote specifically about object relationships or subjectivity, his work is pervaded by the idea of *subject–object relations,* or even *intersubjective relations.* This might need some explaining.

In an examination of the close parallel between the views of Foulkes and those of the French phenomenologist Merleau-Ponty, Cohn (1991) points out that experience of oneself inevitably means experience of oneself in the context of relationships with others – as Foulkes said (1948: 10), the isolated individual is an artificial abstraction. In phenomenological terms, meaning and significance occur not inside people, but between them; namely, in intersubjectivity.   As Merleau-Ponty (1964: 134) puts it: '[The] subject is no longer alone, is no longer conscious in general or pure being-for-itself. He is in the midst of unconsciousnesses which likewise have a situation'. In dialogue between one person and another, 'my thought and his are interwoven into a single fabric, my words and those of my interlocutor are called forth by the state of the discussion, and they are inserted into a shared opinion of which neither of us is the creator' (Merleau-Ponty 1976: 354). Cohn points out the correspondence between Merleau-Ponty's 'single fabric' and Foulkes' idea of the group matrix, 'the common ground which ultimately determines the meaning and significance of all events and upon which all communications and interpretations, verbal and nonverbal, rest' (Foulkes 1964: 292).

Gordon (1991) has recently written persuasively about the role of intersubjectivity in group psychotherapy. This 'union or contact of the subjectivities' demands reformulation of traditional ideas of subject–object, I–you. Gordon writes, 'In the intersubjective realm there is no inner or outer, only a body of contact and experience which expresses itself in a "consummate reciprocity" in which we discover ourselves through the other' (1991: 43). This describes very vividly the everyday experience of life in an analytic group.

In Chapter 26 of his *Selected Papers* (Foulkes 1990), dictated in his last year of life and entitled 'Concerning criticism of inner-object theory', Foulkes argues for a distinction between experiential and metapsychological processes. He states that internal mental processes are not created by individuals in isolation, but originate in the context of a multipersonal network of interaction. The individual is stamped with these experiences in the primary family, and tends to re-experience and re-create them in later contexts. But, Foulkes insists, 'the more mature and free a person becomes to function as a *whole* person in relation to other persons, the more will these processes lose in importance and significance'.

The mediator for the encounter between self and other, Merleau-Ponty argues, is language. This accords with the primacy of communication in group analysis, of making articulate what could not previously be put into words.

It is only retrospectively, when I have withdrawn from the dialogue and am recalling it, that I am able to integrate it into my life and make it an episode in my private history, and that other recedes into his absence, or, insofar as he remains, is felt as a threat.

(Merleau-Ponty 1976: 354-5)

However, as I see it, integrating the dialogue established in inter-subjectivity plays a part in transforming old structures based on rigid internal object relationships, and reduces that threat. Sharing promotes recognition that others are not just objects to be desired or feared. They have their own valid viewpoints and feelings. This recognition opens the way to empathy, withdrawal of projections and stereotyping, and the attainment of mutual concern between members of the group.

George Klein, in his influential attempt to formulate a clinical as opposed to a meta-psychological theory of psychoanalysis, pointed out that psychoanalysts had lacked a concept of 'we-ness'. This has its prototype in the mother–infant unit and continues as an essential part of identity. He states that

The terminology of subject and object has contributed to misleading conceptualisations of selfhood and especially to obscuring its 'we' aspect. The traditional view of man as becoming gradually aware of himself as 'subject' confronting others as 'object' may be applicable *morphologically* but it does not describe dynamic wholes. Identity must always be defined as having aspects of both separateness and membership in a more encompassing entity, and as developing functions that reflect one's role in a relationship to that larger entity.

(Klein 1976:178)

This 'Janus-faced view' of the relationship of the individual to the other contrasts markedly with Bion's view of the inevitable struggle of the individual in the group as corresponding to that of the infant in relation to the breast, and of the group as only an illusion (Bion 1961); a view I have contrasted with that of Foulkes (Brown 1985). One could just as well say the individual is an illusion, or that both the group and the individuals in it are illusions. It is here that the idea of intersubjectivity proves useful. Groups can certainly share illusions, but a therapeutic group provides a way of exposing illusions, and of modifying them by intersubjective validation.

Atwood and Stolorow (1984: 41) have pointed out that individual psychoanalysis can be viewed as 'a science of the *intersubjective* focused on the interplay between the differently organised subjective worlds of the observer and the observed'. Group analysis can also be approached as a study of intersubjectivity, focusing on the interplay of the subjective worlds of group members, including the conductor. According to Atwood and Stolorow (1984: 52), negative therapeutic reactions in psychoanalysis can be seen as 'most often a product of prolonged, unrecognised transference-countertransference disjunctions and the chronic misunderstandings that result'. Just as this can occur in the 'bi-personal field' of psychoanalysis, so it can occur in the 'multi-personal field' of group analysis. But here it is less likely, as harmful collusions between individual patient and therapist can be observed and challenged by others. This might be one reason why groups can help people who have become stuck in interminable individual analyses – intersubjective impasse is open to scrutiny by others.

Intersubjectivity is an important aspect of relationships from early infancy onwards, but the notion of internal object relationships seems unavoidable in the present state of our understanding. To make sense of this, philosophical ideas have to be augmented by ideas originating in infant observation and clinical experience.

## THE DEVELOPMENT OF INTERNAL OBJECT RELATIONS

Turning to the early development of the individual, it is reasonable to suppose that the groundwork of a coherent subjective sense of self precedes the establishment of internal representations of the self in relation to others (Stern 1985). Empathic mirroring and containment by mother precede the infant's experience of her as a clearly separate object. Whether she is the object of instinctual drives or the focus of powerful wishes is a distinction which can still be left open, as pointed out by Greenberg and Mitchell (1985) in their thorough examination of the contributions of the principal object relations theorists – including Balint, Fairbairn, Klein, and Winnicott in Britain, Jacobson, Modell, and Mahler in the United States. It is relationships that are internalised.

Kernberg (1980), attempting to integrate the work of these pioneers with ego psychology, has built up a case for viewing internal object relationships as composed of subject-object-affect units. These units gradually develop into more complex sub-structures, such as real and ideal self and object representations in the internal world. These internal representations and relationships originate in the subjective experience of self with other, in a world not yet sharply split into internal and external. One could add that it is likely that the nascent self, emerging from a barely differentiated unity, experiences objects as essential parts of itself; for example, as the confirming (mirroring) and motivating (idealising) selfobjects, the antagonist and twin selfobjects described by Kohut and his followers (Kohut and Wolf 1978). They continue to influence perception of outside relationships, largely unconsciously, so that inner and outer worlds resonate and mutually recreate each other.

However, beyond the family the personality is sustained, for good or ill, through significant relationships with others. Work and recreation foster linkages and identification through membership of groups that give one a continuing sense of 'we-ness'. Rouchy (1987) has written about the importance of such 'belonging groups' (groupes d'appartenance). These are only now beginning to receive proper attention from psychoanalysts and group analysts. They can be taken for granted until they – and their function for the individual – are disrupted by migration and other exigencies. They can be viewed as serving transformational (Bollas 1987) and transitional functions for the individual (Winnicott 1971), and provide opportunities for sublimation of instinctual drives, and for such necessary functions as reparation and idealisation. But also they act as links with sociocultural norms and values, with the world outside the family. They provide alternative belonging groups.

In the course of development we internalise relationships between important people in our universe: the primary dyad, family and wider social groups, all in turn impregnated by and thus to varying degrees internalising values, customs, standards, history, myths, and aspirations of the prevailing culture or subculture in which we are embedded (see Le Roy, Chapter 12). The individual internalises automatically and unconsciously what is at first neither internal nor external. Culture is both between people and encompasses them, binds them and defines them to one another. However, the significance of each to the other, and thus the nature and quality of the subjective feelings and phantasies evoked by the interaction at any point in time, will depend on the total configuration of relationships within the system – or the matrix within the multipersonal psychological field. Foulkes' way of understanding Oedipal phenomena illustrates such a systemic viewpoint (Chapter 1, page 5). The arrival of an infant leads to regression in *all* members of the family, so that both parents as well as the infant instigate the Oedipal conflict. Moreover, identification is not unidirectional. As Rouchy puts it, 'the subject is created in the desire of the parents and through reflections. A lack or an ambiguity in the eye of the other is a source of deficiencies and disturbances in the constitution of identity and the social link' (Rouchy 1993).

How each family member manages and manifests this regression, and how they look at and respond to the baby, will depend on their own history and personality. What each member has 'internalised' is composed in the first place of relatively fixed mutual relational patterns between self and parents, siblings, and often members of the wider family, family friends, and even pets. Represented as images and phantasies, these are essentially unconscious because of repression and infantile amnesia, but also because their earliest form is adumbrated by purely somatic strivings and experiences, at a pre-reflective stage that Bion (1961: 101) called the 'protomental level of development'. Many people continue to manifest difficulties in relationships at this level throughout life, especially at times of stress, leading to psychosomatic disorders (Brown 1985, 1989; McDougall 1974; Taylor 1987). At this protomental level the infant, or physically ill adult, functions at the level of beta-functions (Bion 1962b) before the alpha-functions of phantasy and imagery appear (see the cases of Richard and the 'drowsy group' below).

It is those relationships which are forgotten, repressed or based on as yet unimaginable, beta-element experiences that increase in power in regressive states – for example, as a result of anxiety and stress, including the given-up/giving-up states of despair and withdrawal that can lead to physical illness (Engel 1962: 392). They are therefore less available for correction and modification by accurate appraisal of external, consensually validated reality. They lead to transference distortion of external relationships, and interfere with individuals' engagement in new and more mature relationships (A. Freud 1965: 39), as will be evident from the clinical material described later.

In a recent examination of the psychoanalytic concept of internal object relationships, Sandler (1990) proposes that our need to cling to the internal object relationship is a source of severe resistance in analysis. This often becomes clear in the matrix of the analytic group as a shared problem. What do we do if our sense of self and safety, or that of another group member depends on maintaining, for instance, the role of victim or of omnipotent controller, of independent coper or entertainer? These and other roles can block the development of the individual or group. For example, mature dependence (Fairbairn 1952) may fail to replace infantile dependence or counterdependence (see the case of Kim below).

## DEVELOPMENT BEYOND INTERNAL OBJECT RELATIONS

These relationships and roles can be incorporated into character traits and inhibitions of personality such as alexithymia (McDougall 1974; Taylor 1987). They become manifest in the therapeutic situation, not as isolated internal objects, but as relationships or 'presences' which allows a reconstruction of each individual's past life and their consequent 'internal baggage'. At the same time, structures based on internalising certain types of object relations that were not present at crucial times in development can be built up later during therapeutic regression (Loewald 1980: 376–7). These include relationships in which other group members and the whole group can be said to function as the selfobjects described earlier. Other new opportunities for identification and internalisation are offered by the therapist's 'analytic attitude', and healthier experiences of mothering, fathering, or sibling relationship that provide a more appropriate balance of confrontation and support, frustration, and compensation.

They occur in a group-analytic group without any conscious 'corrective emotional experience' (Alexander and French 1946); indeed, they are an important part of the therapeutic and maturing effects of membership of an analytic group (Brown 1987). Pines (1990) has argued for replacing the term 'corrective emotional experience' by 'the appropriate response, the good-enough gesture, which enables the patient to move from an embedded defensive position towards intersubjectivity, being with another in a shared state, that is being understood in a proper sense of being with one who stands underneath the other'. This experience enables us to know more about ourselves in a way that makes us better able to make that knowledge part of a firmer foundation for the self as locus of experience. In a therapeutic group, most people want to feel understood and to understand themselves better. Eventually they usually do, and in the process understand others better. Members of a group become more capable of engaging empathically with one another. However, as Nitsun (1992) has emphasised, the empathic gulf can be extremely difficult to bridge, and can be accentuated rather than diminished in groups. Indeed, Nitsun has suggested that such 'misattunement' may lead to the 'anti-group' experiences he has so valuably highlighted (Nitsun 1991). Thus it is important to bear in mind the dangers of failed intersubjectivity at the same time as clarifying the significance of aiming for intersubjective relatedness.

It will be seen that we have now moved through the three stages outlined near the start of this chapter: (1) discovering inner worlds of object relationship; (2) using new opportunities to transcend blocks rooted in them; (3) learning to relate to others in empathic mutuality. In the clinical situation these stages are reached in a fitful and recurrent progress towards intimacy and empathic understanding. When achieved, they carry the group and its members forward towards a greater degree of experienced intersubjectivity.

## CLINICAL MATERIAL

I shall present and comment on clinical material following these three stages.

First, *The Man Who Could Not Understand.* In a recent paper (Brown 1989), I described the struggles of a group with a patient stuck at a protomental level, before any awareness of an inner world. It illustrates the interplay between understanding, being understood, the role of empathy, and the need for *intersubjective validation* to create a solid enough self for interaction with others to be meaningful. It could be seen as a paradigm of the sort of construction through 'transmuting internalisations' (Kohut 1971) that this degree of self-deficit requires.

Richard came to therapy because of his inability to present himself verbally before groups of colleagues at work. He also complained of a constriction of feelings which made his marriage sterile for his wife in a way that he himself *could not understand*, in contrast with his intense emotional attachment and concern for his young son. From joining, his involvement in the twice weekly group was precarious and puzzling. He constantly felt *unable to understand* what 'people were going on about'. However, after a while it became clear that he longed for attention, waited for it, and raged inwardly when it did not come. He came to appreciate his own needs and wishes.

After one such occasion he did not return. In a letter he said he despaired of being able to use the group. I offered him an individual session in which we explored his feeling of being forgotten and defeated in the group. Though formerly denying early memories, he had gradually uncovered some in the group, and this time he talked of being put aside by his mother when his sister was born and father returned from the army; also of mother's suppression of his feeling, saying 'boys don't feel' while the sister was allowed her tantrums. In the session he acknowledged with pleasure my telling him of the projected tearfulness I felt. After recognising the group was experienced as a family in which he could not find a place and afford to be spontaneous, he decided to return to it. He fleetingly appreciated how he had externalised his experience of his internal family.

When he did so, he spoke of realising he *needed the group every day* and feared he would fall flat if not picked up. One could thus see that an important part of his character defence was against dependence and abandonment.

At the next session he reported fury with me for not 'bringing him out' despite my declared knowledge of his need, but did so only after someone else had been talking about leaving and wishing to be special. For a while Richard had been sitting impassively, but flicked a speck off his tie once and glanced quickly at his watch. I withheld indicating that I had observed these signs, and the man who had been talking asked him how he was. Richard replied, 'Furious, there is no point. I nearly walked out'. He could not 'understand' what was being talked about. He saw no point in coming if I was aware of his needs and did nothing about them. Another member expressed his anger at Richard, but explained that he also identified with him, realising that he covered his own needs by *talking* rather than by *silence*. This exposed him to the possibility of intersubjectivity, begun by the other member.

Again, this time in the group, I pointed out my own tears, recognising them, as well as the anger, as his and that of others in the group. At this confrontation with empathy or exchange of subjectivity he was deeply and dramatically moved, felt intense pain in the neck and shoulders '*as though being choked*'. When I commented that he was choking his own feelings, he began to cry. One member passed him the tissues and another put her hand on his shoulder, but he could not talk about it until the intensity had worn off. Asked how it related to feelings in the family, he could clearly see it was, especially in situations of being ignored and overlooked, of which he gave graphic examples. After this opening up, and the discovery that his rage and tears could be accepted and understood, for the rest of the session he was able to keep up with the ebb and flow of conversation and understanding in the group. He left his isolated internal world and joined the intersubjective world of the group for a while.

What happened here seems to correspond with that stage of development of the nascent self calling for a responsive selfobject (Kohut 1971). The group was able to take on an empathic and maternal role, sufficient for Richard to open himself to it. He discovered he had, like others, an internal world, understandable by others, and he was able to take part in the ebb and flow of shared experiences.

This is the basis of intersubjective validation; the person's sense of themselves in relation to others is confirmed by those others' responses in a mutual process of self-discovery. It entails each discovering something new about themselves and the other, which confirms and changes views of self and other. In this way it deepens the sense of relatedness. In a well-functioning group, each member discovers *their* inner world and discerns how it colours their view of others, and their inner worlds. Similarities and differences can then be clarified and respected, as projections are reduced, transference distortions based on internal object relationships are modified, and prejudices transcended in the direction of mutual empathy. Individuals then become less defensively self-absorbed. The negotiation and holding together of deep ambivalences allows the development of concern, which recognises the fragility of these achievements. Working through within the group, or in relationships outside, strengthens confidence in these achievements. But in a group that does not function well, or one that fails to meet the needs of an individual, such intersubjective validation through empathic attunement does not occur, or not sufficiently to promote the developmental spiral. It might require a change of group, move to individual therapy totally or in augmentation, or even acceptance that the individual cannot be helped further at this time.

In fact, Richard dropped out of the group, as he had dropped out of individual therapy before. In a sense he had defeated us. One might question whether his baffled response of 'not understanding', as it were identifying with a misattuned parent who did not understand, was a response to misattunement in his early life, or to disrupted partial attunement – a defensive post-traumatic refusal to trust that was stirred up by the moments of apparent attunement experienced in the group and in his individual sessions.

Nevertheless, in a group one often finds that those members who are most defensively self-absorbed to start with are the ones who are later capable of the greatest empathic sensitivity to others. The opportunity for learning through such experiences in group analysis gives it a special advantage over individual psychoanalysis, where empathy is almost the prerogative of the analyst. The latter then has to rely on changes in the patient's transference, and his or her reports of changes in relationships outside the treatment setting. Indeed, the group setting not only provides the opportunity for observing others in interaction, and of having oneself observed in interaction with others, but it also models the triangulation that is the basis of both Oedipal and social development (see Nitsun, Chapter 9).

Second, *The Woman Who Would Not Feel Understood.* At this later stage of development, experiencing oneself as having a valued place in a family that supports and challenges is also important for development. Individuation involves recognition of others in relation together as well as to oneself. In this stage, late Oedipal and sibling jealousy and rivalry are added to, and to some extent supersede, separation anxiety and insecurity springing from environmental failure, infantile envy of the breast and of mother and the parental couple. In Lacanian terms, *la loi* (the law) and *le nom du père* (the Name of the Father) demand and assist the move from fusion in a dyad into the social world of language and its symbolic order (Benvenuto and Kennedy 1986: 133). The sense of belonging gains new horizons and boundaries. The sense of 'we-ness' develops through extension and differentiation.

Kim was a 30-year old Oriental immigrant, a helping-professional who denied her own needs in the group for a long time. Her counter-dependence was fiercely maintained, as was her single marital status, to such a degree that it stood out at times as a troubling and puzzling foreground to the general background level of expressed neediness in the group. The group confronted her with her extreme position, which she nevertheless clung to, even after she had shared childhood experiences of being dropped as an infant, and choosing after the birth of her brother to spend a lot of her childhood nights at the home of a grandmother.

From early on in the group she attributed to me a dislike of her, which echoed (in reverse) her dislike of men from her country of origin, clearly connected with her father who spent long periods away from home and denied her affection and a sense of being valued as a girl. For a long time she insisted that I was unable to understand her because she came from a different culture.

Her counterdependence gradually softened, but broke down in a group session when intense rivalry emerged between her and another woman member over 'secrets' withheld from me after a session when I had been away. After her rival had told me more about this 'secret', I took the issue up. While I was still speaking, Kim stormed out of the group, leaving us upset and concerned.

Reflecting on this next time, she was able to relate what happened to walking out of the homes of both her parents and her grandmother, making each feel the rejection she found it so painful to feel herself – as in projective identification. Further, she was able to see, and have understood, that the hurt was especially keen because she had felt betrayed by the woman in the group she most liked, and by me for seeming to favour her. Kim's dependent longings were now further revealed also in her painful recollection of seeing her brother breast-fed by her mother; and her telling us that she only went to her grandmother to sleep, as grandmother did not cook as well as mother. In the same session, other group members, associating to these events, and to the discovery of powerful needs behind defensive indifference and detachment, reinforced the awareness of such processes in themselves. Kim had become more human and knowable, more a member of the group, which gained a deeper understanding of the wishes and defences of all.

The example shows how the group can confront strong character defences by stimulating the emergence of repressed object relationships. Here their recognition allowed them to become part of a greater awareness of commonality. This reinforced the sense of empathic attunement, the need for which Kim had previously denied, and unblocked her development.

Third, *The Drowsy Group, Including the Conductor*. Drowsing is a common and insufficiently attended to phenomenon in groups. Drowsiness in the conductor, in individual members of the group, or in the group-as-a-whole, can often be understood as a defensive avoidance of feelings stimulated by the situation, just as disturbing affects provoked by a theatrical performance can sometimes explain the boredom or sleepiness experienced by members of the audience. Drowsing may occur in either patient or therapist, when blocking off their own emotional responses. Equally, however, I often find that my own countertransference drowsiness represents a failure of empathy which can be triggered by a patient withholding from themselves and from me, powerful and often primitive affects. These can be the very early, protomental affects illustrated by Richard; the reason why so many 'alexithymic' patients provoke boredom in their interviewers (Wolff 1977). I have previously described countertransference drowsiness playing a crucial role in individual psychoanalysis (Brown 1977). Until its significance was realised, it was merely a block to progress.

Countertransference drowsiness occurs more often in some groups than in others, particularly those that are emotionally inhibited or in which several people exhibit alexithymic features, but even then it will tend to happen during certain phases in the group.

In one group, I felt intensely drowsy on two consecutive sessions. In the first session, it persisted for a while. It disappeared when John, normally rather bouncy and frequently insisting he no longer needed to be in the group, talked about his mother not having had a photograph of him on her wall. He became aware of a sense of outrage at her omission, which he associated with not knowing why she had agreed to his being evacuated in the war between the ages of 2 and 3. The strength of his feeling seemed to lift my drowsiness, but, surprisingly I felt an intense pain in my stomach.

In the next session, another member, Tom, reported that he had experienced a pain in his stomach since the last session, and felt it had to do with his own emotional deprivation as a child, when he had very troublesome eczema. In his usual emotionally flat way, Tom recounted how he would rock his pram so violently that his father had tied it down and put his hands in splints. Despite the distressing content of his story, the whole group appeared drowsy and inattentive. When I pointed this out, it was acknowledged, and lifted somewhat as members spoke about their fear of expressing dangerous feelings.

This led on in the next session to the group exploring, with considerable animation, issues of power and powerlessness, and the fear of having their emotions 'played with'. It seemed that by identifying with Tom's example, they had lowered their defensive barrier against communicating their experience. Intersubjectivity replaced concealing their individual vulnerability.

Having observed drowsiness develop in individuals who were disturbed by feelings stirred up by another group member's experience, I do not think it is inappropriate to equate this group drowsiness with countertransference drowsiness of the subjective type, contrasting it with Winnicott's 'objective countertransference' (Winnicott 1949). That is, it is particular to that person or group, and is saying something covert about their subjective experience; not something that anyone or any group would feel in that situation. It corresponds to withdrawal in hurt from the 'ebb and flow' of the group, or missing sessions when the longed-for interest is withheld or seems to move to another group member. The difference is that for the drowsing to be evoked, the other person has to be physically there but emotionally and empathically absent.

## CONCLUDING DISCUSSION

The matrix of the group, with its personal, interpersonal, and transpersonal functions, is a multipersonal field in which subjects and objects appear, interact, interchange, and transform. In the early stages of a group, the individual tends to get drawn into anxious opposition or self-denying fusion, treating the group and others in it as objects to be submitted to or possessed. Later, they tend to be desired or feared. As the group and its members mature, this gives way to recognition of similarities and differences, and to a sense of intersubjectivity that permits real communication. The self, or ego, finds itself through communication with others, as the infant finds itself through the mutual attunement of infant and mother. Internal representations of self and objects are recognised through their action and enactment in the group matrix. They emerge there, and can be modified there in the struggle to be understood and to understand. To be growth-promoting, yet allowing benign regression when necessary, the group needs to feel secure and function well. This is the ultimate responsibility of the conductor.

As each member's inner world of internal object relationships is played out in the group, old object relationships (what Kernberg calls subject-object-affect links) are clarified in a public light that makes them less easy to forget. Their modification by empathic understanding and insight is aided by the *new* subjective interrelationships provided in an increasingly mature group. In the process of exposing and clarifying these residues of early experiences, and the sharing of new experiences within the common ground of the group matrix, mutual understanding can develop. At its deepest I believe this is rooted in what Merleau-Ponty called collaboration in 'consummate reciprocity' (1976: 354). As Gordon (1991) argues, this is not only developmentally primitive. Mahler's symbiotic phase (Mahler *et al.* 1975), selfobject functioning (Kohut 1971), and the intersubjectivity of the infant–mother dyad (Stern 1985) may underlie the need and capacity to relate intersubjectively. But intersubjectivity is also part of relating fully in adult life.

At fleeting moments Richard seemed capable of it. Kim increasingly established this capacity, bringing together an enlarged subjective experience which intercommunicated with that of others in the group. The group where drowsiness was a prominent problem, by working through it, functioned more fully, and sharpened its awareness of one another's subjective experience. These changes are subsumed in my understanding of an important aspect of what Foulkes called 'ego training in action', which I call 'self development through subjective interaction'.

Hans Cohn (1992) has questioned the possibility of integrating phenomenological notions with psychoanalytic theory, as the latter is flawed by a Cartesian split that the notion of intersubjectivity overcomes. Am I therefore mistaken in seeing intersubjectivity as providing the first building blocks of the sense of self in infancy, and yet a goal to achieve in mature relationship? I think not, if we take the view that the 'internal world', internal objects, and object relationships reflect subjective experiences that have been split off and 'privatised' as a result of defensive manoeuvres, as well as representing the seat of imagination and creativity. They make the inner world a subjective reality. I think it is reasonable to suppose that while the 'internal world' of psychic reality has been discovered through psychoanalysis, emphasis on it reflects the individualistic nature of modern socio-economic philosophy and *Zeitgeist*, underplaying and even denying the connectedness underlined by existential phenomenology.

Intimacy is often a prominent characteristic in the final stages of development in experimental group dynamic situations, reviewed, for example, by Whiteley and Gordon (1979: 77–83), and seen in group-analytic and other workshops – sometimes as wished-for or pseudo-intimacy. In slow-open group-analytic groups it is more a recurrent phase, repeatedly and more deeply experienced each time round, as in a spiral. My impression of how it progresses is that the experience of mutual empathy allows the development of enough sense of security to promote another turn in exploring and sharing private inner object worlds, and so to allow the middle phase of achieving a more flexible relationship to them. This will often entail turbulent confrontation of transference distortions and projections, but when worked through will lead to a renewed mutual understanding and intimacy.

A once-weekly group had met once in my expected absence. On my return they reported that they had had a good meeting, patching up the violent transference-based confrontation between two members occurring the previous week. Gradually they realised that the apparent resolution had been partly motivated by fear, and that they needed the safety afforded by the conductor's presence to face the potential hatred between members, itself based on intense rivalry for my attention when I was there. My verbal interpretation of the conflict was scarcely necessary, but it helped them to see that the integration of the experience of the 'bad', uncomfortable session with the pseudo-'good' session was necessary to achieve a deeper sense of empathic relatedness, both between the couple and between them and others in the group who could identify the issues as also their own.

The spiral I have described can move in both directions. Members starting in the group with little insight or introspectiveness can begin to develop a sense of their own inner world by witnessing and participating in the moves others make towards mutual empathic understanding, and by tuning in to similarities with them through what Foulkes called 'resonance'. In other words, empathy can come before an awareness of an 'internal world' of relationship.

While something akin to the spiral process happens in individual analysis, the final phase of reciprocity does not fit in with customary psychoanalytic techniques. This might explain some of the caution psychoanalysts show in publicising what they actually do. One of the advantages of group analysis, therefore, is that the final phase can be explored and exploited by the group without the conductor relinquishing a necessary degree of analytic detachment.

In the transitional space of the group there is opportunity for recognition and modification of restrictive or distorting object relationships, and for new identifications and selfobject usage as individuals allow themselves to be seen more fully, and to look at and be seen by one another in different ways through empathic attunement. Much of this is subsumed in what Foulkes called 'mirror reactions', but the wider view allows one to see how object relations theory and self psychology could be integrated into an understanding of 'self development through subjective interaction'.

*In summary*, it is proposed that the process of self development in group analysis is circular and spiral: the experience of being empathised with, and failed enough – as in early infancy – sets in motion the three stages enumerated in the beginning of the chapter: fuller *discovery* of our inner world, which allows us to *discern* the difference between old internal object relationships and new ones, and in a step towards maturity to *learn* to attune ourselves to *other* people's experience as well as our own. On the way to more mature, intimate and reciprocal relationships with others, we mitigate the effects of earlier empathic failure and ossification of internal object relationships. I call this *self development through subjective interaction*, and believe its attainment during group analysis is a test of how well the group is functioning.

## ACKNOWLEDGEMENTS

I am grateful to Hans Cohn, Morris Nitsun, and Louis Zinkin for very helpful conversations and correspondence about earlier drafts of this chapter.

# Chapter 7

# Exchange as a therapeutic factor in group analysis

*Louis Zinkin*

In developing his model of group analysis, Foulkes suggested that there were four group-specific factors. Briefly stated, these were: mirroring, exchange, social integration, and the activation of the collective unconscious (Foulkes 1964: 24). In this chapter, I want to consider exchange in the group-analytic group. The topic is so complex that I will not attempt to do much more than share my own preliminary reflections on it, in the hope that this might at least suggest ways in which we might continue to think about it. My conclusions are based on my belief that Foulkes has provided, in outline, a scheme or model for doing this.

There is so much overlap between the various dynamic psychotherapeutic methods that it is not easy to make a precise differentiation between the factors which are operative in each, though the protagonists of any method inevitably have to make a claim for them. We must begin, then, with the fact that Foulkes regarded exchange as an important therapeutic factor which was specific to his model of group analysis and that this was one of four. At the same time, he appears only to have made a few provisional statements about them. His principal aim was to compare group analysis with the psychoanalytic model as he understood it at the time. Unusually for a psychoanalyst, Foulkes also turned to Jung, whose broader perspective helped him to account for group phenomena not easily encompassed by Freudian theory, and this meant incorporating into his model Jung's difficult and controversial idea of the collective unconscious, as we shall see.

In all the uncertainty that continues to exist on the relative merits of group and individual analysis, these four factors have had little direct attention. There are a number of possible reasons for this. Foulkes' remarks are very brief, which might give the impression that he did not think they merited much thought. He did consider, however, that, of the possible specific factors, these were 'the most important which we could so far discern'. Why, then, did he not write more extensively about them? The main problem may lie in the nature of the distinction he was making. By contrasting the group with the individual method, he was evaluating indirectly between psychoanalytic theory based on the individual patient and sociological theory on the ways in which the individual functions in groups. This involved the comparison between two very different kinds of theory. Foulkes was primarily a clinician – a psychiatrist and a psychoanalyst – and what is striking about his four factors is that they all lie outside the psychoanalytic framework, or at least the framework which was then current.

Group-analytic theory is partly an attempt to extend the clinical insights of the psychoanalytic model developed from the familiar dyadic medical model of doctor and patient into the insights which can be gained by placing patients in a somewhat artificially constructed social system. This seems to require applying knowledge of sociology and social psychology, which is quite a different discipline but is necessary if we are to regard the individual as an abstraction and the 'social' as being of the essential nature of man. Despite his interest in sociological questions, Foulkes may not have felt equipped to explore this area in great depth and it is hard for his followers, who may be even more limited to a psychoanalytic perspective, to do so. Sociologists and social psychologists, on the other hand, have their own difficulties with the psychoanalytic model and do not readily concern themselves with therapy and how it works.

Though I have been intrigued for many years by Foulkes' four factors, my own background, with a formal training in psychiatry and in analytical psychology, leaves me, also, ill-equipped to use sociological concepts. Nevertheless, I think it is important at least to make a start and to start where Foulkes started, with a few simple ideas derived from what he saw happening in groups. It is, of course, also desirable that others for whom social concepts are more familiar to come in the opposite direction, from sociology via social psychology, to consider dynamic analytic concepts. Both paths are quite difficult.

Another problem soon presents itself in any attempt to isolate specifically *group* therapeutic factors. Even if everyone were to agree that one particular list does indeed portray identifiable therapeutic factors, it is hard to regard them as either specific for group analysis or to be sure that they are the only factors which are specific. On the other hand, if Foulkes was right in his attaching importance to them, they could provide the necessary foundations for future development of his model.

It may also be remarked that Foulkes himself indirectly suggested that there were other factors at work, especially in his much-quoted bits of technical advice. These conveyed a notion of the conductor and the way such a therapist could help the group to function, which certainly seems to distinguish group from individual therapy. However, he did not categorically state that these distinctions constituted a major advantage for group over individual analysis. To some extent, this advice expressed a general attitude which the individual analyst might also have. One may ask, for example, why one cannot use the same principles he advocated for the group conductor (leading from behind, trusting the patients' flow of associations, seeing oneself as part of the process) equally well for individual analysis, and it seems likely that Foulkes did so in his individual work. One may further wonder why it is better, therapeutically, to be a node in the network, rather than a participant in a two-person dialogue. But Foulkes, though he clearly thought the group process represented a fuller recognition of the essentially social nature of the human person than classical psychoanalysis did, could only point to four distinct factors which he could claim to be group-specific.

## SPECIFICITY AS A PROBLEM

It is hard to believe, though, that Foulkes could have meant to imply an *absolute* specificity. However I try to understand them, I cannot see that these four phenomena occur only in group and not at all in individual analysis. They are certainly more prominent in the group, but even this depends a good deal on the particular model of individual analysis used for the comparison. It may well apply more to a certain kind of psychoanalysis than another or than it would to my own model of Jungian analysis. It could be generally agreed, though, that there is nevertheless a significant *relative* difference.

Foulkes is speaking of processes which arise naturally between the participants of a group. He is voicing a belief that, if cultivated and allowed to grow rather than being weeded out, these factors will be therapeutic. In psychoanalysis, as we shall see later, there are technical reasons, resulting from the way the process is conceived, why a different view is taken.

## THE ARCHETYPAL SIGNIFICANCE OF THE QUATERNIO

Foulkes' suggestion was that, in addition to there being four therapeutic factors, there were also four levels on which the group functions. In both these descriptions, the number four may seem arbitrary. Why not three or six? One answer is provided by analytical psychology, where the number four is often given a special significance. A double quaternity in which the collective unconscious occurs twice forms a structure which might suggest something of this significance in theory building. The image of a theory as an edifice built like a square or a cube, resting on four 'factors', like four pillars, and there being also four levels, like four floors, is reminiscent of Jung's observation that four is the symbol of wholeness and is therefore frequently found in collective symbolism to represent the archetype of the self, which he defined as being both the centre and the totality of the psyche. To illustrate this he used examples drawn from alchemy and gnosticism, where he showed that the *quaternio* both symbolised and structured in the individuation process. In each case there is an asymmetry in this otherwise symmetrical arrangement of elements, in that the fourth seems to be different from the other three and may be hidden – as, for example, in Christian symbolism the Trinity excludes the fourth, which might be either Mary as a female principle or the Devil.

The fourth can also be regarded as the unity which combines the other three, as in the axiom of Maria, a medieval alchemist: 'One becomes two, two becomes three and out of the third comes one as the fourth' (quoted by Jung 1959, C W 9:2 p. 153). It is therefore striking that Foulkes, perhaps unconsciously (though he was familiar with Jung's ideas), should isolate four (neither less nor more) elements as therapeutic factors which can be arranged horizontally and that this applies also to his four levels of group interaction, which can be arranged hierarchically to form a vertical quaternio. Jung similarly thought that there are four horizontal quaternios arranged vertically (see diagram in 'Aion', Jung 1934, Part 2: 227). The fourth factor – the collective unconscious in Foulkes' model – would seem to be different from the other three. It is the most mysterious and difficult to talk about, and Foulkes did little more than allude to it, but it occurs in *both* groups of four and perhaps is the fourth which indicates the unity of the other three. The fours together would form a balanced pattern of eight, indicating the whole system, and eight is also said to be the ideal number for a group.

Jung has said that there is a natural tendency to establish order by dividing things into four; for example, the four seasons, the four elements, four humours, or his own four functions. However, the quaternio is more than a system of classification: it is a structure which is conducive to change, the kind of progressive growth which Jung termed 'individuation'. This conception supports the idea that the four factors should not be taken separately but that together, they act synergistically. They may be divided into pairs of opposites, but they can also be understood to have a complementary relationship.

## EXCHANGE AND MIRRORING AS RELATED CONCEPTS

One such opposed or complementary pair is the relationship of exchange with mirroring. I have written elsewhere about the ambivalence of mirroring (Zinkin 1983), and exchange too, has ambivalent qualities in that it can take detrimental as well as helpful forms. Unfortunately, although called 'therapeutic factors', they are not like drugs which can be prescribed when necessary by a doctor. They arise spontaneously in the group, and the conductor needs the help of the group-as-a-whole to monitor them.

## SAMENESS AND DIFFERENCE

The key to combining these concepts is that mirroring implies sameness between members and exchange implies difference. People are helped both by identifying with others and by recognising their differences. Exchange is only worthwhile between people if each has something which the other lacks. The concepts themselves can also be seen as similar in some respects and different in others. Principally, mirroring can only take place *if identification remains incomplete.* I can be the same as you only if I remain different in some respect: otherwise I *am* you. And I can only exchange something with you if there is some degree of sameness, some matching between what I give you and what you give me. Attunement between mother and baby, taking the form of each imitating the other, is the condition for exchange – as Stern and others have shown (Stern 1985) – just as the instruments of an orchestra (using Foulkes' analogy of the orchestral conductor) have to be in tune before they can begin their exchanges with one another. Let us begin to examine these concepts more closely and particularly try to refine the idea of exchange.

## FAIR EXCHANGE IS NO ROBBERY

The sense of a fair exchange, where what is exchanged is seen to be of equivalent value, is easier to grasp in the group because the group members are supposed to have equal status. At least, there is no built-in role difference; members are all patients and this undermines the commonly felt sense of hierarchy in the patient–therapist role division. Foulkes seems to have this in mind. In *Therapeutic Group Analysis*, his remarks as to the nature of the exchange are quite brief. He says:

> Explanations and information, for which there is a great demand and surprising interest, are of course not peculiar to the group situation, but in one respect there is a significant difference: there is the element of *exchange*. This not only makes discussions more lively and full, but alters the emotional situation, just as children accept many things from each other which they would oppose if they came from their parents.
>
> (1964: 34)

Though I feel I can get the gist of what Foulkes is saying here, there is much that is not clear. Certainly, anyone who puts people into a group having first treated them on their own (and this is how Foulkes started) would be immediately struck by the fact that they talk to one another in a different way; they exchange experiences and pay attention to one another in a way which reveals almost a different personality from what is displayed in the individual situation. The group personality often seems more spontaneous and shows a much greater range of resources than when restricted to the clinical relationship of doctor and patient. The difference is particularly striking in couples' groups, when the couples are exchanging their experiences of the same problems. Though this exchanging seems obviously beneficial, it is necessary to see more clearly what is the therapeutic factor involved, which Foulkes isolates as exchange, how it works, how to help it working, as well as understanding what goes wrong or how it might act as a resistance to other processes.

A number of questions suggest themselves on reading Foulkes' description. What is meant by explanations and information? What is surprising in the interest in it? Why is the element of exchange significant? Something is being picked out which not only makes the discussion more lively and full but also alters the emotional tone. To illustrate this, Foulkes uses an analogy: *children* have this kind of exchange in that they will accept from one another what they will oppose from their parents. This analogy has to suffice, in the text, as an answer to the questions I have raised.

A psychoanalyst might first consider the case of sexual information or explanations in the form of phantasy-based theories of sexual intercourse and birth. This would readily account for the liveliness, the great demand, the interest, and the alteration of emotional tone. But of course children do excitedly exchange all sorts of other information in a way that is different from the way they talk to adults, and this includes the lore of the playground and perhaps embraces the whole area of learning which comes through children playing together – the serious aspect of play. And children accept one another's explanations in serious discussion of matters other than sex, including death. I imagine that Foulkes had all this in mind. If he had been thinking specifically of sexual fantasies he would probably have said so. To make sense of the passage, then, I take it that Foulkes is comparing group patients with children in that they communicate in special ways because of their equal status. They see one another as being like one another, as thinking in similar ways, as inhabiting the same world. They cannot do this in the same way with their parents. The implication is that individual analysis is more like a child being with a parent.

But this is not Foulkes' main point. He brings out the element of *exchange*. It is not that one child gives something to another but that this is done reciprocally. Again, if one thinks of children exchanging sexual information this becomes abundantly clear: 'I'll show you mine if you show me yours'; there will then be a useful pooling of information. The excitement in this exchange is not only in the mutual increase of knowledge, though, but in the bonding between the two individuals, not least in doing together something forbidden, as in the Adam and Eve myth. But again sexual knowledge is not the only kind which children exchange.

In any case, Foulkes is using children only as an example. He is actually talking of adults in a therapy group. It is not easy to be certain what to make of his choice of this particular example. It may be that he is not just using an illustration but suggesting something more: for example, that there is a regression to a child-like state in the group. If he does mean this, he is thinking of regression as a therapeutically helpful factor, like 'regression in the service of the ego', and perhaps also suggesting that it is helpful to regress to a state of being children together as well as to being like a child is when with an adult. The question of regression in the group is a highly complicated one because child–adult transferences are frequent between the members as well as with the conductor. Again I doubt whether Foulkes wished to lead us into these complexities at this point in his writings. It seems better to abstract from his remarks a schema in which the free exchange (1) of information and explanations (2) between people who see one another as equals (3) goes on to build up a common pool of knowledge and a specific culture, and a sense of doing this together is of interest (4) to the participants. The combination of these four elements (four again) constitutes the particular exchange which is specific to group therapy. Abstracting these elements enables the group situation to be correlated with innumerable social situations (such as the exchange of ideas in this book). Children would then provide a vivid but not unique case and we would be considering a social rather than intrapersonal world.

## WHAT IS MISSING IN CLASSICAL PSYCHOANALYSIS?

Before taking further these group phenomena, it is worth pausing for a backward glance at individual analysis. If exchange is specific to group analysis, why should this be so? Why cannot exchange be a factor in classical psychoanalysis? The short answer is that, of course, it is. On the whole, however, a classical analytic technique is one which discourages the *kind* of exchange Foulkes is describing. Explanations and information are not given freely by the analyst, let alone exchanged with the patient. The formal setting provides a quite different atmosphere or 'emotional tone'. It is understood that the analyst will remain mostly silent while the patient free-associates. In return, the analyst will provide interpretations. It is true that this may also involve explanation but of a rather careful and restricted kind. Thus the exchange is not of 'like for like', and this means that the roles of the participants in the exchange are not equivalent. One is holding back while the other is giving as much as he or she can. One is an expert in the process while the other is not. This sets up an asymmetry which at least seems to the patient like a hierarchical or 'unequal' one. This is the basis of the transference neurosis according to Freud, and is an important therapeutic factor in the classical model. Although this state of affairs is partly reproduced in the group by the difference in roles of conductor and patients, it lacks the centrality which it has in the two-person psychoanalytic situation. It would be wrong, therefore, to consider the specific group exchange simply as an advantage over the individual one. The differences, in fact, might be a factor in determining which form of analysis would be better suited to the needs of any particular patient.

For example, in dealing with delinquent adolescents in an institutional setting I found that most of them who were severely blocked when seen alone became spontaneous and talkative when placed in a group with their peers. It is common to find, in individual work, that one is restricted to working on just one problem which dominates the interaction. It is not simply that this is 'diluted' in the group. With my delinquent group the clash with an older, male authority figure could only be worked with by the group giving one another the support that no one member could feel in isolation. Similarly, a young woman who had been sexually abused by her father could barely speak in individual psychotherapy, regardless of my interpretations (which she agreed with) of the reasons for her anxiety. In the group she could deal with the anxiety with the help of the other members, because she was never actually subjected to the trauma of being alone with me.

Of course, it is frequently the other way round: the patient requires the intimacy and sole attention of the therapist which the individual situation provides. Very often the difference provided by the role differentiation, by the therapist being relatively detached, professional, or even being seen as more experienced or more mature (rightly or wrongly) is enabling in a way that the rivalry or camaraderie of the group is not. My point is that it is the nature of the exchange which is paramount in these two situations, and that each type has advantages and disadvantages which can be weighed up for a particular patient by the unbiased therapist who is familiar with both.

## A SOCIAL PERSPECTIVE

There is another way of looking at the difference between the psycho-analytic and the group-analytic model, and that is by comparing the kind of conversation which takes place with what is commonly thought of as 'social conversation'. Although ordinary social exchanges are dis-couraged in both models and there is a suspension of the ordinary rules of politeness, in favour of an 'unstructured' situation, there is a marked difference in emphasis. In group analysis, the social rules are retained as a basis for the exchanges between the members to a much greater extent because this is seen to be fruitful. The conductor allows the group to start by using them, may from time to time question their usefulness and allows the group to develop its own modifications of these rules so that each group acquires its own distinctive culture. This culture is not something incidental to the therapeutic process: it is a testimony to it. The way the exchanges take place in the group is an essential ingredient of its culture and how far it has developed depends on how far the group has evolved therapeutically.

Even though something of this sort must also take place in every analyst–patient pair, the ordinary social exchanges are not considered to be part of the analytic process: rather than being considered specifically therapeutic, they are held to interfere with therapy. Foulkes' technique, in contrast, is based more on the idea of the essentially social nature of the individual, and he therefore saw *socialisation* as part of the therapeutic process itself. This is why the four factors have a different significance for the group even though they must exist too in the one-to-one model. Exchange and mirroring take place naturally and spontaneously in all social interaction, and the group analyst simply makes use of this fact rather than imposing a substitute.

The group is, of course, helped to become more conscious of social processes and their normative function. They are helped to see how their rules, as they develop and change, are conducive or not to the therapeutic endeavour. They thus become self-conscious to a far greater extent than obtains in any other form of social grouping. The single analytic patient also becomes more self-conscious of what he or she does, but there are great differences. The most important seem to me to be in the degree to which each individual in the group is constantly defining themselves in the light of the group–self consciousness through its awareness of its social structure. Self-definition is an ongoing process in the group, by its very conceptualisation; whereas in psychoanalysis it is only gradually finding a place in a system originally designed for the cure of neurosis, with personality change a secondary consideration. In group analysis each member learns how to relate to the others by developing social awareness. It is this social awareness or self awareness in a social setting that is pooled by the group-as-a-whole. It is for this reason that theoretical models drawn from sociology and related disciplines are required. These disciplines take the group (large or small) as the primary datum, how groups are structured and how they function, and may derive from this an understanding of the behaviour of the individual. This is the exact opposite of the psychoanalytic approach. Exchange is such a central concept in these disciplines that it becomes an almost embarrassingly rich source of information in our understanding of our highly specialised group-analytic groups.

In anthropology, the variety of actual and possible social groups depends on the system of exchange which gives them their structure. The question of exchange, moreover, is one which brings together political theorists, sociologists, anthropologists, specialists in linguistics, communication theorists, social psychologists, and economists. A more abstract conceptualisation is provided by systems theory, in which information has to be exchanged across boundaries, either for the system to be maintained or to change. Exchange in all the fields I have mentioned is inseparable from the system in which it takes place, and therefore all systems can be understood as organisations of exchange.

## EXCHANGE IN THE GROUP CULTURE

Understanding exchange in the group requires, among other things, an understanding of its culture, and in this field anthropology becomes the appropriate discipline and Foulkes' observations might be regarded as anthropological rather than clinical. Although there are some limitations in the analogy, one can imagine an actual anthropologist studying a therapy group ethnographically. Let us imagine this anthropologist doing fieldwork and studying the analytic group as though it were a strange, 'primitive' tribe. The anthropologist would need to ascertain the exchange system and ask a series of questions. These might include: what is the medium of exchange, the 'currency'? What are the rules governing how exchanges are made? What is the function of the exchange, or what purposes is it serving? In what circumstances are the exchanges fulfilling the aims for which the group is brought together? Are there exchanges taking place which are detrimental to these aims? Are the conditions or rules such that the system of exchange does not involve the exploitation of some individuals by others? Is everyone aware of the nature of the exchanges taking place and of the rules governing them? These questions could not be easily answered if they were addressed to the group conductor, the equivalent to the chief of a tribe. The conductor would have to think hard to answer them, and this is largely because understanding what is going on in the group is not usually thought of in the terms of exchange theory, particularly if the main orientation of the conductor is psychoanalytic. Nevertheless, field-work needs to be done and we should make a beginning. With the rapid increase in group analysts resulting from training bodies being set up all over the world, there are now a large number of groups in existence run on similar lines. Furthermore, these groups are small enough for their exchange processes to be easily studied compared with the macro-economics of the large, even global structures of the postmodern age. Hence my justification for using the anthropological parallel.

The most immediate difficulty confronting both the anthropologist and the group conductor is that, apart from money and bills or receipts, no 'things' can be seen passing from hand to hand. All that seems to happen is that the circle of people are having a conversation. There is therefore some sort of conversational exchange, but this tells us very little. One can think, as Foulkes did, of explanations and information on various matters being exchanged, but again is this really the currency? Or rather, surely it cannot be the only currency. It is obviously not primarily an educational group. Is it interpretations, insight, moving experiences, perceptions, intuitions, phantasies, or memories? The conductor would perhaps say: 'Yes, all these things and many more'. But then, what about all the other questions? The great difficulty in answering them, as anthropologists readily acknowledge, is that no one member of the tribe, even the chief or the oldest member, may be able to provide the information. It means explaining the whole society in a novel way and doing so in a language which is not the language of the society but is a sort of meta-language.

This is an area where we have all sorts of unexamined assumptions, an unconscious ideology. It is difficult, in our materialistic society, to begin thinking of exchange other than as the exchange of possessions, and possessions as other than commodities. We imagine that we cannot exchange what we do not already own. We will only exchange if we get back at least the value of what we have parted with and preferably will gain from the transaction. If this is the underlying metaphor behind the exchanges in the group, each individual will be on their guard not to lose out. There will be an insistence on 'fair play' and thus on the rules of the marketplace. These rules are based on the idea of a person's inalienable right to own property, but it is just this right that leads to unfair exchange, as some become exploited by others. It was, of course, Marx who showed how alienation resulted from the commodification of labour. What seems, in principle, to be a fair exchange turns out to be unfair because commodities are given an exchange value of equivalence which reflects their material value in money terms. The labourer has only his labour to give but has to hand over the fruits of his labour and thus loses any sense of a meaning or purpose to it. Can exchange in the group be considered in other terms? One can begin to do so by seeing the group as one which values sharing more than private property. Taking 'explanation' as the currency, the exchange of explanations can be seen to lead to a shared explanation from which everyone gains; everyone knows more than they did before. Explanation, it is easy to acknowledge, is not to be hoarded as private property. It is not usually something to hold on to and be afraid of parting with. It is often considered that everyone in the group will benefit if the members are helped to disclose, to make public what they are holding onto rather than to think that, because it is their private property, it must be kept private and nobody else is entitled to it. If the group goes well, these ideas change. It is realised that nothing is lost by making the private public, and that what is disclosed remains private property, but of the group rather than as the sole possession of the individual. Perhaps it is this communality of property which led Foulkes to choose exchange as a therapeutic factor specific to the group. It is easy to see the value of this idea if 'explanation' is taken as the 'goods' to be exchanged.

## OWNING AND SHARING

However, this communistic ideology clashes with another, in which the right to individual possessions is highly valued as reflecting the autonomy of the individual. This can be seen in many typical remarks which form part of the group culture. Most group therapists will be familiar with the following examples:

'That stuff belongs to you.'
'Don't give me any of that shit.'
'I have to own that.'
'You have to be your own person.' And so on

This is the language of self-possession, of minding one's own business. There is, however, also a 'sharing' language which assumes that there it is good to turn the private into the common property of the group.

'I want to share this with you.'
'Thank you for letting me share my experience with you last week.'

These considerations have gone beyond regarding 'explanations' as the important currency. They would represent just one example of the many sorts of entity that can be exchanged. The language of giving, taking, sharing, and exchanging, robbing and stealing, lending and owing or being in debt, thanking, asking, demanding (the list can be extended indefinitely) is often vague as to what are the valuable objects being discussed as well as to the rights and wrongs of the matter. In fact, it is by being conscious of the need to define more clearly what is at stake that the group finds itself discussing these very questions. As it does so, the group can be said to have raised its level of consciousness or to have become more truly democratic or to have evolved into a more therapeutic milieu (depending on one's metaphorical model). The conductor will help the group in this direction in so far as he or she has thought out the issues involved.

There is often controversy as to what can be shared and thus become common property, justifying statements beginning with such generalisations as 'We are all feeling. . . ' or 'The group has a phantasy that. . .'. It is often not clear, or may be regarded as a matter of opinion, whether one member is speaking for himself or herself or voicing the feeling of the whole group or sub-group. The controversy is not restricted to a question of who begins by owning what but involves, also, discussions on who *takes* what of whatever the group has to offer. In this question, time and space, especially, are regarded as precious commodities which should be shared equally. One must not be greedy with them and one must not take them from others. Or there is an obligation to give them freely: 'Let us give Mary some space (or time).' This is the language of quantity. The more one talks the more one will get out of the group, but the more space one will take up which will deprive others, who will complain that they would do better in 'one-to-one'. Sometimes there will be quite a naked individualism: 'I'm not here to help the group; I'm only here to help myself.'

This sort of statement is often not opposed by the group. After all, the ultimate goal of group analysis is to help the individuals to get better and leave. At this point people will ask: 'What have you got out of it?' Or people will say what they have 'got out of' the person who is leaving. This is a kind of accounting, like looking at a balance sheet. 'Trusting the group' is often not very helpful in this regard. It is like trusting a free-market economy, and a '*laissez-faire*' policy may lead to monopoly, as the expression of the 'group monopoliser' suggests.

It is very hard to find another language, though the idea of the development of altruism has been put forward as a therapeutic factor by Yalom (1975). What seems to be needed is a different concept of exchange which is not based on private property. One does not have to be generous or altruistic. There has to be a notion of giving without losing whatever one has given, or receiving without taking away. This does not mean that property is shared in the sense of being divided. It seems to require a quite different view of property, a sense in which it is not privately owned but freely available to all.

'It costs nothing to smile.' When one says this, one recognises that giving someone a smile does not mean parting with it. 'It gives me pleasure to hear you talk' may acknowledge a gift where there was no thought of giving. Usually people are called 'gifted' when no one has given them anything. So we do have, in everyday language, a notion of giving and receiving not based on property which has somehow to be acquired, looked after, guarded, or exchanged through fear of being lost or stolen. What is hard to explain is how this is possible. Whether it is explained in religious terms as an appeal to man's higher nature or in terms of an evolutionarily determined necessity for co-operation rather than competition, it seems to depend on the individual's realisation of being in themselves, not being (in Donne's words) an island, but a part of a greater whole, a member of a group being like a member of the body.

It is often claimed that group analysis recognises the social nature of the human being whereas the psychoanalytic procedure does not. Such claims are always a gross oversimplification. What truth it may once have had is rapidly ebbing away as the psychoanalytic model changes (see the chapters by Brown and Marrone, for example, for confirmation of this). Psychoanalysts are recognising more and more that their patients develop as social beings and that the model of infantile development on which they rely is largely one of socialisation from the very beginning. This is particularly evident in self psychology, following Kohut, and in attachment theory. Nevertheless, it remains true that there is a marked difference of emphasis in the conceptualisations of group analysis. However much psychoanalysis tries to incorporate a social perspective, it is limited by its underlying model which views the individual as a primary entity, which happens also to live in a society of individuals. This problem is not restricted to the psychological discipline but has been a major epistemological stumbling block in all the human sciences and perhaps in the natural sciences as well (see, for example, Bateson (1979), Prigogine and Stengers (1984), Bohm (1980), and Andrew Powell's chapter in this volume). This mistaken epistemology of course affects not only theoreticians, but also the theories everybody holds in their conception of themselves and the world in which they live.

## UNCONSCIOUSNESS

The group may be unconscious of its values and, in particular, of its system of exchange. Taking a social perspective means studying hidden values and hidden rules, as we found when considering the problem the chief has in describing his community. There is also always an ideology which determines the way things are perceived, a set of hidden assumptions which may never be questioned. This kind of unconsciousness is different from the usual Freudian one, which concerns the repression of what is forbidden. Because both meanings are used by group analysts, who try to combine a social with a dynamic model, group phenomena are hard to describe consistently, and often both senses are confused in the description.

In the case of exchange, there is a particular difficulty. However much the group can understand and frame its own rules, it remains unconscious in both senses. Once we start to move away from Foulkes' own example of children exchanging happily with one another what they cannot exchange with their parents, this difficulty becomes more and more apparent. Most exchanges are not voluntary because they are not conscious, and exploitation and unfair exchanges take place when the degree of voluntariness and awareness of what is happening is not the same for both parties. At times people exploit one another without either of them being aware of it.

Although Freud usefully distinguished the pre-conscious from the unconscious, the unconscious as such was treated by him as a single entity. It is more helpful, especially in a group-analytic context, to speak of 'levels of awareness' and to regard these levels not simply quantitatively as degrees of awareness but as levels in which one is aware of some things and not of others – in other words, of different kinds of unconsciousness, of which the Freudian is only one. Foulkes' levels are of this kind. With this in mind, the relationship between Foulkes' two fourfold classifications, which I earlier compared to the quaternios in Jung's studies of alchemy, can usefully be considered. There needs to be some way of making a conceptual link between the two groups of four. One, the four factors, describes processes: mirroring, exchanging, integrating, and activating. The other describes structure in the form of levels. Every system requires a description both of its structure and of the way it functions. So the obvious solution is to combine these two groups of four.

It is apparent, too, that to discriminate difference as levels is to make use of a metaphor of height and depth or, in other words, of a vertical dimension, while the four factors are described as processes which can readily been seen to be going on in any group at any given time, giving them more the quality of horizontality. Once they are combined, however, the relationship between these two sets of four can be treated more subtly. The four factors could be seen as operating on all four levels but differently at each level. Foulkes himself did not combine them in this way and seems to have been thinking about separate subjects. His description of levels does seem to indicate that he thought of four different sorts of process occurring at each one and these were not in any case to be identified with the four therapeutic factors. But combining them in the way I have suggested might be the most productive scheme for further study of the therapeutic factors, and in conclusion, I should like to illustrate the advantages of such an approach.

As a reminder to the reader, Foulkes described four levels at which the group interacts. They are arranged in descending order of depth as:

1 Current Level
2 Transference Level

3 Projective Level
4 Primordial Level.

(Foulkes 1964: 114–15)

Level three is characterised by projective identification which, in turn, involves splitting. Could this be seen as a primitive form of exchange? There are two senses in which this could be so, even though not originally described as such by Melanie Klein. One is that what is projected is lost to the projector but if the lost part of the self is felt to be 'bad', there may be a gain for the projector. He or she has lost part of the self but feels better off without it. The recipient loses their previous sense of self and has (unwillingly) exchanged it for the bad bit put into them. The other, more systemic, way is the frequently seen case of *mutual* projective identifications, as is commonly described in marriages. Clearly, these exchanges are deeply unconscious. It has not always been easy for theorists to differentiate projective identification from the more simple projections which give rise to most of the transference and which Foulkes assigns to Level two, but if we follow Foulkes in making such a distinction, the main difference may be in the *kind* of unconsciousness (split-off rather than repressed). These exchanges seem to be of such a different kind from that in Foulkes' example (which seems to belong more to Level one, the current level) that they can hardly be called therapeutic factors in the same breath. However, the idea that therapy requires only that the projections be taken back, that the exchanges can be reversed, restoring the *status quo ante*, is again a very limited idea of therapeutic change. To see the exchange as therapeutic, it is more productive to consider that even if both partners do take them back, both gain in the process by acquiring something which did not previously exist, except in another person. Each has gained in no longer being split off from what only the other seemed to have possessed.

Level four concerns an even more fundamentally unconscious level of exchange, where all boundaries seem to disappear. At least at Level three, where projective identification is rife, people are aware that something is going on *between people* even if they cannot quite say what. At Level four, the whole group, including the conductor, may not know that they are all gripped by an archetype. If they sense it at all, it may be attributed to an outside force beyond their control: the institution, state, the gods, or just 'them'. At this level exchanges are a long way from the civilised, polite rules of Level one but take on the nature of sacrifice. Scapegoating would be only one example. Nevertheless, however primitive and barbarous such processes may appear, it is still important to regard them as at least potentially therapeutic factors. Consider what may happen when a patient leaves, to be replaced by another. In a sense, it is necessary for the leaving one to be 'destroyed' to make way for the new one, even though the group at a higher level may be doing the opposite, holding on to the departing member and then ritually making life difficult for the new one. At a higher level still, perhaps Level one, the group may wish the departing member well *and* welcome the new one. Using this framework, one would no longer talk easily about what is defensively being avoided. It becomes possible to see each level as a defence against the other three.

It can be seen that I have considerably elaborated Foulkes' idea of exchange as a therapeutic factor. In my last example, the exchange is *of* the group members rather than between them, and shows that there is no one kind of commodity such as 'explanations' which form the currency. The exchange of members in the slow-open group may perform a function similar to the exchange of women in so-called primitive societies, as Lévi-Strauss has demonstrated. The dynamics of this exchange in group analysis awaits detailed study.

I have also tried to bring out a diachronic as well as a synchronic perspective, incorporating the generally accepted idea that groups evolve and that the therapeutic processes, including exchange, change through time in the history of any particular group.

All these considerations make the topic difficult to handle, but I hope to have shown that Foulkes' ideas, albeit somewhat sketchy, do provide the basis for a developing consensus.

## CONCLUSION

In conclusion, I should like to stress that the overall aim of psychotherapy is, for me, the pursuit of wholeness as expressed by Jung in his idea of individuation. Although wholeness often becomes a rather vague ideal, it is much clearer in group analysis than in individual analysis, because it is easy to grasp that the individuation of the group member depends on the individuation of the group-as-a-whole.

The quaternio structure within which I have sought to understand exchange in this chapter has certain implications with which I would like to conclude it. First, the group hopes to acquire knowledge of the whole system in which they are trying to relate to one another, the processes taking place in it as well as its structure. The four therapeutic factors can be looked at separately, but really they act together.

Exchange requires mirroring and mirroring requires exchange; both require social integration and the activation of the collective unconscious. At any time, one of these may be overvalued at the expense of others, and this leads to loss of balance and then the factors become antitherapeutic.

Second, the four levels, too, are interdependent. Again, each can be studied separately but they are parts of the same structure, and it is only we who have divided them for the sake of being able to discern them. Also, it is wrong to think of any level as being 'better' than another. 'Deeper', for instance, does not mean 'better'. Everyday reality is not superficial in the sense of trivial, and the deepest layer of the unconscious, the primordial, is neither wiser nor more primitive. So although exchange shows certain differences at different levels, there is a place for each. However, the group will only progress in so far as the levels as well as the therapeutic factors are seen as forming a balancing and co-ordinated whole. The exchanges in the group then gradually become both richly varied and integrated as well as fair.

# Chapter 8

# The womb and gender identity

*Barbara Elliott*

It would be foolish to believe that the mind begins to function only at the moment of birth – he must get from his existence the impression that he is in fact omnipotent. . .the feeling that one has all that one wants, and that one has nothing to wish for.

(Ferenczi 1913)

This chapter will explore the regression to very primitive psychological and interpersonal states of mind that occur in groups. I will argue that the experience of being in a group evokes unconsciously memory traces of having been in and of the womb. During this phase of regression both males and females may feel that they have wombs contained inside themselves. I will illustrate these hypotheses with examples from therapeutic and training groups, and will examine the implications of these ideas for theories of the development of gender identity – our sense of ourselves as masculine or feminine.

The notion of the group representing mother's body has been taken up by Schindler (1966) and Scheidlinger (1974) and, more recently, by Hearst (1981), Anzieu (1984), and Prodgers (1990). Foulkes (1964) did not take it very far, yet, he too considered the idea that the group represented parts of the body. He wrote:

The whole group can serve as an imago, a reflection of phantasies of the group which are in everybody's mind. Individual members are used as personifications in the sense of transference figures, substitute figures, but also personifications of the whole self, parts of self and the body image.

(1964: 164)

He further distinguished between the group as a symbol of the inside of the mother as opposed to the outside of the mother. He said of one group:

the group not only represented the mother Image but seemed to represent the mother's inside, the mother's womb, the mother containing the unborn children as it were.

(1964: 260)

It would seem that the idea of the group representing the mother is a complex one, and one which requires a certain clarification between the inside and the outside of the body. One concept refers to the re-enactment in groups of the relationship between the *infant* and the mother, while the other refers to the re-enactment of the relationship between the *foetus* and the mother. It is this later relationship involving experiences in the womb on which I wish to concentrate.

The notion of a memory trace of life in the womb is certainly not a far-fetched idea. With the aid of modern technology, more is being discovered about life before birth. It is becoming increasingly clear that the foetus is not an isolated or passive being. 'Long before birth, a foetus can hear, respond to pressure and touch, swallow, taste, react to pain, choose its preferential position and also have some kind of primitive dream experience and show the beginnings of some kind of learning' (Piontelli 1987: 454). There is little doubt that sensory perceptions occur while the foetus is in the womb, and this will undoubtedly produce some form of memory trace.

How might regression to the phantasy of being in the womb be experienced and re-enacted? I would like to explore this question by turning to a description of a large-group experience. Several years ago, I attended a series of large groups as part of the Introductory Course offered by the Institute of Group Analysis. This encounter made such an impact on me that it remains and continues to affect the way I view both large- and small-group processes.

My first impression of the very first meeting was of the level of noise in the room. I could hardly hear a word that was spoken. I took this to be an inevitable result of placing more than 100 people into a single group and an indication that the experience was destined to be frustrating. There seemed to be considerable excitement and tension in the room and a great deal of activity – shuffling, coughing, throat clearing, head scratching, and heavier than usual breathing. My own sense of excitement had resulted in blood pulsing round my head. The effect was similar to that of putting a shell to my ear and listening to the rush of the sea. I was surprised to discover, that after a few minutes, I could hear every word uttered with absolute clarity. I realised that my inability to hear had not been the result of the size of the room and the number of people taking part but of what had been taking place in the group and within myself. I started to relax, taking in what was around me, and listening to what was being said by the various speakers. I became aware of the sounds of gentle breathing all around, and a pleasant, sleepy sensation began to creep over me. Gradually, I began to experience a sense of disorientation as if I were floating gently in space. I felt surrounded and weightless – a pleasurable sensation. Suddenly I began to feel that I would fall off my chair. My awareness of my position as an adult in a room full of other adults warned me that I would be humiliated if I fell over in the middle of a large group. I clung to the seat of my chair, and through a process of coughing, blinking, and concentrating on what was being said by various group members, brought myself back from my disorientation. I returned, as it were, to the land of the social.

Although I was able to re-experience the sensations of disorientation, confusion, and merging during the subsequent weeks, I was careful not to let them overwhelm me again. I began to wonder what produced such strong and peculiar feelings and whether they would always be stimulated when one was in a large group.

Since that initial encounter in the large group, I have often experienced these distinct sensations in both small- and large-group settings, and have observed what I believe to be the same experiences in patients. I have in fact, seen a member of a small group come off his chair and fall into the middle of the circle during a small-group session.

Such phenomena have often been reported by students of group dynamics, and many clinicians from various forms of group therapy have developed explanations for this lack of differentiation between individual and group. For example, Usandivaras (1985, 1989) has introduced the concept of Communitas, referring to the inevitable regression that occurs within all groups during certain phases of therapy. The patient regresses to time when 'the world is a totality in which everything is related' (Usandivaras 1985: 9). The process involves a paring down to a bare, cognitive, mental structure, including what Jung (1934) has described as the archetypes in the collective unconscious that are then re-enacted in group sessions as rituals and myths. The notion of Communitas refers to phenomena that are similar to those that I have described. This explanation, however, for the tendency to regress in groups is very much rooted in spiritualism, mysticism, and the assumption of the inheritance of acquired characteristics, and as such provides only a piece of this rather complex puzzle.

Numerous other clinicians have also observed that patients do not always meaningfully differentiate themselves from the group and explain this phenomenon differently. For example, Turquet (1975), Anzieu (1984), Wexler *et al.* (1984) and Battegay (1986) focus on fusional processes in groups which are always based on regression. Here is an example of fusion in which a patient I was seeing in a once-weekly analytic psychotherapy group clearly demonstrated his poor ego boundaries: long periods of silence (often punctuated by sudden, frightened outbursts about his inability to settle in the group) were combined with periods of interaction during which he took up communication with others only as a stimulus for what he needed to express about himself. He used the words and ideas of other group members as associative stimuli in order to communicate something about his own experience.

Although it is the borderline patient who typically relates in this manner, I have observed many differently diagnosed patients interact in ways which suggest that at times, the communications from other group members (regardless of the subject) are used only as a background to the speaker and his own experience at that moment. This pattern of fused interaction can be understood in terms of the earliest relationship between the infant and the mother where the infant does not yet view itself as a separate being.

However, the re-enactment of life in the womb – a separate and different kind of regressive experience – may also occur in groups. I suggest that we can, and should, account for both kinds of experience in group life. If we agree on this course, we will soon discover that distinguishing between states of fusion and what can be called womb phenomena is not an easy matter. It involves an attempt at differentiating clinically between the re-enactment of intrauterine life and the re-enactment of the earliest relationship between the infant and the mother. Before attempting to discriminate between these two distinct types of experience as they are re-enacted in groups, I need to outline my position with regard to the development of primitive mental life.

The first problem to address is the timing relating to the establishment of the first object relationships. A debate exists between the Kleinian position that object relations begin at birth and the latter and more popular view that the newborn is for some time in an undifferentiated state of fusion with the mother – a 'normal' state of symbiosis or autism. Recent findings based on infant observation and research challenge the largely accepted view of the infant as psychically undifferentiated from the mother.

In contrast to the concept of normal autism, the concept of emergent relatedness assumes that the infant, from the moment of birth is deeply social in the sense of being designed to engage in and find uniquely salient interaction with other humans.

(Stern 1985: 235)

Stern goes on to suggest that the capacity to experience fusion with another is dependent on the prior existence and development of a sense of self and a distinct sense of the other. The position in this chapter regarding the development of early mental life is consistent with this view. It also incorporates Stern's premise that 'Development occurs in leaps and bounds; qualitative shifts may be one of its most obvious features' (1985: 8).

If we accept that one very significant qualitative shift occurs at birth – the shift that signals the onset of 'interpersonal relatedness' (Stern 1985: 43) – we must also try to theorise about the kind of mental life which precedes it in the womb.

It is commonly accepted that there exists some form of mental life *in utero*. My position is that this form of mental life necessarily excludes object relations. The foetus cannot develop true object representations and object relations because it is part and parcel of the object itself. In the womb there will never occur the absence or loss of the object, both of which are prerequisites for the development of thought and phantasy (Bion 1962b). Yet, we must somehow account for the mental activity which is taking place. We can do this by hypothesising that the foetus will have some kind of mental impression of its experience – a memory trace. The impression which occurs in the womb becomes a memory without an attached instinct or wish. It is the thing remembered in itself without any mind/body interaction. This must be distinguished from a phantasy, which is a memory trace with a wish and some form of object relationship attached to it. I suggest that it is only from the time of birth, after the loss of the womb, and after the first encounter with the breast, that the potential for object relations begins. One must clearly differentiate the state of fusion with a primal object (which comes about as a defence against anxiety such as a fear of engulfment), from memory traces of having been in the womb. The former is based on the prior development of representations of objects and object relations, whereas the latter is a mental image without any wishes or impulses linked to it.

Any argument, therefore, which suggests that the suckling infant re-creates the womb experience through a process of merging and loss of boundary with the mother (Maizels 1985) is confusing two similar but separate states. The experience of the infant at the breast is not the same as that of the foetus in the womb, although, as Klein (1952) points out, it may be the next best thing.

The re-enactment in groups of early object relationships, such as those based on fusion, always and necessarily involves forms of active 'relating to' one another. Some of the most primitive levels of group functioning, such as Bion's (1961) basic assumptions, imply an interaction between separate objects or, at least, an attitude between one object and another. Even when patients are silent, they may be relating directly to an object, as when a group member is actively engaged in what is taking place in a session and monitoring subjective experience; such as, boredom, irritation, excitement, or sense of identification. However, patients in groups do not always and inevitably locate the therapist or other group members in this way, and can regress to a level prior to even the earliest form of object relating. This early form of relationship is primarily concerned with being part of and surrounded by, without being separate in any sense. It concerns an inability to identify or relate to an object as separate from the self. In a group, a patient can be silent while at the same time surrounded by and therefore engaged with various forms of activity involving sounds, smells, and movement (Brown 1985). The living structure of the group embraces all, and makes periods of complete passivity simultaneously active. The patient is joined to a life force which is greater than the self. I suggest that this level of functioning is more primitive than even the earliest form of object relating based on orality and is directly related to the womb memory trace.

If we accept that patients in groups have access to memories of intra-uterine life, then the notion of the womb as an introject needs to be explored.

In 1928 Melanie Klein wrote on the Oedipus complex, saying:

> The dread of the mother is so overwhelming because there is combined with it an intense dread of castration by the father. The destructive tendencies whose object is the womb are also directed with their full oral and anal-sadistic intensity against the father's penis which is supposed to be located there.
>
> (1928: 190)

Later, in 'The emotional life of the infant' (Klein 1952), while writing about the powerful and overwhelming feelings the infant is subject to in relation to the good and bad breast, she writes, 'We may also assume that the infant hallucinates the longed for pre-natal state' (p. 64).

Klein was not arguing for the existence of true object relations prior to birth. Yet her theories seem consistent with my earlier suggestion. While the womb does not exist as an object in pre-natal life (because there is as yet no separation from and loss of the womb), at the point of birth and the moment of encounter with the first object, the womb memory can then be related to as an object. Just as pre-verbal experiences can be verbalised and made meaningful by a process of working backwards in time, so too can experiences which are pre-object, by acting upon them with the same psychic mechanisms. This would mean that the womb memory could be introjected in the same way as any other primal object.

The following illustration could be understood in a number of ways, one of which is as a description of the loss of an introjected womb object based on a memory trace.

> A pregnant colleague reported that her son of $2\frac{1}{2}$ years had recently fallen into a deep depression. The boy had earlier shown an active and lively interest in his mother's distended abdomen and had spoken to her repeatedly about his wish to grow a baby inside. He was resistant to her attempts at explaining that boys did not have wombs and could not produce babies, even when they became men. When at last the resistance gave way to acceptance, the boy entered into an acute despair which lasted several days.

My hypothesis is that the memory trace of the womb experience is subject to mechanisms of early psychic life. As an image, perhaps an image of space, the womb can be introjected and internalised by the neonate. At the earliest phases of development, both boys and girls have the capacity to internalise the womb space phantasy which is based on their own direct experience of it. This means that both men and women have the unconscious phantasy that they have wombs inside their bodies. This phantasy becomes dim with time as the sphere of interpersonal relationships begins to dominate. The boy infant will abandon the internal phantasy womb for something that is much more tangible and immediate – his penis. The girl will become increasingly more aware and preoccupied with the real womb. However, these early images and phantasies, while superseded, are never entirely lost, and on this level the mental representation of a womb inside belongs equally to the man as to the woman.

This has major implications for gender identity formation and for our understanding of it. We can expect to see expressions in group life of the unconscious phantasy that men and women have wombs inside themselves. We can also expect to see expressions of gender-identity confusion around this issue which may be of great importance in the therapeutic setting. Before examining the role of the womb in the development of gender identity, I would like to turn to some earlier work on this theme.

During times of group stress, patients in a once-weekly psychotherapy group often divided themselves into male and female subgroups from which clearly defined patterns of interaction arose. The women were on the whole, direct, forceful, and dominant, while the men were quiet, withdrawn, and passive. From the beginning most women seemed to know immediately and intuitively how to 'proceed' in psychotherapy, which gave them an edge and an advantage over the men. Group therapy, I began to think, was being experienced as a feminine activity.

> women are given a familiar model while men are exposed to the unfamiliar. Therapy deals with the unseen, with emotions and thoughts that cannot be physically touched, that come from inside the mind and body. I suggest that the group-analytic process corresponds unconsciously to the little girl's discovery that her reproductive organs lie not outside the body where they can be seen and touched but inside where they can only be fantasised or talked about.
>
> (Elliott 1986)

The way the women expressed their competence, however, and the response of the men to them, created a flurry of confused and frightening phantasies about the nature of maleness and femaleness. When women were viewed by one another and by the men as powerful and competent, I discovered that they were not always necessarily experienced as the pre-Oedipal, controlling mother (Alonso and Rutan 1979). They were sometimes experienced as masculine and phallic beings. In other words, an unconscious equation was made between competency, potency, and masculinity. The intuitive feminine aptitude for the penetrating insight often experienced as masculine, became the phantasy phallus, which is consistent with Klein's (1952) theories regarding the infant's phantasy of the penis contained within the mother's body.

This is one example of how various parts of the male and female body with their accompanying images were experienced as belonging to an individual of the opposite sex. Beyond this phantasy of the phallus, which was attributed in this case to a woman, many other phantasies exist about the nature of the body and relationships to it. It can be argued, for example, within the framework of gender-identity confusion, that a man who is perceived as powerful in the group may be experienced not as a penetrating phallus but as a nipple with an executive function of gatekeeper to the breast and the contents inside. Not only is there confusion brought about by phantasies of the phallus being contained inside the mother but also by phantasies about the nature of the nipple as a prototype of the phallus (Meltzer 1967).

It would appear that these unconscious phantasies about parts of the body are experienced both by males and females, and are only later superseded by less chaotic and fragmented images of maleness and femaleness. Within the group setting there exists an interface between levels of primitive functioning where there is no differentiation between the sexes, and levels of social Oedipal functioning where there is a clear distinction made between male and female and masculine and feminine.

If we accept that men and women engage in these unconscious phantasies about the breast and penis and that these images of parts of the body are incorporated into the primitive psyche, then interesting possibilities arise in relation to the psychic representation of the womb. I do not, of course, refer here to the womb as the mental representation of a part of the body that is contained within the woman, but rather as a representation of something both males and females were at one time attached to and therefore, something which was, and is, experienced as part of the self. It is within the womb that men and women have actually shared identical sensations, and it is worth speculating about the implications of this common experience as expressed in groups. For example, we could expect to uncover some deep-seated confusion and insecurity in the men who do not have a physiological womb which corresponds to the phantasy. Alternatively, issues around womb envy and fear of becoming engulfed by a ravenous, greedy space might usefully be explored by both male and female patients.

In one long-established out-patient psychotherapy group, I once had occasion to introduce two new male patients together. The group was in a phase where prolonged (although not uncomfortable) silences were the norm. When the two new males dropped out fairly soon after joining, I was puzzled. I considered the possibility that the sudden departure of one and then another man from the group might be explained by relating it to the natural discomfort which accompanies long silence in everyday social intercourse. Perhaps these patients had been unable to contain the anxiety which was aroused by the silence. However, both patients had received what seemed like adequate attention and space from the group, and I could not somehow justify their sudden and abrupt departures by explanations of social discomfort or anxiety at being in a new and unusual situation. I began to search for other explanations. A more meaningful although untestable hypothesis seemed that the terror motivating the 'escape' from the group originated from a much more primitive fear. This might be the result of a symbiosis anxiety (Stoller 1975), but equally could be explained in terms of a terror of engulfment within the womb.

In another group, made up of individual psychotherapy trainees, a young male student found himself overwhelmed with anxiety sometimes bordering on terror from the very first session of a one-year experiential group. This student was reasonably confident and unusually articulate in his normal day-to-day life, of which we occasionally were allowed to see glimpses. However, when in the group setting he habitually became pale, inarticulate, and troubled. We attempted to look at the sources of his anxiety and his discomfort with specific group members to no avail, and often he was simply unable to speak. After some months of his alternately suffering or sleeping in the group, I began to interpret his behaviour in terms of feelings of being totally overwhelmed in the womb. He found this specific interpretation very useful. It brought relief and was used to explore certain aspects of his early life, including a deep-seated confusion between him and his mother, and the resultant confusion between his sense of masculinity and femininity. We had insufficient time to explore the conflict produced by the phantasy of an internalised womb, but I would suggest that this has particular relevance for male psychotherapy trainees who may experience confusion brought about by the mismatch between phantasy and reality with regard to the presence and absence of a womb. This is particularly stimulated by the identification with the role of therapist or caretaker.

The effects of the womb space as a container and as an introject in group therapy are not always easy to observe. The most intense experiences of being contained occur neither during periods of active interaction nor during periods of what could be termed 'active listening'. The experience occurs when a patient is engaged in a deeply regressive state and is silent. Although it is never possible to be sure of what a patient is experiencing during periods of silence, it would not be unreasonable to assume that there can occur a particularly intense form of regression under certain circumstances and at certain times. Of course, it would be naïve to assume that all sensations in the womb are pleasant. The foetus may also have many kinds of painful, negative experiences in the womb. It should be possible therefore to distinguish between these negative womb memory traces and the later defensive states of alienation and fragmentation which are expressed in the group processes of aggregation and massification (Hopper 1991). Equally, the regression could be experienced as something restful and potentially healing. This might indeed explain why quiet patients often make such dramatic strides forward in groups. These patients will, of course, inevitably derive benefit from what they are witnessing in a group – what they see and hear. However, a model of experience which takes into account active engagement, active listening, and a deeply regressive, restful state, more closely reflects the curative elements to be found in groups.

The idea of the group as mother and the idea of the group as womb are not new and can be found throughout the group-analytic literature. I hope to have argued that the two concepts should be kept clearly separated. One refers to the relationship between the infant and the mother, and the other refers to a relationship between the foetus and the mother. The re-enactment in groups of the earlier mental state can be understood in terms of a particular type of regressive phenomenon which is partly based on a memory trace of having been inside 'mother's womb'. The memory trace will be subject to all the mechanisms of early psychic life, including projection and introjection, and this will have implications for the development of gender identity.

Within the group setting we can always expect to witness a certain amount of confusion about maleness and femaleness. Some of this confusion occurs as a result of conflicts between groups culture and the wider society. But further confusion will arise as a result of the regression to levels of unconscious fantasy which is dominated by the part objects – breast, penis, and womb – and operates regardless of the sex of those involved.

The notion of the womb as part object as well as a space and container in group life can be useful in the overall exploration of the nature of patients' maleness and femaleness. It is within the group structure that men and women have the opportunity to engage with one another simultaneously on the most sophisticated yet the most primitive levels, and this provides them with unique opportunities for exploring the fantasies and the realities of their relationships with one another.

## ACKNOWLEDGEMENTS

My thanks to Karl König, Diana Birkett, and Louis Zinkin for their helpful comments and suggestions. My gratitude to Earl Hopper for his encouragement, constructive criticism, and generosity.

# Chapter 9

# The primal scene in group analysis

*Morris Nitsun*

What is at the centre of the group? Ever since I started training as a group analyst and through my years of qualified practice, a question something like this has nagged at me. Is there a centre to the group and if so, what is it? I needed something substantial to put there. The familiar symbol or logo of group analysis is a circle of squares surrounding a central object representing a table. Of course, in reality most of us use a table, but this is a concrete thing. What, metaphorically, humanly, is at the centre of the group?

The question is associated in my mind with some dissatisfaction with Foulkes' concept of the group matrix (see Chapter 2). This is a valuable concept in many respects, emphasising the overall containing network of the group in a way that gives us a broad framework for understanding group process. But it sometimes seems to me too diffuse, too global, too all-containing to be of immediate use. Also, it is associated almost entirely with the feminine principle in group analysis. The matrix is the mother, the womb specifically (Foulkes 1964; Roberts 1982), perhaps also the early mother–infant relationship (James 1984; Nitsun 1989), but what about the father? How does he enter the scene? I link this question not so much with familiar issues about leadership and authority in the group, which are often interpreted in masculine terms, but in a more fundamental way with the matrix itself. How does the father, symbolically the penis, enter the mother, the matrix, in our conception of the group? How do male and female come together, not only in the interpersonal sphere in groups but in the unconscious creation of the group and in our meta-psychological understanding of groups? Increasingly, this question has led me to the psychoanalytic notion of the primal scene as an explanatory paradigm for the group. The primal scene is generally regarded as portraying 'the sexual relations of the parents both as perceived and imagined' (Britton 1989), but I prefer the extended definition given by Joyce McDougall, which refers to 'the child's total store of unconscious knowledge and personal mythology concerning the human sexual relation, particularly that of the parents' (McDougall 1980).

In this chapter, I will argue that the primal scene is at the centre of the group, that in order to understand the complex development of the group and its many obscure and difficult manifestations, such as periods of regression, excessive confusion and even disintegration – processes I have referred to as the Anti-Group (Nitsun 1991) – as well as periods of dramatic growth and excitement, recognition of the primal scene and its derivatives may be essential. The concept of the primal scene is derived from individual rather than group analysis, but I hope to show that it has considerable relevance to groups and that its elucidation through the group-analytic process can extend our understanding of the phenomenon, thereby embracing individual and group development on a single continuum.

## THE CONCEPT OF THE PRIMAL SCENE

The concept of the primal scene has a universal significance (Laplanche and Pontalis 1980), reflected in its wide representation in the realms of psychoanalytic discourse, where it crosses many of the usual boundaries of theoretical and ideological difference. Freud saw it not only as an expression of the child's view of parental intercourse but as a vehicle for the child's understanding of its own origins and that of the family. In Freud's theory, the primal scene was a precursor to the Oedipus complex, which, as we know, he saw as an organising principle – if not *the* organising principle – in psychosexual development.

Freud (1908) described several versions of the primal scene, with some emphasis on the view of parental intercourse as a sadistic act, specifically an attack by the father on the mother. Much of the subsequent analytic literature contrasted the sadistic view of parental intercourse with the view of the primal scene as a loving, creative act, indeed the supremely creative act. Jung (1913) emphasised the constructive: the archetypal image of parental union symbolises the union of opposites and thus facilitates the individual's potential for integration and individuation. The image of the parents in bed is seen as a container of parts of the individual's own psyche, so that the child discovering the parental union is also discovering itself and recovering what has been projected onto the parents. Further, Jung believed that differentiation of the parents in bed encourages looking beyond or through the real parents to membership of the human race and to issues of ontology, purpose, and meaning (Samuels 1985).

This is very different from the view of Melanie Klein, who saw the primal scene as a focus for intensely aggressive fears and phantasies. She argues:

> the Oedipus conflict begins under the complete dominance of sadism ... the attack launched upon the object with all the weapons of sadism rouses the subject's dread of analogous attack upon himself from the external and internalised objects.
>
> (Klein 1929: 212)

Klein differed from Freud in believing that the Oedipus complex started very early in life, in the first few months, and was associated with part-object relations to breast and penis and relationships between these two objects, as contrasted with the classical view of the Oedipus complex of the two parents perceived as whole objects in genital terms. According to Klein, the perception of parental union originates in the phantasy of a monstrous, fused figure of mother and father, later moving on to a sense of partial parental differentiation. This stimulates very primitive responses of hatred and envy, which through projective identification contaminate the part objects and make them dangerous and retaliatory. Recognition of the primal scene may be so fraught with anxiety that the infant resorts to ways of totally denying the reality of parental intercourse or of mentally fracturing their relationship in such a way that their creativity is (in phantasy) destroyed.

Klein believed that some resolution of these early phantasies is necessary in order for the child to proceed to the more mature Oedipus complex. This is achieved, in part, through the depressive position, in which separation and differentiation are dealt with. Through reparation, the infant imbues the primal scene with constructive qualities and eventually introjects a harmonious parental couple.

Some psychoanalytic theorists, like Chasseguet-Smirgel (1984), emphasise that the position the child takes in relation to the primal scene – and the level of implied psychic integration – is a crucial determinant not only of the child's sexual development but of its overall psychological adjustment. For example, the nature of an individual's thinking may be linked to this phenomenon. Klein (1926) referred to the 'epistemophilic impulse', or the urge to learn, which she saw as strongly influenced by curiosity and anxiety about the mother's body and its relationship to the father. Britton (1989) suggests that the capacity to differentiate the self from the parental couple in intercourse, as opposed to being merged with an undifferentiated parental couple, is linked to the ability to take a reflective, outsider's position in observing relationships – 'a constructive mental space within the boundary of the oedipal triangle'.

Another derivative of the perception of the primal scene is the capacity for creativity in the general sense rather than the procreative sense. Daniel Dervin (1990), an American psychoanalyst and literary critic, gives this a major focus. His thesis is that the child's construction of the primal scene gives form to some of the deepest questions about human origins and the destiny of the family (not unlike Jung's view). This early psychic elaboration is seen as a natural stage of creativity, a precursor to later forms of creativity, both artistic and otherwise.

Both these derivatives of the primal scene – the capacity for reflective thought in observing relationships and the early stage of creativity in constructing a form of social meaning – have clear and important implications for group life in general and group analysis in particular – points that will be developed later in this chapter. But as part of this consideration of the wider implications of the primal scene, I wish to offer a personal view that in some respects conflicts with those psychoanalytic theories described above, particularly those of Klein.

Klein's view of the significance of the primal scene rests heavily on an intrapsychic model of development. Although I accept this in some respects, I also believe that the intrapsychic version of the primal scene cannot be separated from the real family and social histories of the parents. Each partner brings to the primal scene a distinctive personal history. This has genetic, family, and cultural components, and the act of sexual penetration between the parents is at the same time an *interpenetration* of two individual histories. In this sense, the phantasy of the primal scene can be viewed not as a fictional construction but as an intense mirroring of complex social and genetic factors in a state of convergence. I believe that in forming its version of the primal scene, the child intuitively picks up the influence of the biological and social pasts of its parents and adds to these its own subjective perceptions, borne out of its possibly witnessing and/or phantasising about the parents' relationship. So, the primal scene, like the dream, is a *condensation* of reality factors linked to parental history, mediated via the child's conscious and unconscious interpretations and imbued with the child's search for its origins and its quest for identity. *It is this extended version of the primal scene, viewed as a link between intrapsychic and external reality, that I see as appropriate to the group-analytic endeavour.*

## BION AND FOULKES: CONTRASTING APPROACHES

No consideration of psychoanalytic thought as applied to the group is complete without reference to Bion and Foulkes. How did they view the significance of the primal scene in relation to groups? Of the two, Bion comes much closer to the model I am developing. In fact, it was a statement that he made in his classic text *Experiences in Groups* (Bion 1961) that stimulated my thinking. This is a statement that I consider to be of major significance to our understanding of groups but one that has received surprisingly littler further attention, although Brown (1985), in an evaluation of Bion's contribution to group psychotherapy, made an important attempt to address the issue and I return to this below.

Bion's pivotal statement arises in the context of a discussion about the origin of the basic assumptions in groups:

> It will be seen. . . that the basic assumptions now emerge as forma-
> tions secondary to an *extremely early primal scene* worked out on a
> level of part-objects, and associated with psychotic anxiety and
> mechanisms of splitting and projective identification such as Melanie
> Klein has described as characteristic of the paranoid-schizoid and
> depressive positions.
>
> (Bion 1961: 164)

Klein's influence on Bion's thinking is very clear, both in his overall view of the early primal scene and in his taking up the notion of an 'epistemophilic impulse'. Bion sees groups as arousing enormous anxiety about the very process of enquiry that is intrinsic to psychotherapy. This, he argues, is because the group evokes very primitive phantasies about the contents of the mother's body and is linked to the early primal scene in so far as it 'seems to assume that part of one parent, the breast or the mother's body, contains amongst other objects a part of the father'. He adds that this constellation exists in all groups, although it may be closer to the surface in groups of very disturbed individuals. Furthermore, he emphasises that it is essential for the constructive development of the group to work out very thoroughly the primitive primal scene as revealed in the group.

When I first read these views some years ago, I was struck by the conviction with which Bion expressed them, as if they were not just ideas but imperatives. I was also frustrated that no more was said about them. Brown, in the paper referred to above, explored more closely the link between the basic assumptions and the primal scene, presenting convincing evidence for the link, and showing how each basic assumption state provides a defence against the deep ambivalence experienced when confronted by the parental couple. Notwithstanding this elucidation, I was left with several further questions. Is anxiety about the primal scene more pronounced in a group than individual analysis? Does it apply only to the basic assumptions or to the overall development of the group? How does the individual–group distinction influence the expression of the primal scene in the group, and what *are* the consequences of it not being worked out very thoroughly, as Bion suggests?

When I turned to Foulkes to see how he dealt with these issues, I found an odd ambiguity. Foulkes repeatedly emphasised the Oedipus complex in his writing and devoted one of his later papers to the subject: 'Oedipus conflict and regression' (Foulkes 1972). However, much of this is a general theoretical paper, related more to family groups than to analytic stranger groups, and where he did relate it to psychotherapy groups this was as an interpersonal dynamic in the group rather than as a possibly fundamental determinant of the nature of the group. Foulkes tended also to focus on the 'classical' or later Oedipus complex. He recognises that very primitive material is stirred up by Oedipal phenomena; for example, in family groups he described the whole family as regressing when one child is in the Oedipal stage (see Chapter 1 for reference to Foulkes' view of the Oedipus complex as contributed to by all the family members). But he is very ambivalent about whether this material could be handled in analytic groups. At one point he says that such material is best left to individual analysis; while at another, he suggests that groups can be 'more tolerant and less afraid of these reactions' than a patient in individual therapy and can be more 'mature and grown up' about the subject (1972: 242). There is an uncomfortable, contradictory quality about his position, which leaves unresolved the conceptualisation of parental sexuality in groups.

Foulkes uses an analogy in his paper which rather sums up his position: 'It seems to me that the insight we get in a group into the oedipal conflict situation comes to us from a distant lighthouse, each patient having, as it were, his own signals' (1972: 246). But whereas Bion emphasises the importance of getting to grips with these 'signals', so that they can materialise more fully in the group, Foulkes concludes on an uncertain note – as if 'from a distant lighthouse'.

Interestingly, Bion's strong conviction about the primal scene and other aspects of group functioning did not serve to hold his interest and involvement in groups, since he thereafter withdrew from the field of psychoanalytic group work. Given his withdrawal and Foulkes' pre-varication on this particular issue, we may wonder whether something about the intensity and complexity of material connected to the primal scene in the group was problematic for *both* Bion and Foulkes.

## THE PRIMAL SCENE IN GROUP ANALYSIS – A CONCEPTUALISATION

In this section I aim to draw together the previous thinking described and some of my own ideas, in an attempt to formulate a hypothetical schema of how the primal scene occurs in the group and to highlight some theoretical and technical issues that apply to group-analytic psychotherapy. I do this in the form of several propositions.

First, the significance of the primal scene must be linked to the very start of the analytic group. A collection of individuals coming from their separate worlds is required to establish a potentially intimate social group. But there are no clear structures or guidelines within which to do this. The group occurs within a physically boundaried space, but the mental space or group space is wide open to projection and interpretation. The anxiety in such a situation can be profound, throwing participants back onto very early experiences and phantasies (Nitsun 1989). Consciously, members struggle to establish working ties in the group, forming the first affiliations and identifications which define the initial stages of the group. But unconsciously there is a very different level of cognition about the group, and this, I propose, is linked to the primal scene. The genesis of the therapy group provokes far earlier conceptions of origins, stirring very early phantasies of the primal scene as the archaic reference point for the formation of a sexual union and the generativity that leads to a new beginning, a birth.

Second, far more than in individual psychoanalysis, with its dyadic relationship, the group comprises situations which stimulate actual and phantasied triangular relationships. In a mixed sex group, which is usual in group-analytic psychotherapy, the presence of males and females is immediately a potential trigger for Oedipal longings and rivalries, al-though wishes and tensions between members of the same sex should not be under-emphasised, particularly since these are likely to reflect some version of the primal scene. The presence of the therapist, in phantasy the parent or leader of the group, creates further triangular relationships, such as that between the individual member, the therapist, and the rest of the group, and these arouse strong emotions, often sexually tinged. All of this sets the scene for the revival and re-enactment of early sexual relationships, including the phantasy of the primal scene with its considerable threats and potentials.

Third, as in all psychotherapy, the analytic group stimulates a process of enquiry and exploration. Although the aim of this is thera-peutic – that is, the development of the individual in the group – it can none the less be highly anxiety-provoking, especially since it occurs in the open, unstructured mental space of the group. I find some con-gruence in the view (interestingly shared by Bion *and* Foulkes) that the group is unconsciously equated with the mother's body and the search for the contents of the mother's body. I agree with Bion that this includes evidence of the primal scene, in the discovery of a part of the father inside the mother, and that this may be associated with fears of attack and retaliation. The group is therefore likely to erect defences aimed at repressing or denying the primal scene, although the pressure of enquiry in the group and the therapeutic momentum of the process is likely to open doors to the revelation, in some form, at some time, of the primal scene.

Fourth, the process is complicated by the presence of *several* group members, including the conductor. How exactly the separate primal constellations of these members come together and what combined effect they have on the group is fundamental but difficult to com-prehend, since there is a many-sided intersection of personal histories contained in several versions of the primal scene. My own proposal is that in much the way that there are shared phantasies between marriage partners, so the group members share phantasies about the primal scene. This includes the extent to which the scene can be disclosed in the group, *how* it will be disclosed, and whether it will permit of a con-structive development for the group or not. Within this shared phantasy, individual members will take particular positions in playing out roles that open or obstruct the disclosure of the primal scene and that facilitate or foreclose the *reworking* of the phantasy in the interests of a therapeutic outcome.

Fifth, the process of working-through requires a form of healthy idealisation of the group. Most group members bring a spirit of positive motivation and expectation, but this is often countered by resistance, therapeutic pessimism, self-destructive tendencies, and doubt about the value of the group. In my paper on the Anti-Group (Nitsun 1991), I explored the important part played by envy in the genesis of destructive group developments. There, I tended to emphasise envy of the breast as the paradigmatic problem. In this context, the focus must shift to envy of the parental couple and their creative capacities. Meltzer (1973) has explored this phenomenon, suggesting that in addition to the usual protagonists of the primal scene, there enters another member: the 'outsider', 'the stranger to the family, the enemy of parental creativity, of familial harmony, of love'. This figure, usually represented as a part of the self, is malevolent in its intent towards the idealised family and sets out to destroy it. I believe that a similar process occurs in the group as a growing entity and that a part of the group represents this kind of malevolence, often unconsciously or barely expressed, but aimed at undermining the group. If this is successful, the group will get stuck or regress into chaos and despair, and instead of a birth, there will be, symbolically, a miscarriage or a death.

Sixth, how then *are* phantasies of the primal scene revealed in the group? I suggest this can take several forms. It may be expressed in a direct evocation of parental sexuality and the emotional constellation surrounding this. But it is more likely to be expressed indirectly, through male–female interactions in the group or through the way male and female are dealt with as personal attributes belonging to either sex. Also, in a more indirect way, it could be expressed through the nature of awareness and commentary in the group, in which the quality of understanding (or the struggle to understand) may be a product of the reflective capacity described by Britton as an achievement of the mental space occurring in the triangle of the Oedipus complex. But these indirect expressions draw further and further away from the actual 'scene of the event', and, in my view, the most important channel for communication about the primal scene is the disclosure of sexuality in the group. By this, I mean the present-day sexual relationships and phantasies of group members. These are clearly likely to be more consciously preoccupying than past scenes of parental sexuality, but at the same time they are essentially derivatives of the original primal scene and reflect the individuals' later developmental solutions and adaptations to the dilemmas posed by the primal scene.

However, these are also not revealed with ease. In fact, my impression is that of all subjects dealt with in groups, sexuality is the most highly charged and most difficult for many participants. Quite often, when people are invited to join a therapy group they show reluctance, and will say that there are certain things they just cannot talk about in a group: very often they mean (and say) '*sex*'. It is not difficult to see why. For most people, their sexual relations, and especially their phantasies, are intensely personal and private experiences. These may be difficult enough to talk about in individual therapy, but how much more so in a group? Since present-day sexual preoccupations tap directly into the primal scene, there is anxiety about unwittingly revealing the darker recesses of the primal drama. The usual embarrassment and shame about disclosing sexual details in a group is a reflection of this deeper anxiety and, for this reason, open discussion about sex is often avoided in groups. The problem is that these sexual secrets are important clues to the underlying primal constellation, and so there are important technical questions about how best to tackle this: whether through direct confrontation or interpretation. This is a sensitive area of intervention, since it may unwittingly repeat some aspect of the primal dynamic, such as an unwanted exposure or intrusion, and merits careful consideration.

Seventh, I have throughout this chapter described the primal scene in heterosexual terms, focusing on the confluence and conflict between male and female in the parental relationship. But this should not preclude a full awareness of the homosexual counterpart in development and in the group. Whether this is represented in the group by homosexual members as such, or by homosexual phantasies and inclinations in heterosexual members, this area of sexuality can be seen as a particular version of the primal scene or as an adaptation to the disturbing impact of the scene. It amounts to what Freud described as the 'negative Oedipus complex', a natural variation of the Oedipus complex in which the same-sex parent is the object of desire and the opposite-sex parent regarded as the rival. The exclusion or avoidance of this version of the primal scene in the group could conceal important material, whereas its recognition may lead to a fuller understanding of sexual origins and outcomes across a wider spectrum.

Further, I am not suggesting that the only way to be psychologically healthy or to develop a healthy group is by adopting heterosexual procreativity as an absolute criterion. Psychological health often requires symbolic and reparative adjustments that are specific to the individual, rather than conformity to a rigid ideal. One of the strengths of group analysis is the value it places on human difference, and I would want the model of group development I am proposing to support that openness of spirit. In fact, I believe that the constructive handling of the primal scene in the group may have precisely this value: to free personal potential from the yoke of archaic sexual phantasy, reflected in either the individual unconscious or in social repression concerned with conformity to accepted norms.

Eighth, there are some remaining questions about developmental sequences that require clarification. In an earlier paper (Nitsun 1989), I proposed the mother–infant relationship as an essential paradigm for the first stage of analytic groups, largely because holding and containment are so important in the early period of the group. Given that in this chapter I am presenting the primal scene as a core element in the life of the group and one that may be triggered at the very start, there may appear to be a contradiction. But I would suggest that both phenomena apply and are linked. The group as mother, providing sufficient attention to early dependency needs and the containment of excessive anxiety, is all the more important in the context of the primal scene, which can provoke a dramatic resurgence of anxiety with potentially fragmenting effects on the group. The thesis of my earlier paper therefore remains, strengthened if anything by the considerations of this chapter. If this implies a prescription for the handling of the group, it may be that early dependency needs at the start should be given priority and that the working-out of the primal scene should not be emphasised until the group has acquired sufficient strength and resilience. But thereafter it is important to facilitate the transition from the relation to the nurturing mother to the challenging relationship with mother *and* father, in which father's more active input needs to be encountered, assimilated, and introjected.

## CLINICAL EXAMPLES

This brings me to the clinical material. I propose to compare two different psychotherapy groups I have run that dealt with issues connected with the primal scene in very different ways. In the one, the material manifested itself in a difficult but accessible way, so that the important issues could be recognised and worked with, and this was linked to a constructive outcome for the group. In the other, there was considerable defensiveness in this area, making the material particularly difficult to deal with analytically, and, in my view, limiting the development of the group. The material is obviously selective and simplified for the purposes of illustration.

### Group 1

In this group, I wish to explore the development from an anxious and depressive preoccupation with the group as mother to an eruption of material connected with the primal scene.

In the very first session of this group there was material that came strikingly close to the primitive phantasies I have previously described. Gillian revealed how she had had cosmetic surgery to enlarge her breasts but that the prosthesis left inside her had resulted in an unpleasant hardening and lumpiness of her breasts. This distressed her deeply because she feared that any man in intimate contact with her would discover her deformed breasts and recoil from her.

Apart from the personal significance to Gillian of this revelation, I suggest that she was presenting a problem that could be interpreted in group terms: her fear that the group might damage her. Furthermore, I believe it is possible that she was signalling, on behalf of the group, the dreaded situation in the very early primal scene, postulated by Bion, in which the father's penis (represented by the surgeon's prosthesis) is discovered inside the mother's breast. This group was in fact extremely anxious in its initial period, as if something very disturbing had to be confronted.

There was for a time an atmosphere of manic flight and pseudo-group formation that appeared to be ways of defending against this anxiety. But gradually the group settled into a more reflective mode in which anxiety could be contained and the emergence of very early symbolic material facilitated. Throughout this period, the material suggested an infant exploring the mother's body, particularly the womb. For example, Jean described with great distress how many years ago her father had been buried in an anonymous communal grave. She had become very preoccupied with the grave, a number of times referring to it as a 'group grave' and bringing to the group phantasies of what was inside the grave. I did not interpret this to the group but saw it as possibly symbolising the mother's inside with the dead babies; by association, the group might also represent the dead babies in the mother's womb. Through talking about this, the patient was eventually able to reach a point of considerable reparation, and the group, by grappling with the very anxious, depressive theme of loss and damage, gradually gained a sense of safety about the very early relationship with the mother.

It seemed that this enabled the group to talk more freely about adult sexual relationships and ties to the past that might have influenced the present. Martin had recently suffered the sudden collapse of a twenty-two-year marriage; his wife left him for another man. He was the group cynic, the voice of the anti-group, very much in the way that Meltzer described 'the outsider' in the primal scene. But, in spite of himself, Martin made use of the group and in one session spoke about the deterioration of his sexual relationship with his wife earlier in the marriage and his sense of a dwindling hold on the marriage and his family. He described rather movingly how he had thought of adopting a child as a way of bringing warmth and cohesion back into the family. In the group, he had established an ambivalent relationship with Jean: they were attracted to each other but also easily irritated each other. In one session, following a misunderstanding on Jean's part about some of Martin's communications (in fact, about the adopted child), a vicious fight broke out between the two. Members of the group were taken aback, but listened silently until one member asked Martin whether he might be displacing his anger towards his wife onto Jean. His retort was 'If she were my wife, I would have her on the floor!'

The remark suggested both sex and violence. This whipped up further aggression on Jean's part, but the group began to intervene in a constructive way, helping the two to disentangle themselves by seeing what they were projecting onto each other. Although very disturbing at the time, the event helped Martin and Jean to get closer, to understand each other better, and the group felt stronger for having witnessed and contained a scene of potential violence.

Although this 'scene' took place in the present and its immediate link in the past was with Martin's failed marriage, there was a sense that it was a re-enactment of a much earlier scene, perhaps a sadistic primal scene between the parents. It is an example of how the primal scene could be disclosed in the contemporary material of the group; further how the group, by providing a holding and an understanding function, could help to transform a potentially dangerous primal scene into an opportunity for growth for the protagonists and for the group-as-a-whole. A genuinely creative intercourse was achieved.

Gradually, the group freed up and members were able to talk more and more about some of the most difficult aspects of sexuality, some of which must have had primal origins – incestuous feelings between parents and children, previously undisclosed sexual abuse by parents, sado-masochistic phantasies, and so on. This was a group that worked very well as a therapy group, with members making substantial progress in their personal lives.

## Group 2

This group started with members adopting strongly defensive positions about their personal relationships. Several members had had disappointing or traumatic relationships in their adult lives that were presented to the group in very fixed terms, such as 'You can't trust men. Either you get the better of them or they get the better of you,' or 'I have never had a proper relationship with anyone and I know that I never will.' The group often showed an apparent openness about sexuality that seemed a defence against real openness. On one occasion, there was a prolonged discussion about parental inter-course (something that, interestingly, never happened directly in the first group). The form it took was of a chat, a bit of a nudge-nudge, wink-wink type exercise, emphasising at the same time that it was unimaginable that parents might have had – or worse – still have sex. Liz remembered as a child walking into a room and finding her parents in bed having sex. She was startled and outraged by this and still felt this way. The group appeared to identify with her. The same patient, Liz, also described how, in her early teens, she tormented her father by going out with much older men. She described how she would sit in the car, watching her father fussing and fuming in the house and how she enjoyed the sight. This was also unchallenged by the group. Liz's Oedipal triumph, in which she succeeded in re-versing roles with her father so that he became the helpless outsider, overwhelmed by his jealousy and rage, was received by the group as if it was perfectly fitting for parents to be put in their place.

This striving to triumph over the parents was also evident in the group's relationship to me as conductor. I was frequently invited to intervene in the group, but when I did was more often than not shot down in flames. At some point in the group I introduced a female co-therapist. When material came up suggesting fantasies of my relationship with her, I commented on this. My comment was met with massive denial, coupled with a scathing attack on me for making such an odious interpretation. I was accused of using my position as conductor to stir up jealousy and to test the group's reaction in a taunting, belittling way. Any further comment I tried to make, such as the suggestion that the group's intense reaction to my comment suggested that *perhaps* I had touched a raw nerve, only led to increased scorn. Defeated, I shut up. Ironically, at the end of the group, a female member, Cathy, turned to me very directly and hissed, 'Well, what sort of a relationship *do* you have with Georgina?'

There was some movement in the group: some people appeared to be making progress in their lives and, at a certain point, two members decided to leave the group at the same time. These two, a male and female, had both been very dominant members of the group, strongly rivalrous with me, as well as with each other, but in their last group they presented themselves as if a loving couple. They sat very close to each other, his arm seemingly around her shoulder, both looking smugly pleased with themselves. It was as if they had prepared for their exit by forming a pair. This whipped up enormous envy in the group, evident particularly in the anguished tears of one woman who thought that she would never get better or succeed in having a relationship with the man she wanted.

In this group there appeared to be a determined and partly successful attempt to reverse the impact of the primal scene, so that parental sexuality and power could be denied and painful feelings of exclusion avoided, together with the sadistic hatred that could be unleashed towards the objects of envy. Instead, the sadism was directed into the group against members themselves, and, I believe, against the group itself, since the group – and the conductor identified with it – presented the challenge of revealing the vulnerability and shame connected with the early primal scene. It is not as if material about the primal scene was absent from the group – if anything, it was more directly expressed than in the first group – but it was enacted in the group in a way that made understanding and working-through very difficult. The group, I felt, had markedly anti-group tendencies, as it struggled to form and endure as a group, as if the refusal to accept parental responsibility and authority meant that the group, like the child in the repressed, avoided, or even obliterated primal scene, could not fully be born or develop.

In presenting these two groups, I have, no doubt, simplified the material for the sake of illustration, with the result that one emerges as the 'good' group and the other as the 'bad' group. In reality, it was, of course, not as clear-cut as this, but overall I think the groups represent two contrasting approaches to the uncovering and working-through of the primal scene in group analysis.

## CONCLUSION

I began this chapter by commenting on my need to place something at the centre of the group. No doubt, this was in response to the great complexity of the group process. I am often baffled by the many strands of conscious and unconscious communication that occur in groups, and struggle to piece these together in terms of the group-as-a-whole. Perhaps my wish to put something in the group centre is an arrogance –

it may be necessary to accept that there is no one centre. However, I would argue that there are certain universal themes that occupy a more or less central position in the group and that the primal scene is one of the least recognised of such themes. In the chapter, I have suggested that it has considerable generative power in the evolution of the group, and that the way it is disclosed – or not – may have a major influence on the development of the group. In my own work, I have found it helpful to consider the primal scene as an organising theme in groups, in the different settings of both psychotherapy groups and staff support groups.

Locating the primal scene in the group-analytic context has also provided an opportunity to review the concept itself. I have suggested that it be viewed not so much as a theory transposed from individual to group analysis, but as a concept that deals intrinsically with the child's early attempts to understand the nature of group and social processes. It involves a diametric shift from the exclusive mother–infant relationship to the recognition of the two parents with their own relationship, involving a differentiation of the self from the parents, and beyond that, to a conception of the nuclear family and the extended family with its generational history. This sequence is repeated in group-analytic psychotherapy, in which the therapeutic setting necessitates – and usually facilitates – a movement from the conception of 'self' to 'other' to 'self-and-other' to 'group' (see the chapters by Dennis Brown and John Schlapobersky for further expositions of this theme).

Some conceptual issues remain unanswered in this chapter, including the extent to which the concept is given a literal or a figurative meaning in the group. Perhaps both apply in different ways. I see the phantasy of the primal scene in much the way that Ogden (1989) described it – as a *psychological deep structure*, a psychological readiness to organise experience along specific predetermined lines. How exactly this is manifested will vary from one group to another. In many cases it may form a backcloth of understanding, rather than requiring specific interventions on the part of the conductor, but in other cases it may require a clear focus of interpretation.

Finally, I have also suggested in this chapter an interpretation of the primal scene as a bridge between the intrapsychic world and external reality, by which I mean the parents' actual relationship at a moment of intense convergence or conflict. As such, the illumination of primal scene phantasies in analytic groups may be especially valuable – groups are so much about the friction between history and biology, inner and outer, the private and the social, and, as in the primal scene, about the creative achievement of people in intimate contact. The Jungian analyst, Andrew Samuels, in his paper 'The image of the parents in bed' (1985), describes the concept of the primal scene as being essentially about the conjunction of opposites, especially male and female, but also the mythological themes of the grotesque and the divine. In some ways, we seek the divine in our groups – by striving to create a group that will bring people out of their isolation into a sense of communion. Yet, we cannot do that without confronting the monstrous and the grotesque.

# Chapter 10

# Attachment theory and group analysis

*Mario Marrone*

## AN OUTLINE OF ATTACHMENT THEORY

Attachment theory was first proposed to explain observations made in the course of research on maternal deprivation, but its subject of study has now widened considerably to include other issues in the fields of psychoanalysis, developmental and cognitive psychology, social psychology, psychopathology, and psychotherapy.

Attachment theory emerged in the context of psychoanalytic ideas and particularly of object relations theory. It was formulated by John Bowlby (1907–90), a British psychoanalyst. Attachment theory is the result of the convergence of psychoanalytic formulations with several important trends in the biological, psychological, and social sciences. It might be best described as 'programmatic' and open-ended in the sense that it does not intend to be a tight system of propositions but a new paradigm. The aim of this paradigm is to create new areas of scientific insight within a conceptual system rather than to replace the system completely. This new paradigm (attachment theory) expects to be assimilated into an old and wider theoretical system (psychoanalysis) on the assumption that the old system is capable of assimilating the new paradigm.

This new paradigm has six areas of application: (1) psychoanalytic meta-psychology; (2) psychoanalytic epistemology; (3) methodology of research in early social development; (4) psychopathology; (5) therapy; and (6) prophylaxis.

1 *In terms of psychoanalytic theory, it formulates a new meta-psychology.* Following Rapaport and Gill (1959), who have classified Freud's theory of drive, instinct, and motivation into five viewpoints (structural, genetic, adaptive, dynamic, and economic), Bowlby (1969)

endorsed the first three viewpoints but replaced the dynamic and economic by a cybernetic model which contains new propositions about
instinctive behaviour. Once the dynamic and economic viewpoints –
together with traditional instinct theory – are abandoned, the use of
terms and concepts rooted in them become redundant.

2 *In terms of psychoanalytic epistemology, this paradigm concerns
itself with issues such as the object of psychoanalytic study and the
nature and scientific status of psychoanalysis.* Bowlby proposed four
fundamental ideas:

(a) That any science is defined by its object of study and not by any
    particular ideology, theory, or method; therefore what defines
    psychoanalysis is its object of study and not any school of thought
    or any particular and exclusive method of collecting data;

(b) That the objects of study of psychoanalysis as a science are the
    unconscious mental processes of the individual in a developmental
    and social context. In other words, the individual's system of un-
    conscious processes that has been called 'the inner world' *together
    with the interactions between the inner world and the environment
    (or social context)* are the object of study of psychoanalysis.

(c) That, in psychoanalysis as in any other science, there can be various
    ways of acquiring information, not only that of treating a patient
    psychoanalytically. However productive any method may be, it is
    bound to have its limitations, while there is always a prospect that
    some other method may compensate for them. Therefore, there is
    no reason to exclude complementary methods of obtaining data,
    such as baby observation, observation of families as well as others
    derived from neighbouring disciplines such as social psychology,
    ethology, developmental psychology, and so on. The object of
    psychoanalytic study can be regarded as a complex non-linear sys-
    tem. The analysis of this system may require multiple approaches
    and may not be expressed canonically. This is so because even the
    simplest of non-linear systems can behave in a complex dynamic
    way at any given time and the study of this behaviour cannot be
    effectively done with only one method.

(d) The epistemological problems of psychoanalysis can only be
    productively approached if the discipline is regarded as a natural
    science as opposed to a hermeneutics. Because Freud drew so much
    of his scientific inspiration from late-nineteenth-century biological
    thought, Bowlby felt justified in trying to find inspiration in con-
    temporary biology and ethology. In 1980 he wrote:

To accept that psychoanalysis should abandon its aim of becoming a natural science and instead should regard itself as a hermeneutic discipline has seemed to me to be not only a result of obsolete ideas about science but also a counsel of despair; because, in a hermeneutic discipline, there are no criteria by the application of which it is ever possible to resolve disagreement.

3 *In terms of methodology of research in early social development, an enormous amount of work has been accomplished.*  Bowlby's work has generated an ever-expanding field of study. The list of contributors is too long to be mentioned here, although the name of Mary Ainsworth has a place as one of the most creative pioneers. Research guided by attachment theory is branching out in exciting new directions, including attachment issues across the life span, across generations, and across cultures. *The central point here is the development of a set of methodological tools to investigate and assess how relationships are internalised and how these internalisations predict future outcomes.*

In addition to the notion that attachment behaviour represents an independent, biologically based system that does not derive from sexuality or other sources, there are three important propositions which have been validated by empirical research:

(a) That the quality of primary attachment relationships depends on the degree of empathy and responsiveness of the caregiver (or parental figure) as it is subjectively experienced by the growing individual;
(b) That the quality of primary attachment relationships strongly influences early personality organisation, especially the child's concept of self and others (normally known as self and object representations or *internal working models*);
(c) The organisation of social behaviour is an ongoing process that depends on the interaction between the person's self and object representations and the individual's adaptive reactions to their interpersonal environment. Early experience is of basic importance because each successive adaptation is a product of the new situation and of development to that point (Shoufe 1986).

4 *In terms of psychopathology, a variety of evidence also attests to the significance of attachment relationships.*  Prospective studies inspired by Bowlby's original ideas suggest fundamental links between insecurity of early attachments, anxiety, and later psychopathology.

5 *In terms of therapy, the main task of the analytic process is seen as*

*that of eliciting, integrating, and modifying internal working models of oneself and others.* This is an issue that we shall explore later.

6 *In terms of prophylaxis, accumulated knowledge about the trauma resulting from separation, insecurity, and lack of empathic responsiveness will help to prevent such ill effects.* Bowlby's 1951 report for the World Health Organisation, *Maternal Care and Mental Health,* served as a guideline for the organisation of paediatric in-patient care, social services policies, and educational systems in a good number of countries and institutions. Appreciation of the fact that optimal personality development depends on the continuity, nature, and quality of child care should make us aware that the improvement of these conditions (even if they may be difficult to achieve) have expectable positive outcomes.

## JOHN BOWLBY

Bowlby began his psychoanalytic training when he was still a medical student. He had analysis with Joan Riviere and qualified in medicine in 1933. He worked for two years at the Maudsley Hospital and moved later to the London Child Guidance Clinic where he worked as a child psychiatrist until the outbreak of war. On the basis of case material that he saw in this clinic he wrote his paper 'The influence of early environment in the development of neurosis and neurotic character' (1940). He found that mothers of neurotic children tend to displace hostility originally related to their own parents onto their own children, and that these mothers may also attempt to satisfy previously unmet affectional needs by making inordinate and inappropriate demands on their own children. In this early paper, Bowlby showed his concern with family interaction and intergenerational phenomena. Whereas in this paper, Bowlby referred to the pathology of a mother–child relationship, in later papers he showed increasing concern about the ill effects of early separation, loss, and deprivation of maternal care.

In 1944 he published his paper 'Forty-four juvenile thieves', in which he suggested that the 'affectionless character' was rooted in early deprivation. In this way, he offered a systematic alternative to the ideas of those analysts who, having been so intensively preoccupied with the individual's intrapsychic life and his world of unconscious phantasies, have shown little interest and belief in the patient's account of his real past experiences.

Between 1946 and 1956 Bowlby dedicated a great deal of his time and energy to build the Department for Children and Parents of the Tavistock Clinic. His clinical experience confirmed his idea that continuity of maternal care is essential for the psychological well-being of young children. Research done by his associates Joyce and James Robertson supported this view.

Until the mid-fifties only one view of the nature and origin of affectional bonds was prevalent among psychoanalysts: the attachment between child and mother – it was said – develops because the child discovers that in order to reduce instinctual tension (for example his hunger), a maternal figure is necessary. According to this view, the child needs to be fed and gratified orally, but the specificity of his relationship with a single maternal figure was not sufficiently taken into account, let alone explained.

The work of some British object relations theorists, like Bion, recognised that the child's first contacts with his mother and other persons of his immediate environment have a special quality that has profound importance for his later development. But often too much emphasis was put on orality, and the relationship of the child not with mother as a whole human being (capable of all sorts of responses) but with her breast. This could be seen as an important metapsychological problem.

At this point, Bowlby, through discussions with Robert Hinde and Julian Huxley, became interested in the contribution that ethological studies could make to resolve this theoretical problem. Studies on imprinting – and particularly filial imprinting – and its biological function (protection and survival) were relevant. Consequently, Bowlby thought that some parts of psychoanalytic theory could be rewritten in the light of ethological principles. He concluded that the child's tendency to form a strong and fundamental bond with a maternal figure is part of an archaic heritage whose function is species survival (protection from predators in the environment of evolutionary adaptedness) and that this tendency is independent from libidinal or sexual urges.

In 1958 Bowlby sketched the outline of a theory of attachment and introduced the term in his paper 'The nature of the child's tie to his mother'. In 1956 he began working on what was going to be his seminal work, *Attachment and Loss*, which appeared in three volumes in 1969, 1973, and 1980.

Throughout the 1960s Bowlby repeatedly convened the Tavistock Mother–Infant Interaction multidisciplinary seminars, whose participants included Mary Ainsworth, Robert Hinde, and many others, a group quite diverse in background and theoretical orientation. The first pieces of attachment-orientated research were engendered by these seminars and included Ainsworth's Baltimore study. In the 1970s research in mother–infant attachment began to accelerate, particularly in the United States, and many insights gained from these studies were incorporated into the general body of attachment theory.

Meanwhile, Bowlby continued to have a dialogue with clinicians and to think about the possible application of attachment theory to clinical work. Emanuel Peterfreund, an eminent psychoanalyst from New York, became very sympathetic to his ideas and was one of his good friends and interlocutors.

Although Bowlby was not a group analyst, he became interested in the theory and practice of group analysis through conversations with Liza Glenn and myself. In the early 1980s, I convened yearly series of seminars on the clinical applications of attachment theory and its position in the context of contemporary psychoanalytic thinking, which were held at the Institute of Group Analysis (London). Bowlby attended these seminars as main speaker or discussant of other people's presentations. These group discussions generated a great deal of interest and enthusiasm. Since then, attachment theory has been included in the curriculum of the Institute's Qualifying Course in Group Analysis.

Bowlby died quite suddenly of a stroke in September 1990, shortly after he published his last book *Charles Darwin: A Biography*, at a time in which, in spite of his advanced age, he was still working a few hours a week at the Tavistock Clinic and maintaining a high level of intellectual productivity.

## SOME KEY ISSUES IN ATTACHMENT THEORY

One of the major features of attachment theory is the concept of a behavioural system. It assumes that there are several mental systems which lead to certain kinds of behaviour. Each one of these systems is designed to serve a particular biological function and has a particular set-goal. Feeding, sexual, affiliative, exploratory, and caregiving functions are served by respective behavioural systems. Any one of these systems can be activated in the presence of certain conditions. When the attachment system is activated, the individual needs to gain proximity or contact with a preferred individual, who is usually conceived as stronger, wiser and/or better able to cope with life. The individual has formed with that preferred individual 'an attachment', which is specific to that person and durable. Each individual has attachments with different persons but only in accordance with a scale of priorities (some persons are more important than others). Activating conditions of attachment are strangeness, hunger, fatigue, and anything frightening. We must make the distinction between 'attachment behaviour' – which is an organised set of emotional, cognitive, and behavioural responses – and 'attachment' itself, attachment as a bond.

Attachment behaviour interplays with exploratory behaviour: the first is related with seeking proximity to the person one is attached to, the second is related with trying to gain distance from that person in order to explore other areas of interest.

Sexual behaviour can be complementary to attachment behaviour but they are not the same thing. In maturity, a person may establish a specific relationship with somebody who is also the primordial object of sexual interest, yet, sexuality and attachment should be distinguished one from the other instead of being put together under the term 'libidinal'.

Attachment theorists assume that individuals, from infancy on, are capable of experiencing reality at a subjective, cognitive, and emotional level. Their experience suffers no distortion by virtue of wishes, phantasies, or defences, but only those made inevitable by immaturity. This contrasts with a predominant view in psychoanalysis that the most relevant subjective experiences of the infant are reality-distorting phantasies. However, attachment theorists do allow for the fact that reality is interpreted from a subjective perspective, but they understand this experience as the result of an interactional process whereby inter-personal communications can be misconstrued in its semantic meaning.

## DEVELOPMENTAL PATHWAYS

Early experiences of loss and deprivation on the one hand, a whole range of pathological patterns of relatedness and communication in the intact family on the other, can produce a deviation of psychological development from an optimal pathway in childhood and adolescence. The concept of developmental pathway was proposed by the biologist, C. H. Waddington (1957). Within this framework, human personality is conceived as a structure that develops along one or another of an array of possible pathways during all the years of immaturity from infancy to late adolescence. An important variable that determines the pathway an individual is taking at any given time of his development is the way his parental figures treat him. According to this view, pathology is not explained as the result of 'fixation' or 'regression' but as the outcome of the individual having taken a deviant pathway at some early stage.

## INTERNAL WORKING MODELS OF SELF AND OTHERS

A central point in attachment theory is the concept of *internal working model*, formulated by Bowlby (1969) and Peterfreund (1983). This is a concept that developed from two main sources: (1) the psychoanalytic notion of self and object representation, particularly as it was defined by Hartmann (1950) and Jacobson (1964) and (2) Piaget's (1954) theory of representation. Indeed, the concepts of internal working model and self and object representation are almost identical, although – in my view, as I shall explain below – the latter is a special type of the former. However, it seems that Bowlby formulated the concept of internal working model while being inspired by a book by Craik (1943), in which mental representations of external reality are seen as the base on which a repertoire of possible and quick adaptive reactions is organised.

As Bretherton says,

> As a conceptual metaphor, the term 'internal working model' has several advantages. First, the adjective 'working' draws attention to the dynamic aspects of representation. By operating on mental models, an individual can generate interpretations of the present and evaluate alternative courses of future action. Second, the word 'model' implies constructions, and hence development, with later, more complex working models coming to replace earlier and simpler versions.
>
> (Bretherton and Waters 1985: 74–9)

Working models are cognitive maps, representations, schemes, or scripts that an individual has about himself (as an unique bodily and psychic entity) and his environment. Such maps can be of all degrees of sophistication from elementary constructs to complex ones. A working model is a selected representation of whatever is mapped: aspects of a person, aspects of the world (anything that may be the object of knowledge or psychic representation). There is a complex set of notions or 'concepts' about oneself, other people, and any other object of knowledge that the individual builds, stores, ascribes meaning to, and uses at various levels of consciousness or unconsciousness.[1] This set of notions acts as reference framework to organise responses to the world (that is to say, to organise adaptive behaviour).

Initial working models of something that was experienced in the past may mismatch what one is confronting in the current reality. In other circumstances, working models can be corrected or updated by experience. If a pre-existing model is to be used in a novel situation, and if this model does not fit with the reality of the new situation, one of two things may happen: (1) the new situation is perceived with distortions created by the pre-existing model, or (2) the new situation is perceived correctly and the pre-existing model is modified or 'fine-tuned' by experience (that is to say, by means of error-correcting feedback).

As Peterfreund (1983) puts it, from childhood to adulthood we understand the world through our constantly changing working models. We each interpret existing information in our own way, selecting and processing it to arrive at our particular view of the world, our individual 'reality'. It is through those interpretations that information attains meaning. Our working models enable us to rearrange the world we know, imagine new contributions and possibilities, imagine how things would appear in different circumstances, predict the possible consequences of action to be taken. If this model is to be successfully used in novel situations, it must be extended imaginatively to cover potential realities as well as experienced ones. Thus, working models provide a platform to test and evaluate.

Internal working models are emotionally charged. In other words, there is an emotional component to the cognitive system. And this emotional charge is more marked in self and object representations, which are highly specific forms of working models.

The possibility of updating, correcting, integrating, and synthesising working models depends on the availability of these models to consciousness. Only if we are aware of their existence can we modify them. Representational models may remain unconscious for a variety of reasons, but one of these is the need to set defences against painful or unpleasant emotions associated with them.

When multiple models of a single attachment figure are operative, they are likely to differ in regard to their origin, their dominance, and the extent to which the subject is aware of them. A person may be in a particular mental state under the influence of a particular working model – whose influential position has been re-activated by a particular environmental trigger – without being aware of the existence of this working model and its dominance and without identifying the trigger that has reactivated it.

In terms of Bowlby's theory of defensive processes, incompatible models of attachment figures are understood as the product of incompatible interpretations of experience that may become defensively dissociated. Such dissociations are more likely to occur when the child cannot cope with viewing rejecting parents in an unfavourable light or when parents try to persuade the child that their rejecting behaviour is legitimate and justified (often inducing guilt if the child reacts) or even a particular form of loving. Defensive exclusion from consciousness of negative representations of parents may provide emotional relief but creates two sets of problems: (1) the person has to work with an inadequate model of reality, leading to inappropriate, perhaps even pathological, behaviour; and (2) because the model is defensively excluded from consciousness, it cannot be reconstructed or updated as a serviceable model should be.

Depending on the organisation, integration, and quality of self and object representations, the individual develops to a lesser or greater degree his capacities to form and sustain discriminatory attachments, to manifest warmth, concern, and empathy, to experience, contain, and tolerate ambivalence, to maintain a certain degree of emotional stability despite stresses in everyday life, to be able to be creative, resourceful, self-confident, and thoughtful in coping with and mastering the environment. Seen under this light, transference is one direct manifestation of self and object representations.

## GROUP ANALYSIS AND ATTACHMENT THEORY

Group analysis and attachment theory share some essential principles. Foulkes, founder of group analysis in Britain, believed that the proper study of the individual is within his natural groups, particularly his family. He saw group analysis not only as a method of treatment but also as an ever-evolving theoretical body based on the confluence of psychoanalysis with sociology and other disciplines. The main concern of this theoretical body is the location of psychic functioning in a developmental and social context.

Group analysis makes use of psychoanalytic insights without being applied psychoanalysis. Group analysts have tried to integrate into their theoretical body ideas taken from different schools of psychoanalytic thought. If we examine the extensive literature on group analysis we realise that this discipline has never cut its umbilical cord from psychoanalysis. In other words, even if group analysis is a theoretical body with an identity of its own, still, its theoretical foundations depend to a large degree on psychoanalytic thinking. If we accept this fact, then our task is: (1) to incorporate meta-psychological and developmental concepts drawn from psychoanalysis, which are compatible with basic group-analytical principles; and (2) to apply to our work a way of clinical understanding that emanates from such a theoretical approach.

## GROUP ANALYSIS AND INTEGRATION OF WORKING MODELS

Once a small group of people gather together and begin to communicate and meet on a regular basis, one of the dominant phenomena that occur is that a new micro-social system is established. This new system is a place in which, inevitably, individuals' existing working models are used and brought to play. In this way, each group member presents different notions and ideas, different perceptions and ways of understanding the world. These are manifested implicitly or explicitly. These notions, ideas, and so on can refer to a wide range of themes, subjects, ideologies, and areas of knowledge.

The fact that these working models are brought for analysis in a group context can be very productive because the group provides richness of experience and, at the same time, many minds to think. For instance, as has been done in Argentina (Adamson *et al.* 1985), a group of architects can do this type of work in order to elicit the working models they use in their profession, working models related with styles, symbolisms, conceptions about structures and functions, and so forth. Consequently, the analysis of working models can facilitate the movement from hypothesis to thesis, from thesis to antithesis, from antithesis to synthesis.

In therapy (and more specifically, in terms of attachment theory), the main tasks of the group are to elicit and explore one type of working model: models of oneself and significant others (self and object representations). Since transference is a direct manifestation of self and object representations, a good part of the group analytic process consists of analysing transference as it occurs in the group context (Marrone 1984).

A group analyst orientated by attachment theory has four main tasks to accomplish:

*Task 1.*   To increase (through analytic means) cohesiveness and a sense of affiliation in the group so that the group can become a secure base from which it is possible to explore the members' inner worlds.

In my experience, the sense of closeness and togetherness that makes the group feel like a secure base is most effectively achieved when the group members can relinquish their false self and get in contact with one another through their true self. I use here the metaphor formulated by Winnicott (1960) and adopted by Bowlby (1980) as a key point of attachment theory, which refers to the false self as a defensive armour that the individual builds in compliance with parents' expectations, which covers and denies access to the true self: the needy, authentic, and emotionally ridden core of oneself.

> *Task 2.* To assist the group members in exploring their present circumstances: what situations they find themselves in, what role they play in creating these situations, how they choose people they form relationships with, how they respond to them, and what the consequences of their behaviour are. These explorations usually involve making correlations between the patient's possible behaviour outside the group and their behaviour as it can be seen in the group.
> *Task 3.* To assist the group members in finding out how they interpret one another's behaviour (including the group analyst's behaviour) and explore their expectations about the quality of responses they expect to get.
> *Task 4.* To assist the group members in making links between past and present and to consider how the internal working models they built in the past influence the way they behave, react, interpret responses, and forecast outcomes in the present, both in the group and outside it.

In order to do this the attachment theory-orientated group analyst used a technical device which Bowlby called 'informed inquiry'. The group analyst, being acquainted with the possible repertoire of pathogenic situations in childhood and adolescence, construes a set of hypotheses on which to guide his enquiries. Following the patient's own associative path, he may take certain opportunities given by the group and by each individual patient and ask certain questions about past events. In this way, he also offers a model that group members can use to mutually facilitate reliving and reviving experiences in the recent and remote past, focusing on a process leading to discovery and insight.

Placing the analytic work in a historical context is advantageous for two reasons: (1) it increases areas of awareness in terms of eliciting information about one's personal history which would be lost if the analytic interventions were otherwise only confined to the 'here and now'; (2) it helps to provide a corrective emotional experience because when a patient talks about past events (particularly if they were painful and the patient can talk about them with emotion) the group tends to respond in an empathic, friendly, and supportive manner.

These questions are aimed at eliciting memories of attachment events and evaluations of experience in two contrasting forms: overall evaluation of experience, and specific biographical episodes. This is based on a piece of scientific knowledge. Bowlby (1980), using data provided by cognitive psychologists (Tulving 1972), makes the distinction between 'episodic storage' (storing information according to personal experiences, autobiographically), and 'semantic storage' (storing it according to its meaning, its global appreciation, its contribution to personal knowledge).

Bowlby says:

> My reason for calling attention to the different types of storage and the consequent opportunities for cognitive and emotional conflict is that during therapeutic work it is not uncommon to uncover gross inconsistencies between the generalisations a patient makes about his parents and what is implied by some of the episodes he recalls of how they actually behaved and what they said on particular occasions.

After explaining this point in greater detail, Bowlby says that, similarly, it is not unusual to uncover gross inconsistencies between the generalised judgements a patient makes about himself and the picture we build up of how he commonly thinks, feels, and behaves on particular occasions. He adds:

> For these reasons it is often helpful for a patient to be encouraged to recall actual events in as much detail as he can, so that he can appraise afresh, with all the appropriate feeling, both what his own desires, feeling and behaviour may have been on each particular occasion and also what his parents' behaviour may have been. In so doing he has an opportunity to correct or modify images in semantic store that are found to be out of keeping with the evidence, historical and current.
>
> (Bowlby 1980: 61-3)

I have tested the effectiveness of this technical approach, in my own clinical experience as a group analyst and also in experiential workshops for trained psychotherapists who wish to gain a clearer understanding of attachment theory and its clinical applications. In these workshops, I initially ask the participants to pair off and apply to each other a version of the Adult Attachment Interview. This is the scheme of a moderately structured interview which includes features of both the high structured 'questionnaire' and a much more open model of a clinical interview. This scheme was devised by Carol George, Nancy Kaplan and Mary Main (March 1985) of the Department of Psychology of California University in Berkeley, as an instrument of research about the organisation and origins of internal working models in cross-sections of the adult population. The interview contains questions which are asked in a set order. Specific probes are used when questions are not answered. The interviewing technique creates space for free association. In other words, the interviewer follows the associative path that is more evocative in reviving past experiences and in discovering unique and personal meaning.

In summary, the first questions concern issues such as the subject's early family situation and interpersonal network, deaths in the family, early separations and losses, and so on. There are also questions aimed at (1) eliciting the subject's overall evaluation of their relationships with parental figures and important others during all the years of immaturity and; (2) visualising the subject's conception of each individual parent's availability and responsiveness to care-eliciting communications. Next, there are questions regarding the subject's perception of changes in their relationship with their parents over the years, from childhood to the present. This may lead to considerations regarding changes across the life cycle, adolescent rebelliousness, reparation, and forgiveness. Finally, there is a set of questions about the subject's own children, their feelings and long-term expectations about them and their capacity to learn from experience and use this learning for the benefit of the relationship with the child.

My own version of the Adult Attachment Interview is adapted to: (1) making it more congenial with a clinical interview; (2) applying it to teaching rather than research.

In my workshops, once each pair of participants has interviewed each other, we all come together as a group and have an unstructured group discussion to share, evaluate, and integrate the material that emerged in the first part of the session.

In these workshops, participants seem to be able to understand in both a cognitive and emotional level the following points:

1 One's whole attachment history, from birth to the present time (not just earliest events), is relevant to understand internal working models.

2 Some pathogenic patterns of interaction between parents and children tend to extend from early times throughout the whole duration of the relationship.

3　One's appraisal of one's attachment history is often organised according to a clear split between a 'semantic' view of important relationships and 'episodic' recollection of past events.

4　The episodic recollection of past events tends to evoke associated emotions in a way that semantic recollection does not.

5　Internal working models are formed in the course of episodes or scenes of one's life and can only be modified if these episodes and their related emotions are revived and relived.

Of course, what can be gained with trained psychotherapists in one intensive workshop is very different from what can be gained through years of psychotherapeutic work in an ongoing group. Any significant modification and integration of internal working models is part of an unfolding process which, in optimal conditions, takes place over several years in the context of a stable group.

## CLINICAL IMPLICATIONS

The group analyst who is informed by attachment theory still places their work in the general context of compatible ideas taken from group analysis and psychoanalysis. In their interventions they are inspired by a number of concepts and experiences which constitute a wide spectrum of working models which, it is hoped, they may have been able to integrate to an optimal degree. The group analyst focuses on a process leading to discovery through free-floating communication, following the associative path that is most evocative at any given moment. Yet, they use some opportunities, offered by the group, to investigate the attachment history of each group member and to offer a model of enquiry that members can apply to one another. This involves relating present experiences with past events, eliciting and comparing semantic and episodic memories, discovering unique and personal meanings, scanning for significant transference phenomena which are then placed in a historical developmental context, making links between cognitive findings and emotional contents.

Often a group session is initiated by a story that a patient gives, which normally consists of an account of their recent or present circumstances, perhaps an episode of every-day life that is charged with anxiety. This anxiety is a manifestation of conflict. As the group session develops, other patients react to this story in many different ways. This interaction becomes a scene of the group life that necessarily involves transference phenomena. Members unconsciously take one another, the conductor, and the group-as-a-whole as transference figures.

The group analyst pays attention to the story the patient is telling the group and its possible significance for understanding the patient's representational models, ways of relating, and conflicts. He may detect anxiety and/or defences against it (which may take the form of denial, projection, and so on). He may try to elicit transference phenomena. He may also try to define the present group scene as a manifestation of a 'latent scene', a scene that belongs to the realm of memory and hence belongs to the past. In making this sort of scrutiny, the group analyst can indeed formulate a hypothesis regarding the nature of the anxiety that those patients who are actively involved in communication in the group may be manifesting; the transference situation that reactivates this anxiety and the pattern of parent–child relationship that may have given rise to this type of transference reaction.

If the group analyst believes that the timing of his intervention is appropriate, he proceeds as follows: first, he assists the patient to recognise the presence of excessive anxiety (or anxiety-ridden feelings) and – if pertinent – the operation of defence mechanisms. Secondly, he draws the patient's attention to the fact that the present situation that the patient is describing, or is involved in, does not warrant such an amount of anxiety. Thirdly, he explains that, in fact, the present or recent situation only reactivates an anxiety that – because of its intensity – is likely to belong to the past. From that, the group analyst may suggest that this anxiety may have been induced by a particular type of early parent–child interaction and can help the patient to reconstruct pieces of their attachment history.

Often, once the anxiety or anxiety-ridden feeling has been recognised in the here-and-now, the analyst needs do no more than ask, 'Is this feeling familiar to you? Have you experienced it before?' in order to elicit a relevant response. If the patient is open to further explorations, the group analyst may try to bring to the surface episodic memories and their associated affects.

While all this is going on, other group members may help the group analyst or even take the lead to advance the analytic process. When a group member is able to recall painful episodes of his life together with the emotions linked to them, other group members – by way of a mechanism that Foulkes called 'resonance' – recapture similar experiences of their own lives and/or develop insight into the nature of their anxieties and defences. When pain and tears are shown and shared, one can say that group members, instead of relating with one another through their 'false selves' are now relating through their 'true selves'.

They are discovering and acknowledging their pain, their despair, their neediness, their sense of vulnerability. They discover that they can fruitfully use one another and the group experience. Consequently, a sense of cohesiveness develops. Attachments between group members consolidate, and members are more prepared to extend their membership over a long period of time, as long as necessary, in order to reorganise their internal working models to a more satisfactory degree.

## NOTE

1 Pichon Riviere (1977), in Argentina, quite independently, formulated a very similar concept, ECRO, which in Spanish stands for 'conceptual, referential and operative scheme'. This concept is well known in the Spanish-speaking world and has been applied to group therapy and learning in groups.

# Chapter 11

# Families and group analysis

*Harold Behr*

The family is a group, subject to group dynamics in much the same way as a typically constituted therapy group, but complicated by other powerful interpersonal factors which are intrinsic to family life. Family therapy is in fact a form of small-group therapy. As such, it falls technically within the purview of group analysis. Yet it is not easy to discern a distinctive group-analytic approach to family therapy which could stand comparison with other significant models of family therapy, notably those derived from systems theory.

## S. H. FOULKES ON FAMILIES

S. H. Foulkes remarked only briefly on family therapy in his writings. He recognised the family as a 'life group', a naturally occurring network, or 'plexus', as he called it, in which the members were 'vitally interrelated' and interdependent, but having no single occupation as a group. Although speaking positively of family therapy, Foulkes acknowledged that his own experience in the field was limited. 'I myself have treated families only off and on', he wrote (Foulkes 1975a: 13), 'sometimes with considerable success and in a very short time, relatively speaking'. But we are left in the dark about his technique. He makes the point, however, that although the family is a group, it does not follow that we should address and treat it all the time as a whole. 'On the contrary', he states, 'here as at any time we treat the individuals composing this group in the context of the group' (p.14).

Having given family therapy his blessing, Foulkes retired from the fray. He was more enthusiastic about the 'psycho-diagnostic' value of family interviews. The nuclear family, 'with its intimate, inter-linked system of interaction and transactions', provided him with a special opportunity to study transpersonal processes and to discover patterns of interaction in their chronological sequence, passed down from one generation to the next. But such study had to await the individual's emergence from childhood.

> As far as I can see, this primary family is best studied at a later stage when the children are more or less adolescent, or even adult. One can then get a clear picture as to the way in which they have been moulded and forced into shape by the conditions prevailing in the family into which they were born, and of which they form a part.
>
> (1975a: 16)

There is little else specific to families that can be gleaned from Foulkes' writings. However, he does make one essential point: the family group is the exact opposite of the standard group-analytic group in terms of the ideal criteria for classic group analysis.

## GROUP ANALYSIS: THE DIALECTIC BETWEEN PSYCHOANALYSIS AND SYSTEMS THEORY

Several factors have militated against the emergence of a specific group-analytic school of family therapy. The contrast between a family presenting itself for therapy and a therapy group made up of individuals who have never previously met (a so-called 'stranger' group) is so great that it is not surprising that entirely different techniques have evolved in each case. In family therapy, approaches generally reflect the need to engage the already established family group as quickly as possible. In stranger-group therapy, issues of change are addressed within a gradually unfolding context. The stranger group, carefully assembled by a therapist and unencumbered by a shared past, is immediately a well-functioning group. Such disturbance as there is, is initially contained within the individual members and only later shared within the group-as-a-whole. The pace of engagement can therefore be much slower, governed in the early stages by all group members' mutual ignorance of one another, and the need to reduce the anxiety of unfamiliarity (actually, the anxiety of not being in one's own family).

The core of the group-analytic training experience lies with the stranger group. Although Foulkes could be regarded as having adumbrated a systems approach to groups, his model of small-group psychotherapy derives largely from the psychoanalytic perspective which has had little impact on mainstream family therapy approaches. On the other hand, systems thinking, a relatively undeveloped strand of thought in group analysis, has had a profound influence on the family therapy world, leading to the development of highly specialised interventions, techniques, and schools of practice built around the notion of the family as the prototype of an open system (see, for example, Minuchin and Fishman 1981; Hoffman 1981; Haley 1976; Palazzoli *et al.* 1978). Richly developed models of structural, systemic, and strategic family therapy hold sway, and have created a climate of practice in family therapy which has made it difficult for psychoanalytically orientated family therapists to assert their position.

The systems, or structural, approaches to family therapy primarily emphasise the current, interactional, interpersonal structure of the family. Issues of power and control, boundary maintenance and the achievement of separation are addressed within a here-and-now context. Psychoanalytic family therapists tend to focus on historical aspects of the family such as unresolved mourning, obsolete intergenerational attitudes based on family myths, and failure to negotiate crucial transitions in the family life cycle. The literature contains plausible efforts to reconcile psychoanalysis with systems theory (Dare 1979; Cooklin 1979). A. C. R. Skynner, a group analyst who worked closely with Foulkes, has openly embraced systems theory, and has extensively developed an integrated model of family therapy which adheres closely to the Foulkesian spirit of group analysis (see, for example, Skynner 1981, 1987).

## THE FAMILY GROUP AND THE STRANGER GROUP

If it can be postulated that the nature of the group determines the style and technique of the therapy, it will be apparent that the family, as an already established group, will require more vigorous interventions to bring about change than those generally associated with classical group analysis. The traditionally reflective, non-prescriptive, non-directive posture of the group-analytic conductor, appropriate for the slowly unfolding therapeutic context of the stranger group, is a formula for therapeutic failure in the face of the family, a group consisting of individuals with a deep mutual investment in one another which has grown organically over a long period of time prior to entry into therapy. In addition, family members have vastly different levels of maturation and development, and usually bring with them divergent attitudes towards the therapeutic process. Thus considerable technical problems would beset any group analyst determined to pursue, without modification, techniques applicable to the carefully composed, well-prepared group of individuals meeting together in an attitude of analytic contemplation. While the untempered analytic attitude is inappropriate for family work, it is perhaps true that some of the mechanistic techniques inspired by systems thinking can be leavened by exposure to group-analytic ways of thinking and working.

In essence, group analysts who intend to work with families have to adjust to a foreshortened time scale for the therapy. They have to be prepared to intervene in highly structured, directive ways without feeling that they are doing injury to the group-analytic ethos.

## THE FAMILY: A GROUP WITH CHILDREN AND ADULTS

The group analyst working with families is faced with the complication posed by the coexistence of children and adults in the same therapeutic setting. Family therapists need to have in mind a model of therapeutic communication which takes account of the different developmental stages of children, adolescents, and adults communicating within a fraught, often crisis-ridden context. This introduces yet another dimension of specialised practice involving an understanding of childhood language and logic, play and activity, and the ability to interpret and translate developmentally governed modes of communication into meaningful signals both within the family and to and from the therapist. The fact that group-analytic training is based almost entirely on experience with adults puts the onus on those whose primary training is as group analysts to acquire their skills in communicating with children along a different professional pathway.

The group analyst's capacity for using metaphor and symbolic language finds considerable application in a family therapy interview where small children interact through the medium of drawing, play, and the obligatory logic of childhood cognition.

## THE LONELINESS OF THE FAMILY THERAPIST

The Foulkesian tenet that the conductor can for the most part entrust the task of therapy to the group-as-a-whole, does not apply to families. As Foulkes observed, the family, by its very nature, fails dismally to meet the criteria for selection which would apply to the composition of a well-balanced stranger group. Its organic growth over a period of years, fuelled by primitive affinities, could not provide a more striking contrast with the stranger group created 'at a stroke' and whose individual members are carefully chosen and matched for complementary personality traits and a diversity of symptoms. Roles, which are relatively fixed in a family, have yet to be negotiated in a stranger group. The language and patterns of communication within the family accommodate to members at vastly different levels of maturation, while the language and patterns of communication within a stranger group confer on all the ability to give and take in equal measure, to analyse and be analysed, each to contribute his idiosyncratic style towards the enrichment of the group-as-a-whole.

With the stranger group providing its own social microcosm, the therapist can afford to be relatively unobtrusive. In the case of family therapy, the therapist, faced with a dysfunctional group, shoulders the responsibility of becoming the agent of social reality. Single-handedly, the therapist may hold up a mirror to the family, turning it this way and that, to reveal to the family their collective and individual identities. The therapist may of course make use of a therapeutic team to conduct a carefully planned programme of interventions designed to tilt or un-balance the family system. But the principle of a therapeutic sub-group consisting of professional or professionals, engaging with a family group which is essentially dysfunctional, underlines the point that it is the family therapist alone (or in consultation with the team) who in the first instance has to perform all the numerous tasks designed to achieve therapeutic change.

## THE 'OUTSIDER' DYNAMIC

An interesting perspective on the contrasting techniques of family and group therapy is obtained by looking at the group which is formed when the family is joined by a therapist. This new group, which might be called the 'family therapy group' ('the therapeutic system', in systems parlance) provides a striking contrast with the stranger group, which is also strictly speaking a group of individuals who have been joined by a therapist. With this tilt of the lens it becomes apparent that the therapist within the family therapy group is much more conspicuously the out-sider than the therapist joining the stranger group. Therefore, whether intuitively or by training, the family therapist mobilises techniques designed to counteract a group dynamic by which the group copes with an outsider. The stranger-group therapist grapples with the problem of retaining outsiders, retrieving potential drop-outs, and averting scape-goating situations. From the outset the stranger-group therapist works to create a climate in which outsider characteristics are minimised.

## GROUP TECHNIQUES FOR DEALING WITH OUTSIDER DYNAMIC

In a stranger group, all are in one sense outsiders. The therapist is one among several, and although he or she is somewhat distinguished by virtue of a known professional role, can afford to be far more leisurely in moving towards the other members of the group, since all are moving cautiously towards one another in their efforts to communicate. The therapist has also to be careful to avoid introducing to the group anyone who will conspicuously assume the role of an outsider, or group deviant. Such a person, who deviates from the rest of the group in any single characteristic, is at risk of dropping out or being excluded from the group, or becoming the group scapegoat.

The group analyst works constantly to discourage a scapegoating climate by encouraging the circulation and redistribution of 'outsider' characteristics. That which is alien to the self is ultimately owned, contained, and shared by the group. The group analyst therefore works to instil an affirmative, supportive mode of communication in the group as a background against which more painful feelings and phantasies can be allowed to surface. Because of the extreme suggestibility of the stranger group, who look towards the therapist for cues on the shaping of the group culture, this task is relatively easy to achieve in a stranger group.

## THE THERAPIST AS 'OUTSIDER' IN THE FAMILY THERAPY GROUP

Engagement of whole families is more likely to occur when the outsider dynamic is constantly borne in mind. Techniques for dealing with the outsider dynamic are implicit in many family therapy approaches. They consist of either deliberately accentuating the role of the outsider, drawing a sharp divide between the 'self' and 'other' of the family therapy grouping, or rapidly diminishing the distance between the outsider and the rest of group (namely, the family itself). They often involve highly active strategies aimed at exchanging information between family members and the therapist, 'joining' the family, overcoming mutual ignorance between family and therapist, and redefining problems in interpersonal language which includes the therapist.

The family therapist is at a disadvantage not only by virtue of the outsider status conferred on him by the group, but because of the timing and circumstances of his entry into the group. It is quite likely that the therapist will be encountering the group at a moment in its life when great stress, possibly crisis, is impinging on the group. In addition, the therapist is not only entering the group but also attempting to influence it significantly, to change its culture even, or to restructure it in a radical fashion. Looked at in stranger-group terms, the therapist is also asking that the group assemble at a time and venue of the therapist's choosing. The therapist is, moreover, the only member of the group who does not continue to participate in the life of the group between the therapeutic sessions.

In effect, the therapist is only too well placed at the outset to become the group scapegoat, and to suffer the fate of expulsion from the group, which of course in practice means that the family fails to engage or drops out of therapy.

Groups under stress tend also to adopt another solution to the problem of the outsider. They may invest them with tremendous power, lavish them with magical expectations, and adopt a correspondingly dependent, helpless, and compliant posture in relation to the outsider. The family therapist therefore sometimes finds himself coping with feelings of exceptional power within the family therapy group. The success of the therapeutic encounter largely depends on how the therapist divests himself of this power and uses it to imbue the family with its own power for change. All too often the family group swings from exaggerated attributions of power to a scapegoating mode.

The family therapist, unlike the stranger-group therapist, therefore finds himself buffeted by strong group pressures early on in the life of the therapeutic group. The techniques of family therapy can be regarded as having the implicit and explicit recognition of the need to compensate for these pressures. This is expressed, for example, in Minuchin's ideas on 'joining' and 'accommodation' (Minuchin 1974; Minuchin and Fishman 1981). The techniques of stranger-group therapy have evolved around the need to wait, in calmer waters, for the emergence of the inner world and its reflection in the group.

## GROUP-ANALYTIC ENGAGEMENT OF FAMILIES

Bearing in mind the outsider dynamic, the race against time, the crisis atmosphere of many families presenting for therapy, and the complex arena of different developmental and motivational attitudes, the group analyst wishing to work with families is faced with a group where the usual techniques of stranger-group therapy are likely to be of little use. It is possible, nevertheless, to retain the group-analytic framework while accepting the need for a vastly modified set of techniques. In effect, the therapist has to reframe the therapeutic situation as an anxiety-laden group consisting of two sub-groups; the family itself and the therapist, or therapeutic sub-group.

## SYMPTOM FORMATION IN FAMILIES

The unifying principle of group-analytic technique, regardless of the group, lies in the promotion of a network of communication to counteract the effects of isolation. In Foulkes' terms, isolation is synonymous with symptom formation. The one cannot occur without the other, and communication is the antidote to both. Group analysis rests on the belief that man is a social being. Disturbances which have arisen in social groupings such as the family, can be re-experienced in the therapeutic group and corrected through the process of communication. Through this participation in the group the individual is slowly helped to yield up his isolation. The symptomatic, incommunicable parts of the self are translated into communicable language, a process which in stranger groups may run to months and years.

Language is the key which unlocks the individual from his isolation. Each individual in the group, by talking and listening, contributes uniquely to the network of communication which springs up instantly at the beginning of the group. Each member helps to diminish the isolation of the others, yet each protects their own area of isolation, surrounding them with highly charged affective barriers. With the passage of time the areas of isolation are thrown into greater relief. The individual experiences an insistent pressure to find words with which to express their isolation.

Where isolation persists, a focus of irritation develops within the social group network. The therapeutic group is a contrivance to coax the individual into dialogue with the group about his isolation. Translated into families, the collective response of the family has been to nominate its own symptomatic area which may be lodged in an individual such as the child, or within a dysfunctional dyadic or multiperson relationship. It is as if the family is functioning with one mind, like an individual, while the therapist, paradoxically, has to function as if he were an entire group.

Since the family generally presents itself with its disturbance crystallised into a symptom located within one member, who is nominated by the family as the patient, the therapist is obliged to address the symptomatic area head-on without the luxury of a gradual development of the non-symptomatic context which characterises stranger-group therapy.

Families often hold a shared view of the whole child as the symptom, or they may see the symptom as residing within the child, such as a psychosomatic problem which renders the whole family dysfunctional. For example, the family may believe that a wetting or soiling problem reflects a disturbance of bladder or bowel in isolation from any other aspect of the individual or his network. Families functioning at a more integrated level of communication may locate the problem within a relationship. An example of this might be a family which recognises that difficulties in the relationship between the parents are affecting the children and creating disturbance in other parts of the network. Some families are even able to acknowledge at the outset that the disturbance is located within the family network as a whole, and they are prepared to let the therapist join the network and to communicate with him as the person who can help the family to change their own pattern of relationship. Yet other families come into therapy with disturbance located within the family's relationship to the outside world. The boundary between the family and the wider network may be the focus of disturbance, and effective therapy may need to involve, as part of the minimum sufficient network, individuals or agencies (for example, a school) over whom the disturbance is dispersed (Skynner 1971).

Unable to bypass the symptom, and remembering that each family is unique, the therapist attempts to identify the interpersonal ramifications of the symptom as quickly as possible. Without any group to assist him, and without a great deal of time before the 'outsider' dynamic begins to drive him towards the periphery of the group and possibly exclude him, he has to identify the symptom and immediately begin the process of translating it into interpersonal language. Again, he does not have the support of the group here. At the same time he has to make himself known to the family so that before the end of the first session, the family's anxieties in relation to the therapeutic situation will have been reduced to a point where the family will return or at least accept the therapist's recommendation for alternative ways of helping them. The therapist functions as the host to the family, and observes social courtesies which serve to close the gap between himself and the family, reduce anxiety, and create a climate in which the family story can be told.

Successful engagement is likely if the therapist responds promptly to the multiplicity of cues which the family will be offering him through both verbal and non-verbal communications. Questions are readily answered and readily asked, exchange of information takes place at a rapid rate, and the therapist works swiftly to contain anxiety, and especially anxiety-driven activity on the part of children, by structuring the interview with words and objects. Silence in early family sessions, however empathically intended, is likely to be construed in a negative light, raising rather than lowering anxiety.

Family disturbance generally declares itself quite conspicuously at an early stage, and the therapist may need to provide a counterbalancing influence by drawing the family's attention to his awareness of their strengths and assets, as well as their obvious shortcomings.

Family members who have come reluctantly, without seeing themselves as involved in the disturbance, have to be acknowledged as important participants and helped towards an awareness of their own part in the family network. They may need to be helped to verbalise their resistance to coming, and to be shown that their own perception of events and relationships is valued. The therapist will have taken account of each family member's role within the family and will have attempted to engage each member individually before the end of the first session.

After exploring the symptom with its interpersonal ramifications, the therapist traces communication from the symptom to the emotionally charged interactions which generated it. This is a to-and-fro exercise which may lead periodically back to the symptom, but may, if the family is amenable, open up the way to a deeper understanding of the problem in a way which renders the symptom redundant. The group-analytic family therapist is comfortable exploring the past, using metaphor and analogy, interacting playfully with the family but at the same time being prepared to apply specialised strategies such as task setting, derived from systemic practice.

## ADOPTING THE SYMPTOM

By listening to the group, the therapist discovers that the symptom drifts towards him. In the first place, information about the symptom is automatically directed towards him. Whether in a chorus or a cacophony, the family demonstrates the symptom to the therapist. But the process goes beyond this. The therapist attracts not only the symptom but the feelings attached to it. He begins to experience, in the counter-transference, the missing dimension of the group which has led to symptom formation. To a greater or lesser extent the therapist may even take on the symptom, perhaps intentionally cultivating it in order to facilitate the process of change within the family. Skynner has drawn attention to the important therapeutic dynamic whereby the therapist intentionally becomes the group scapegoat, relieving the nominated scapegoat within the family of that role, and by virtue of the therapist's articulate authority and nurturing capacity, being able to reflect back to the family the meaning of their choice of scapegoat. Projections onto the therapist are thus redistributed onto the group-as-a-whole (Skynner 1979).

Taking on the role of the scapegoat is only one way in which the family therapist adopts or absorbs the dysfunctional, symptomatic element of the family. Usually within a short space of time, the therapist accumulates a charge, so to speak, which until that moment has clustered around the symptomatic part of the family. He comes to acquire the symptom in a shared relationship with the symptomatic member or members of the family. By feeling the pressure to which the symptomatic member is subjected, the therapist forms a subtle alliance with that member and allows himself to be manoeuvred into the symptomatic relationship. The therapist may, for example, come to feel a sense of sadness in the midst of a lively discussion in which jokey denial is operating to keep depression at bay. As another example, the therapist may experience a sense of mischievous playfulness in a sombre, intense, or depressed family atmosphere. Often the therapist comes to experience himself as the container of anxiety, or the longed-for agent of control in an otherwise uncontained family system. Another frequent experience for the group-analytic family therapist is an ill-defined urge to 'mother' or 'father' the family or individuals within it. Feelings of perplexity, apathy, or anger may also gather in an aura around the therapist, who, by opening himself up to these feelings, completes the new therapeutic group and sets the stage for the process of translating the symptom out of its isolated state.

## MIRRORING AND RESONANCE AS THERAPEUTIC INSTRUMENTS

An important therapeutic element in stranger groups is the mirroring function provided by the group (Pines 1982). Individuals become aware of hidden aspects of themselves which they see reflected in other members. The group-as-a-whole may reflect back to the individual aspects of himself of which he was previously unaware. A sense of shared identity and commonality emerges with the passage of time. The family can be a grotesquely distorting mirror, reflecting ugly images, freezing images in time, imposing the features of the dead on those of the living, turning the young into the old, the old into the young, or, like a vampire, failing to reflect an image at all. The family may be collectively blind to many aspects of its own identity.

The therapist is, in a manner of speaking, the mirror to the family. For some families, particularly the isolated, emotionally blind family, the mirroring role is specially significant. The therapist may simply describe what he sees at first, deepening the communication later to reflect the deeper, hidden layers of meaning within the family communication network.

Resonance calls for the therapist to fall in with prevailing patterns of communication within the family in order to become accepted by the family. In stranger groups, each communication resonates at some level with the group matrix, opening up further opportunities to communicate at any of the levels (Roberts 1984). In families, resonance occurs when the therapist mingles with the family in its style of language and expression, making it easier for any member of the family to express a hitherto unexpressed thought or feeling. The therapist sounds a note, as it were, which echoes through the family and triggers off other notes. Mirroring and resonance may have to be introduced quickly into the family as techniques of engagement, while in stranger groups they evolve slowly over many weeks and months, affecting all group members simultaneously.

**FROM SYMPTOM TO STORY**

For many families the act of telling their story to a stranger is in itself therapeutic. Families often remark with gratitude on the unexpected benefits of talking for the first time about issues which have been harboured silently within the family, or displaced into symptom formation. The authority of the stranger who assembles the family and (in a manner of speaking) forces them to talk openly provides a significant impetus for change. Whether fluent or halting, strung out over weeks or months, or poured out in bursts over a short period of time, the tale of each family member unfolds in a climate of acceptance. Each story is listened to and responded to, perhaps with silence, but more often helped along by questions and reflections. Working with children and relatively inarticulate adults, the therapist frequently has to find words to put to the family which can be accepted or repudiated. Sometimes the therapist offers a tentative challenge, speaking first for one family member then for another, moving deftly between question and statement. The struggle to find words for the family's story is a therapeutic task in itself.

The family story is presented in many guises. For some it begins with the current relationship. With the help of the group a picture is built up, examined and turned around for the story-teller to reflect upon. For others, the first chapter of the story lies in the past, a traumatic event, perhaps, or a phase of life. Again the therapist painstakingly assembles the picture, analyses it, and returns it to the family.

The therapeutic situation forces family members to listen to one another, perhaps for the first time. Parents listen in surprise to their children as they discover the unknown self of the child they thought they knew. Not uncommonly, parents are astonished to hear their child's piping voice announce fears and wishes previously unexpressed, reveal memories of events previously unacknowledged, display affections previously unrecognised, or confess to grievances previously unimagined by the rest of the family. Conversely, parents are sometimes able to tell each other, and their children, stories about themselves previously untold.

The therapist listens to the stories and occasionally translates them to other members of the family. The rendering of private thoughts into public communications is often accompanied by anxiety and painful feelings of grief. The therapist has to work sensitively with these feelings, sometimes speaking for the person, drawing comparable experiences from other members of the family, underlining the shared nature of the feelings evoked, and occasionally helping the speaker to remain silent, to contain the thoughts and feelings, or to express them in different language.

For some families the story-telling forum is enough for them to undergo considerable relief. These are families with relatively low levels of intrafamilial conflict, attempting to come to terms with traumatic events in the past, or attempting to integrate new members (for example, a step-parent or adopted child). In group-analytic terms these families may be regarded as having a well-developed group matrix, and a sensitive capacity to resonate to one another and mirror one another. The therapist merely provides the containing environment and gives permission to talk with appropriate affect.

## FAMILIES IN CONFLICT

In a stranger group, conflict between group members occasionally flares up and gains expression through violent language in both form and content. The anxiety attached to these confrontations often discourages the group from talking openly, and although at the time there may be a sense of excitement or vicarious satisfaction from such exchanges, in the long run they tend to be counter-therapeutic unless immediately addressed as a problem for the whole group. Powerful expressions of affect erupting into the group have to be contained and moderated by the therapist. The group has to be assisted back into a working mode in order to examine the meaning of the conflict for the group-as-a-whole. The isolation of the protagonists is thereby diminished and the cohesion of the group protected.

In many families, conflict is uncontained and frequently discharged into action. The group-analytic family therapist envisages the therapeutic setting as a container, discouraging high anxiety states which drive family members impulsively towards either escape from the situation or attacking behaviour (so-called 'fight-flight' action). The therapist works to translate conflict behaviour into communicable language. He finds himself reformulating communications in more temperate language, identifying first with one, then another protagonist in the conflict, drawing the conflict towards himself. Sometimes he breaks up the family into therapeutic sub-groups, to work piecemeal with family members as a prelude to reuniting them.

## ENMESHED FAMILIES

The boundary around a group sometimes becomes so impermeable that very little communication flows between the group and the outside world. The sense of cohesiveness within the group gives way to an oppressively close, mutually interdependent network of relationships in which individual boundaries weaken and dissolve. The inner self is breached inappropriately, communication becomes highly charged with strong affects binding individuals to one another and limiting the capacity to think. The entire group becomes symptomatic, and in that sense, isolated. Primitive, repetitive patterns of communication prevail, devoid of mental imagery, and the task of the therapist is impeded by the deceptively facile use of language as a means of warding off incursions from the world outside the group.

In group-analytic terms, the therapist has to increase the flow of communication from the outside world into the group, and the reverse. For the time being he is the representative of the outside world and as such comes to experience the projections from the family of unwanted elements which are thought to threaten the integrity of the family. In practice, this means that the therapist is perceived as thoroughly alien, and powerful in a destructive way. To join with such a family the therapist has to introduce a modicum of structure into the communication system. He may, for instance, adhere scrupulously to a model of addressing each member of the family in turn, thereby creating some degree of interpersonal distance between the family members. Interventions are likely to be presented as clearly understood or concrete tasks relating to the presenting problems and delivered with all the authority with which the family have imbued the therapist. Sooner or later individuals within the enmeshed family may have to be diverted into alternative therapeutic situations, such as individual or stranger-group therapy, to facilitate the process of separation and individuation.

## FAMILIES WITH SECRETS

The deliberate withholding of information within a group, for fear of the destructive consequences of its disclosure, creates an area of isolation in the group which disturbs the network of communication. The isolated, or symptomatic, area becomes walled off by a barrier of tension across which thoughts and phantasies are projected. Individuals in a stranger group harbour secrets until the levels of tension accompanying them have dropped to a point where they feel safe enough to disclose the secrets. Again, this may take many months, or even years, during which time the individual becomes known and accepted in other aspects of himself. The disclosure of a secret and the attendant feelings of shame or guilt are compensated for by the understanding that all communication in the group is shared. One member's shame or guilt becomes the whole group's shame or guilt.

In families, the pressure to disclose secrets is often more marked, with a greater sense of urgency. The price of disclosure is often greater, and the therapist may be faced with a silent, hostile, vigilant group of family members, prepared to resort to guile, subterfuge, and frank aggression to keep the secret from the therapist.

Under these circumstances the therapist becomes an unwanted member of the family therapy group. His best prospect for bringing about change lies in the formation of a bond with a sub-group within the family which lies outside the secret area. From this position he may be able to acknowledge to the family the fact that a secret exists. Subsequently, the family may be able to talk about the social repercussions of their secret, their fears of what disclosure would entail, and the imagined benefits of retaining secrecy. Once again, the therapist might have to aid the process by speaking for the family.

## FAMILIES IN CRISIS

Occasionally, a stranger group enters a crisis, but this is rare. The setting of a stranger group is scrupulously constructed in order to minimise the development of a crisis atmosphere. Sessions are carefully spaced at regular frequencies, with an open-ended time perspective, or a precisely determined end-point in mind. Individuals may from time to time be in crisis, but the group-as-a-whole, with its predictability and its capacity to absorb anxiety, usually manages to contain the crisis and slow down the interpersonal transactions which generated the crisis. Everything about a group-analytic stranger group militates against the kind of rapid change that makes up the substance of a crisis.

The family therapist, is, however, often faced with a family group in crisis. Entering the group and completing the missing dynamic, he experiences strong anxiety which impels him to act. He often has to expand the group, to bring in more members, other professionals from other agencies, for instance, to contain the anxiety and reduce it to a level where interpersonal communication can be expressed in words. Crisis work demands attention to the here-and-now of the group. Panic is reduced by putting words to the immediately present feelings. Only later can the group move into the past tense, or focus on the world outside the group.

## GROUP-ANALYTIC FAMILY THERAPY: THE NATURE OF THE BEAST

In group-analytic terms, both stranger-group therapy and family therapy take the individual on a journey from isolation to communication, from telling the story of the symptom to telling the story of its meanings. In both types of group the individual members listen to one another, helped along by the therapist and the setting. In both types of group the symptom and its affects are ultimately shared by the whole group, translated into communicable language and dispersed into the group matrix.

However, the strange paradox of the therapist of the family having to act as if he were a group, to perform the manifold tasks which in a stranger group he could leave to the group itself, imposes on the family therapist a pace and style which rests uncomfortably with the therapist schooled in stranger-group therapy. Family therapists can retain a group-analytic perspective alongside techniques derived from systems theory. This means that the therapist can step mentally in and out of the family and move between foreground and background of the group which the therapist has created, and of which he is potentially the most powerful and most vulnerable member.

It is perhaps premature to postulate a distinctive group-analytic section of family therapy. In so far as technique is concerned, group-analytic thinking, elaborated largely in stranger groups and larger social groups, is not sufficiently specialised to provide a specific repertoire of interventions in family therapy. Group-analytic family therapists must look for technical inspiration to those schools of family therapy informed by systems thinking. Conversely, the systemic therapies may have become too focused on technique at the expense of a broader perspective, and could be enriched by an infusion of the more analogical, analytic, and group-dynamic way of thinking which colours group-analytic theory and practice.

# Chapter 12

# Group analysis and culture

*Jaak Le Roy*

## CULTURE AND IDENTIFICATION – CULTURAL FOUNDATION OF THE SELF

Culture is already there before a person is born. An individual's identity develops within a cultural framework and cannot be separated from it. Throughout this chapter I will focus on the two-way passage between culture and self. The group has an intermediary position, containing both the socio-cultural and the intrapsychic, individual dimension, and linking them.

My interest in this area, designated by Foulkes as the 'foundation matrix', has developed through experiences of workshops held by the European Association for Transcultural Group Analysis (Brown 1987, 1992a, 1992b; Kaës 1987; Le Roy 1987a, 1987b, 1991; Rouchy 1987); and in anthropological fieldwork in Zaïre, Central Africa, in conjunction with René Devisch of the University of Louvain, Belgium (Devisch 1990, 1991). In the workshops I was especially impressed by how the intercultural group-analytic setting provided space in which to bring out denied or split-off family and cultural experiences. The traumatic impact of historical social events on the individual, the family, and on the cultural group to which one belongs can be explored in depth, as well as the way these events can serve metaphorically to organise intrapsychic distress and trauma. In Zaïre we studied prophetic healing churches and considered the healing function of these groups in the context of a social situation with extreme cultural changes, migration and breakage of the traditional containing family structure and cultural institutions. In these transitional healing groups early family traumas of the participants are activated, experienced, and given meaning.

In making sense of these experiences, in addition to many of Foulkes' ideas, I have gained a lot of help from certain writers outside the mainstream of British group analysis, particularly from French work. I wish to point out how this both concurs with and diverges from group-analytic theory.

In this chapter I wish to share my conviction that the foundation matrix is a highly complex but meaningfully structured field, disruptions of which can be highly pathogenic, and which at times of social change, trauma, and migration, needs special consideration.

The contributions of several French workers have thrown light on the link between culture and self. Kaës (1987) has distinguished four major psychic functions for culture: (1) maintaining the individually undifferentiated basis of psychic structures necessary for belonging to a social whole; (2) guaranteeing a set of common defences; (3) giving points for identification and differentiation which guarantee the continuity of the distinction between the sexes and the generations; and (4) constituting an area of psychic transformation by providing signifiers, representations, and modalities for treating and organising psychic reality.

In theoretical writing about the functions of culture for the individual one can discern two simultaneous but seemingly antagonistic functions. On the one hand – functions (1) and (2) – culture contains the undifferentiated and syncretic aspects of the individual psyche, and on the other hand – functions (3) and (4) – it promotes the structuralisation of the psyche through its introduction into a series of symbolic orders.

Inside a culture a person will develop their identity, defined by the symbolic marks conferred on them inside the primary family group, and subsequent social groups. Culture makes differentiation possible, giving markers without guaranteeing its realisation. The ultimate and specific identity of a subject will largely depend on how the subject and the different persons of the family group, as a result of their own psychic development, live the positions provided by the symbolic order.

In functions (1) and (2), described above, culture links each subject to a common non-differentiated entity, that serves as a collective basis common to all the subjects inside that culture. This collective cultural basis has become part of our body and self. It is incorporated in each of us and continuously mirrored and reflected among us. It functions automatically, unconsciously and it produces simultaneous interactions. It is evident that we become aware of this incorporated culture only when it is no longer reflected by others around us; for example, when alone in a strange cultural context.

The common cultural basis includes codes of behaviour, life

rhythms, eating customs, bodily contacts, and preferred distances. They are culturally marked with a given signification. By shaking hands or embracing somebody we use bodily codes to convey a meaning which can only be understood by the other if he also knows the code. These cultural codes concern the relationship to time and space and the relationship to the soma as described by Hall (1971). Rouchy (1987) emphasises 'the physical, bodily, somatic dimension of the cultural investment of the senses: sight, smell, touch, voice and its modulation, style of hearing and listening, gestures and mimicry, fantasies about the erogenous zones' which are part of a shared cultural basis. They are incorporated and function automatically in us, and they are continuously and synchronically at work in our interactions with others. They create the possibility of belonging to a common cultural group life.

Anthropology studies the characteristic way a culture defines time, space, body, health, disease (Devisch 1990), relationships, groups, sexual drives, aggression, birth and death, and we can use these insights to understand how a given culture protects its members against primitive anxieties, represses the expression of desires, and so on. An area of research important for group therapists concerns the basic representations which exist in a given culture about a group. These include the myths, legends, and tales which have been produced in that cultural area. They form a commonly shared internal representation which sustains the creation and functioning of a real group, such as a therapeutic group. Some of these basic representations have been studied in training groups by Anzieu (1984), and often appear in the phantasies of participants in small and large groups during experiential workshops.

## INCORPORATION OF CULTURE – THE FOUNDATION MATRIX

The double dimension of culture which *defines* and *contains* a person is transmitted in groups, the family group and socially organised groups or institutions.

The cultural models as described are transmitted during the first months of life through holding, nursing, songs, rhythms, bodily contacts, and games. It is incorporated in the communication of mother and infant. Several psychoanalysts have described communications in a fusional, archaic phase of the infant–mother unit where psychosomatic contents are exchanged or transmitted directly between child and mother (the dual-unity of Hermann, the primary object-love of Balint) before differentiation of self and object takes place.

In this early communication, culturally coded models are incorporated directly by the infant, and this establishes a state of indistinction and of fusion with others in the unit which will bind the infant and the later individuated person with the group to whom he belongs. This cultural basis continues to function during our whole life, it forms the frame of the feeling of 'us', as a part of our self, and of the phenomenon Foulkes called 'resonance'.

It would be too restrictive to conceive of the unit in which the common cultural base is transferred as limited to the infant and the mother. According to experiences with group analysis, and the development in the understanding of psychopathogenesis of early pathology, the functioning of the mother is embedded and influenced by the primary family group of which she is an essential element. This family group, its members and positions, are not universally defined but differ according to the culture to which the family group belongs. The family group also contains persons and the history of preceding generations. Therefore I continue to use the term 'family group' and not 'family', which is too easily associated with the actual nuclear family.

This is very clearly indicated in Foulkes' (1975a: 15) central concept of transpersonal processes. The individual is 'penetrated' in an interactive unconscious process within a longitudinal network. We can again distinguish a double level, one differentiating-personal and one undifferentiating-transpersonal. At the differentiating level, as Foulkes said, no individual person has the same position in the family plexus as another person, and this specific place will enable this child to individuate inside the total network. At the undifferentiating level there is something independent of the person and common to all the members. This 'something' contains general, transfamilial cultural codes transmitted unconsciously through the longitudinal family plexus. But the 'something' can also contain transgenerational stories, secrets, behaviour, and interpersonal pathologies which will be repeated unconsciously in the following generations.

## INDIVIDUATION AND NON-INDIVIDUATION IN THE PRIMARY FAMILY GROUP

Individuation and development of a psychosocial identity are based on a double transpersonal foundation: the cultural foundation matrix and the family group matrix which links the individual to their cultural and to their family group.

Complete individuation into an autonomous independent being from both the mother–child unit and the family group is an illusion. It should be considered as a process of more articulate differentiation of the self. The individual continues to be transpersonally linked through the interiorisation of the collective aspects of the culture and the family group. We will consider further the theories of Bleger and Jaques about the way cultural institutions and groups are based on this transpersonal dimension and why they can serve in the defence and containment of the self.

Individuation from our culture and from our families are of a different order. First, we will consider the individuation and identification process in the family group. An internal differentiation and the creation of safe boundaries of the self are achieved when the child has had enough experience of being in a safe place and of 'a sense of being held' (Winnicott 1960), in an envelope (Bick 1968) or a skin (Anzieu 1989), and to have felt a coherent inner meaning. Bion's (1962a) concept of container-and-contained to describe a maternal function, fulfilled and supported also by the family network, helps us to explain the achievement of an internal envelope and a coherent sense of meaning. Using Klein's concept of projective identification and the projection of parts of the infant's psyche into the breast of the mother, he describes 'the idea of a container into which an object is projected and the object that can be projected into the container; the latter I shall designate by the term contained'.

This process of containment, which produces awareness and meaning about the internal somato-psychic sensations and enables the development of a secure boundary for the self, requires a mother who is receptive and who allows herself to participate in that shared containment function. Individual and group-analytic work have clarified that the mother can only participate and be receptive if her own psychic structure and the family network allows for it. The outcome of the process will depend on the three interacting factors: the inborn disposition of the individual, the capacity to contain of both the mother, and of the family group. This third factor is related to the psychic structure of the father and his capacity to support the mother, to disruptive unconscious secrets, roles, scripts passed on from earlier generations onto the mother–infant unit (in the transpersonal family matrix), and to other traumata in the family group. Continuous disturbance of the containment will lead to a fragile identity and self boundaries as well as incapacity to manage internal changes and growth, and to what Bion calls a 'psychotic personality'. Such an individual organises his life and his private relationships in a way that ensures continuous dependence on others to keep the self unfragmented and free of anxiety, particularly through the use of rigid and extensive splitting and projective identification. Growth and further individuation is impossible; changes in or loss of the receiving object produce large amounts of fragmentation anxiety and psychopathology. In groups, participants tend to feel and phantasise according to archaic modes based on the reactivated experiences of the early individuation period. Several group analysts (Rouchy 1982; Gillieron 1990) consider the presence of pathology on this archaic level as a positive indication for group-analytic treatment. They tend to consider that pathologic development in this early individuation phase resulting in fragility of the self or a psychotic personality can exist together with a largely neurotic personality organisation. Group analysts in France who consider the presence of pathology on this archaic level as an indication for group analysis, tend to see the interactions and transference in groups mainly influenced by these archaic pre-Oedipal mechanisms of the patients.

The inadequate introjection process has also been described by Abraham and Torok (1978), who used Ferenczi's work to distinguish introjection from incorporation as a *failed* introjection. Their work has been used by Rouchy to understand the function of adequate handling of the group-analytic setting, and of acting out in groups as well as the role of primary belonging group (family group) and secondary belonging groups (social groups).

According to Ferenczi, introjection forms an important early part of identification. It is a process of enlargement of the self towards the external world. Primitive auto-erotic interests are invested in an external object, which then becomes a love-object and is consequently introjected into the self. As such, the process of introjection is not merely a compensation for the loss of an object, as Freud maintained (Freud 1915b), but has to be understood as a growth of the self. It is not the object which is introjected, but the totality of the unconscious wishes and impulses for which the object served as a mediator.

Incorporation is a mechanism used when introjection fails. This failure happens when the loved object, which carries the desires, for some reason disappears and is lost – when the object is absent, or seductive in order to get love for itself, or unreliable – before the cathected desires have been detached from the object and have been introjected into the self. In other words, the desires cannot be introjected when the object functions insufficiently well as a narcissistic self-object for the developing self. They are not accepted into the self and will be repressed. Incorporation of the object is the outcome of this blocked introjection and narcissistic loss. As a consequence of this, the self will repeatedly re-create a dependency to external objects onto which earlier lost and incorporated narcissistic objects will be projected.

One can conclude that the capacity of the mother and the family group to provide an adequate context for the development of identity is a crucial factor. Incomplete individuation results in a dependency on external objects and structures in order to enable support for a fragile identity. As Foulkes puts it, the family group can use the individual not as a nodal point in the system, but as a focus of the disturbance. This deficiency blocks the introjection and identification processes and is due to structural deficits in the parents or to transgenerationally transmitted traumas, which have been censured and excluded from the family history.

## PRIMARY AND SECONDARY BELONGING GROUPS: INTERMEDIARY STRUCTURES LINKING THE INDIVIDUAL TO CULTURE

Let us now consider the individuation and non-individuation of a person belonging to their cultural environment and institutionalised groups. We have seen that in the building of the identity of an individual, personal and transpersonal elements become part of that individual. A person never individuates completely and remains connected to transpersonal entities, the family, and the culture group. So the development of identity as well as the functioning of the person through it in his actual life depend on the link between the personal and the transpersonal, between the individual and the collective, the internal and the external. This linking and intermediary function is the group. As Rouchy (1987) writes, 'It is impossible to declare our identity without naming one of the multiple groups to which we belong'. Although we may not always be conscious of it ourselves, from an outside perspective it is often clear to what groups we belong; for example, our nationality, religion, profession, or social class. We share with the members of the same group and mirror unconsciously a number of common characteristics, which are part of our identity.

The common transpersonal elements of culture and family are strongly enmeshed, and are incorporated inside that family unit by the individual person. Persons of the same class or nationality can easily recognise one another. We all know that in our families some words, tones or styles are the cues for the feeling of belonging to that family, not understandable to outsiders. The function of the primary family may be described as triple: first, the receptive, containing function which enables the child to create boundaries and to find meaning in what happens inside him; secondly, interwoven with the first, the primary group provides an intersubjective space where the subject is subscribed in the lineage and in the double function son/daughter and future father/mother; thirdly, by participating in secondary groups, the family establishes a matrix incorporating cultural codes and rituals. These provide the basis for community feeling (Puget 1989) and citizenship and koinonia (De Mare *et al.* 1991 – see Chapter 13 in this volume).

Rouchy clearly distinguishes this *primary* belonging group from *secondary* belonging groups. The latter

> are very different from the primary group because their institution presupposes that individuation is sufficiently advanced so that an object relation exists, and relationships of an individual to another individual. It is the case at the beginning of primary school and even in daycare. Secondary groups complete the cultural interiorisation and concretize the grasp on space and time.
>
> (1990: 52)

Using this model we can more easily understand how secondary groups of all forms have created ways of behaviour, rules, and rituals which in reality are accepted inside the group but whose additional unconscious function is the organisation of repressed desires and tendencies. This is exactly what Bion (1961) has explored and defined as the basic assumption groups. The dependency, fight-flight, and pairing mechanisms are modalities of using a secondary (work) group to defend the self against psychotic anxieties, which I would see as products of failed introjection. We can also name here Jaques's concept about the defensive function of the institution and the institution as safeguard for the integrity of the self. The secondary group offers a number of positions, relationships, space and time, and rules to its members for these defensive functions.

Individuals who become patients in a group-analytic group will tend to repeat exactly the same modes, and attempt to transform the group into a familiar secondary group. The therapist will be confronted with it when he wants to explore behaviour which may be acceptable or usual in the external cultural group; for instance, coming late and irregularly to sessions. The possible metaphorical value of this act – for example, as hidden expression of anger towards a parental figure – is totally lost when this behaviour is shared and more or less a part of the secondary group.

We may summarise the important functions of the primary and

secondary groups of their relationship for the constitution of identity
with a statement of Rouchy:

> In the primary group as well as in the secondary group, the glance of
> the Other is constitutive of the self-image and of the rapport of self
> to self. The glance of the father, of the mother on the boy and on the
> girl constitutes them in their masculinity and femininity as man and
> woman, son and daughter, future father and mother. The identifica-
> tion is not in one way, from the child to the parents: in the primary
> group the subject finds itself in the desire of the parents and in the
> mirrored reflections. A lack or an ambiguity in the gaze of the other
> is the source of disturbance in the constitution of identity and the
> social link. This is without doubt one of the main therapeutic func-
> tions of group analysis (Pines 1982). The transfer of the same
> process in the secondary belonging group (with the containing frame,
> the transitional space and the substitutive identification figures) gives
> them, in a permanent back and forth movement, a function of con-
> tinuity of the confirmation, protection, institutionalisation, of the
> identifications and the individual sketched in the primary belonging
> group.
>
> (Rouchy 1990: 54-5)

We now understand that disturbance of the identification process can be
situated in the inadequate functioning of the primary family group, in
the continuity or discontinuity between the primary and secondary
group, and in the secondary group itself. Secondary groups are instituted
groups. We call them 'social or cultural institutions' when they have an
organised system of roles and positions, and when the relationships are
regulated by a number of rules, conventions, taboos, or customs. These
institutions can be defined independently of the particular individuals
who take up the roles. But the real existence and life in them depends on
the real persons who use these cultural mechanisms inside that social
structure. It is clear that the unconscious functions of an institution, or a
less structured secondary group as described earlier, are specifically
determined by the particular individuals who occupy the role. Kaës
(1987a and b) has described this intermediary function of institutions in
terms of an unconscious pact which provides for the individual narcissistic reinforcement, identification, defences, and the continuity of this
common psychic space. This pact, with its members, guarantees the
institution its survival and continuity. We have learned from research
and work in institutions that individual distress will develop in institu-

tions when this pact is becoming too rigid, and changes in the institution or in the individual are not allowed or integrated.

Bleger (1966, 1987) has developed the idea that an organised and stable frame – it can be the setting of the analysis, a partner relationship, an institution – acts for every individual as a repository for the psychotic part of the self. This psychotic part which he also calls the 'not-self', is the non-differentiated and undissolved part of the primitive symbiotic links. 'We have to admit that institutions and the frame constitute always a "phantom world", the primitive and the least differentiated one. What is always there, is revealed when it does not exist any more' (Bleger 1987). Every variation in the frame – changes in the regularity of the analysis, for example, due to holiday breaks, the loss of a partner, a change of social status and function due to retirement, the adolescent leaving home, a separation in a couple relationship – leads to a state of crisis of the not-self which is no longer safely contained and can flood the self and its boundaries. In the case of a person with a fragile identity structuration, the self can be flooded in a psychotic episode by the no-longer-contained omnipotent phantasies, destructiveness, and so on. The not-self and the frame have also a bodily dimension; it is 'the non-differentiation of the body-space and of the body-setting'. Through this body dimension of the not-self one is also linked to the containing frame, institution, and human relations. Some analysts are focusing on this factor in order to understand the sudden somatic changes and severe pathologies occurring after a crisis; for example, development of cancer after the loss of a partner.

The basic idea is that institutionalised structures are the safeguards for the development and equilibrium of the individual because they contain the remains of early (un)differentiation, the psychotic or archaic parts of the self. Breakages of the frame provoke crisis and the urgent need for redepositing these parts in a new containing structure, or the transformation and further integration of these archaic elements in an analytic treatment. The group-analytic setting has specific characteristics which makes it the most adequate setting to offer a temporary, stable, containing frame and the possibility of a transition to further individuation and boundary creation.

## MIGRATION: RUPTURES, CRISIS, UNCONTAINMENT

We may differentiate several causes of disturbance to the structuration of the self and its cultural foundation. As we have already described, a good-enough containing frame offers security and continuity to the self. When there is a rupture in this frame, the human being is in crisis. Even when no psychopathological status develops, the human being feels this as a discontinuity, a breakage in himself, in the relationship with the environment, with his history. Anxiety is inevitable when the individual does not find new containing groups, and this crisis becomes traumatic and disturbs the identification process. Every person in a radical transition from one culture to another is for a certain time helpless, whether a migrant from one country to another as a result of deliberate choice or in exile; from one culture to another in mixed marriages a second generation migrant moving from one generation to another; and from one culture to another; from the traditional countryside to urban society, like the migrations during economic crisis in underdeveloped countries; from one social class to another through jobs or marriage.

The basic helplessness can be understood as the result of difficulty in articulating this experience, and in resolving the crisis without the help of their own cultural group. If the person in a situation of radical change has no familiar primary or secondary group around him, he cannot use their coded rituals to give sense to and integrate the loss of the container. This crisis will be felt as a rupture in the natural, ongoing process of life. During this radical transition, and afterwards, the person finds himself between the old and the new social and psychic space. He will have to connect his old space to the receiving culture, country, language, and codes of behaviour. He misses the 'place where we can put down what we find' (Winnicott 1971).

It is logical to suppose that the loss of the container, the existence in that no-man's land, and the transition will be managed by the individual according to their established psychic structure. If the introjection-identification processes and the early loss of the containing primary object have evolved well enough, later the falling away of a traditional cultural container will be well tolerated. But if not, the loss will echo the primary object loss. In that case the transition to the security and the codes of a new environment will be difficult, even if the new environment is welcoming. The migrant remains dependent on the old frame, keeping the incorporated object in his internal graveyard and projecting it into the new frame instead of being able to use it to grow.

If we consider that the cultural environment and the institution always contain and articulate archaic non-individuated parts of the Self the loss of this containing object produces a double loss: the loss of the object itself but also the loss of the parts of the Self which are deposited into it and contained. The result is an impoverishment of the Self.

(Kaës 1979)

The containing object or group may be the family group, the partner, the village, the ethnic group, or the country.

The consequences of this radical change will be experienced in different areas: continuity of the self, the body image, organisation of identifications and ideals, the use of defence mechanisms through depositing of the non-differentiated archaic elements of the self, the reliability of the link of belonging to groups; the coherence of personal modes of feeling, acting, and thinking. It is very important for a person to migrate to a new culture with his whole family or with persons of the same cultural group, because they then have the possibility of sharing the familiar cultural frame and can rely on the support of those who are in the same transitional position. When they do it alone, they have to rely on their internalised matrix and lack the daily support of a familiar group.

A solid family group will remain a safe container to manage and articulate the radical transition. On the other hand, when this family group closes itself up and isolates itself from exchange with new secondary groups and new cultural spaces, this retreat will be pathogenic, because

> the secondary belonging groups cannot play their role in continuity with the primary group, provoking conflicts of belonging, splitting and fragmenting of identity. Individuation from the primary belonging group is difficult to realise, enclosing its members in an eternal fascination of a fantasy about the family fixed to its history.
>
> (Rouchy 1990: 59)

We recognise here the problems inside migrant families between the first and second generation. Members of the first generation remain relatively safe inside the family, which in the new country continues to live according to the original cultural codes, and interact with this new environment from their secure basis. The members of the second generation are living in two cultures, the old at home and the new at school, and they will be able to make the integration of the two only if some permeability between the old and the new is allowed and possible.

The receiving environment has to provide the possibility to form what Kaës (1979) calls a 'neo-frame', a 'neo-group', offering 'an object to the pulsion to be something. . .the protection against the return of the

archaic trauma. . .assure the continuity of existence. . .and the capacity
to rely on a good enough container'.

The receiving culture asks for the impossible when it understands
integration as a substitution of the original codes by the new ones.
Often, in that case, a false integration takes place inside the migrant,
with inevitable splitting between the treasured and defended old matrix
and the necessary and dominating new matrix. On a societal level, there
should be the possibility of neo-groups, intercultural groups, organisations, and spaces.

## SOCIAL TRAUMA: WAR, TOTALITARIANISM, AND RAPID SOCIAL CHANGE

We will consider finally traumatic sources in the cultural container
itself. These traumatic configurations of the cultural container interfere
with the functioning of primary and secondary groups. Nations and
other instituted communities sometimes provide anxiety rather than
security. As we have seen, the members of a cultural group commonly
identify and incorporate codes and norms. Inside the culture individuals
in a common pact renounce those parts of the self which do not coincide
with what this culture prescribes. As Puget has described:

> this trans-subjective agreement is based on solidarity. This is a type
> of link which has not received a metapsychological status. . . . We
> have proposed the hypothesis of two sides of the sibling relationship.
> The classical one which helps us to deal with the primal scene and
> which causes sibling rivalries; the other which depends only on the
> recognition of the equal, of the alterity, the difference. The first refers
> to the family structure, the second to the social structure.
>
> (1989: 142)

In nations, ethnic groups, and societies, this trans-subjective agreement
is guaranteed by the state, on the basis of laws, providing citizenship.
The basic value is the defence of life. This organisation normally allows
the possibility of differences, and it organises fundamental destructiveness and hate (Kaës 1987a and b; De Mare et al. 1991).

In authoritarian states based on a singular and fixed ideology, the
fundamental possibilities and rights to differ and to think autonomously
inside that culture are denied. 'It provides generally anxieties of chaos,
of end of the world fantasies, the experience of inexistence in the form
of anomie or marginality' (Puget 1989). In such a culture, deliberate
massification, violence through torture, censorship, and exclusion

annihilate individuality or its potentiality. Autonomous secondary social groups opposed to the ideological 'truth' are forbidden. The authorities use their power to impose silence about the consequences. Such regimes try to invade the private sphere of the family group, split families or generations, and undermine the safety and containing capacity of the family group. The state and its institutions do not safely contain the fundamental split-off destructiveness of its members; it breaks this frame by attacking and destroying itself. The individuals who participate in this organised violence and destruction will have to split off this part of themselves – the violence against the (br)other – and hide it in the family group, its life and its history. It has to be encapsulated, it remains unspoken in the present and in the following generation, but everyone 'knows' that something dangerous or bad has to be denied forever. This silence and the encapsulated destructiveness will be transmitted in the family matrix and in the common cultural matrix (Le Roy 1987a, 1991; Brown 1992a). Often this culturally repressed content is manifested by individuals in later generations, where it is not understood because it is 'demetaphorised and objectified'. (See the first example in the next section.)

Finally, there is also the area of major changes and developments affecting the cultural codes and norms in a given culture in a certain period of time and history. Currently, rapid changes are taking place in all cultures. The set of rules, norms, and symbolising rituals develops continually. Psychosociologists and anthropologists have described the tendencies of dilution, fragmentation, weakening, making inconsistent the symbolising and containing structures. As a result of this, they do not offer to the primary family group a coherent basis for the roles, positions, and relationships in the family structure. Access to symbolisation and a safe identity will be hampered; for example, in current western society, by blurring of sexual differences, enmeshed relationships of generations and sexes, a lack of the containing function of the parents for the developing child.

> This loss is a trauma which will never more be spoken of and elaborated in the family and it will provoke fragmentation anxieties, the development of a false self, and a myth of self-creation in the next generation. This fantasy can be embodied as: being the first in a new lineage denying the loss, in an objectified and demetaphorised world, characteristic of the effects of the incorporates.
> (Rouchy 1990: 54 and see the second example in the next section)

Let us summarise the loci of disturbance. The primary family group structures and functions can be disturbed as a consequence of parental and transgenerational family pathology and further damaged by fragmented or weakened cultural codes. The secondary groups or the societal institutions as a whole can be disturbed as a result of current or historical traumata (wars, civil wars, state violence, Holocaust, migration) or as a result of rapid cultural changes.

The outcome of the resolution of crisis during the development of a child, or during adult life, will largely depend on these two factors and on the continuity between the two types of belonging groups. Will the second take over, confirm, repair failures, metaphorise the individuation processes of the first one?

We have discovered in the intercultural workshops of the European Association for Transcultural Group Analysis that this continuity has offered the possibility not only of repair, but also that cultural traumata or historical events can be used by the individual as a metaphorical carrier for trauma in the primary family.

## TRANSITION

On the basis of the above concepts we can distinguish the *containing* from the *transitional* function of secondary groups. We know that hierarchical institutions, like the army, the church, the classes, even very rigid ones, can provide a safe and stable frame. They offer a containing function but they resist a person's internal changes if these fundamentally undermine the unconscious structure of the institution. If the unconscious contract between the individual and the institution no longer fits, the individual has to re-adapt to the institution, change it, or leave it.

On top of its containing function, a stable frame can become a transitional space for the development of the individual if it is 'able to receive, tolerate, elaborate and restitute' (Kaës 1979).

A group-analytic group is such a frame. Stability is guaranteed by the setting, the basic rules and agreements, the boundary and space. It re-establishes a sense of continuity by replacing or substituting the dysfunctional primary and secondary groups. In it are deposited the not-self elements, and the undifferentiated cultural parts of the matrix. This containing function will be realised and safeguarded by the therapist's adequate management and administration of the setting and the frame. Or, as Foulkes used to say, 'If the conductor takes care of the group, the group will take care of its members'. The setting of a group-analytic group can be enlarged towards a transcultural group-analytic setting. In such a setting participants and/or conductors are of different cultural backgrounds. It can be created in order to experience and study the above cultural foundation of the self and the function of the cultural institutions. This experiential setting has taught us that a transcultural group-analytic setting is an adequate context for therapy for persons who suffered cultural traumata during their development into adult life. Finally, the group-analytic perspective offers us tools to investigate how real 'neo-groups', like healing groups, function as containing and, to some degree, transitional structures for persons in actual combined social and individual crises.

## Example 1: a transcultural workshop

1   The participants in this workshop found themselves without pre-scribed language or organised translation, with their familiar second-ary groups, confronted with the 'stranger' and the group-analytic rule of free speech. This situation of loss of the cultural container prod-uced anxieties and early defensive mechanisms like splitting, pro-jective identification, and idealisation. The fact that the workshop was held in Heidelberg, that the German language was spoken in the large group and that several participants came from families which had suffered under National Socialism and the Holocaust, greatly influenced the processes in the groups. As part of the splitting defences induced by the transcultural experience and the loss of the familiar container, the suffering of the Nazi period expressed in the *large group* served as a metaphor for their suffering and anxieties in the here-and-now. A historical reality had been mythified in stereo-types in order to create a feeling of collective transcultural unity: they (the staff) treat us (participants) as the Nazis did the Jews. On the other hand, by talking in the large group about the traumas of the Nazi regime, participants expressed fears, family suffering, and hatred related to that period, and by doing this participants could address this historical cultural trauma. Feelings and thoughts, un-expressed and encapsulated in the families, were brought to life in the large and small groups. They were actualised first by splitting into sub-groups between Germans and non-Germans, or between the victim-patients and the victimiser-staff, who were experienced as cold and oppressive.

Later in the workshop, the encapsulated feelings and thoughts about family suffering – for example, feelings of hate, aggression, loss, shame and guilt – were openly and personally expressed in the large group. Some people realised that in their original family group it had been forbidden to talk about the collective suffering and about what their parents and grandparents had been doing or not doing during the war. This had forced them to evacuate feelings and memories. As the large group worked on this double level – their current transcultural experience of being lost, and the suffering, of an earlier cultural trauma – the large group became a new containing and holding secondary group in which it was possible to feel, think, and talk about these experiences. The meetings of the *national* groups enabled the participants to recover from time to time from these anxieties and to feel and enjoy the secure familiar cultural basis. In these meetings one discovered the illusion of a pure nationality, and explored their stereotypical attitudes towards the other national groups.

In the first part of the workshop, as a result of loss of the familiar cultural frame and of the experiences of common feelings concerning cultural trauma (annihilation, segregation, exclusion, persecution), the processes in the *small groups* were very regressive. The small group became for most of its members their re-actualised primary family group. They offered the security and holding to express them-selves more personally than in the stressful large group, but on the other hand they regressed to traumatic experiences of being under-fed, left cold and alone. Later, the wish to receive more help from the conductor was explored, as well as the denial of the aggressive feelings in the small group towards him. This brought several group members to re-experience feelings of helpless dependency and of strong narcissistic frustrations to an early sadistic mother figure. The somatic feelings of inner emptiness, cold, and hunger were trans-formed into more articulate wishes to be fed, filled, and loved by a loving mother. Significant moments in this relationship were ex-plored with great distress. Sharing early experiences of their primary family group revealed that this had not been containing enough and that all primitive aggressive tendencies had to be repressed. The group discovered that this inadequate containment was due to the fact that they themselves had to fulfil mother's own internal needs and that the family container had not been supportive enough, often as a result of some cultural breakage (for example, conflicting cul-tural backgrounds of the parents).

2　A parallel development took place in both large and small groups where denial of aggressive tendencies and loss was worked through; in the large group this concerned historical traumas and conflicts between secondary groups of people, nations, ethnic groups, linguistic, or religious groups. The total setting of the workshop, after the initial paranoid anxieties and the splitting defences, became containing and holding enough for a further elaboration of cultural differences and conflicts between groups and a 'more depressive recognition of mutual responsibility, guilt and concern' (Brown 1992a and b).

3   Often to their own surprise, some people could understand profoundly their interest in transcultural phenomena, their choices in relationships and the links or difficulties they had with some languages or countries. The discovery of links between personal family trauma and cultural trauma or crisis were at the core of the experience in the large and the small group. Some short examples can demonstrate this. Many participants tried to understand why some aspects or crisis of their cultural container – migration, war, multicultural and multilinguistic family, second or third generation, ethnic conflict – had had such an impact on their development, or had not had any; the large group in particular helped to clarify this, because through mutual identification in sub-groups it was possible to differentiate between the suffering of the cultural group to which one belongs, and the suffering of the family and individual. For example, one could understand that not talking about the atrocities in the war and the harm that was felt in the family (shame about fascist attitudes of members of the family, or loss of part of the family in the Holocaust) was a form of group denial that served to hold the narcissistic balance of the group and its members safe. One could differentiate this from the fact that for some persons and families, such a trauma and its subsequent denial or particular attraction served the function of channel or metaphor for a trauma in the family group. By avoiding the cultural trauma in the family (for example, by changing a name or migrating with a part of the family), a corpse could be kept in the cellar, related to an interpersonal disturbance between some family members (hatred of a father or mother, a symbiotic or incestuous relationship, or other family traumas). The cultural crisis or changes, and the subsequent defensive ways of dealing with them can serve as a model or an instrument to hide, to channel, or to integrate them in one's life. The cultural container serves as a repository for feelings and thoughts which have to be kept outside the awareness of the self. There are numerous examples in such transcultural workshops of how in their small groups partici-

pants have discovered and clarified this link for themselves.

To conclude, these transcultural workshops allow exploration of the non-individuated parts of the identity (cultural and familial) and how they are supported in groups and cultural institutions. As the cultural container and groups cannot function in the habitual way in a transcultural group-analytic setting, they intrude into the self and the relationships. When the setting is transformed into a containing and transitional space, these experiences can be given meaning and integrated. Historical events can have a traumatic impact on the individual and the group, and they provide them also with metaphors for the organisation of intrapsychic distress and trauma.

## Example 2:  A prophetic church group in an urban African society

I have used a similar perspective in a medical-anthropology research programme in the Central African country Zaïre, directed by R. Devisch. In the multicultural context of the capital Kinshasa the project aimed at understanding the health behaviours and therapeutic activities in relation to the cultural backgrounds. In traditional medicine, curing the symptoms and the disease is always based on a diagnosis of the cause. Generally the patient is seen as the carrier of a dysfunction outside himself and his body. For example, the relationships between the actual family or village and the ancestors is disturbed. Often something in the earlier family generations had been done which was a transgression or a non-realisation of a social code; for example, the cultural codes ruling the life of the generations, the sexes, the social structure, and the boundaries between private and public life. According to this diagnosis, a defined ritual of the patient and his family is conducted by the healer and produces a new dynamic and healthy equilibrium of the patient and his group. Traditional healing of the individual is also healing of the social group and a dynamic restoration and restrengthening of the cultural codes.

Besides the traditional healers, there are autonomous healing churches, a relatively recent phenomenon. These communities are organised around a man or a woman, who is called a prophet. They are outside the Catholic, Protestant or official Kimbanguist church. The Holy Spirit is their central reference. Their goal is to help and cure all people coming to them with a variety of symptoms and complaints, from severe mental, somatic, and psychosomatic illnesses to problems in relationships, unemployment, and bad luck. In the words of the prophet: if you open yourself to the Spirit, through praying and participation in the rituals, you will be cured.

After a 'diagnostic moment' or 'revelation' during a consultation with a prophet, the patient will be integrated in the community life or will be asked to come back regularly to attend the ritual sessions. Sometimes he will be prescribed to go to hospital first for a bio-medical or surgical treatment.

In a trance-like state and without taking a history from the patient, the prophet declares in the revelation (1) what is happening with the patient – for example, what part of him or of his body is ill; (2) why this is happening to him – for instance, a disturbance in the relationships between family members, with colleagues in the workplace, or because he did something wrong in his actual life; (3) what he has to do – such as participate in the ritual, rest, pray, go to the hospital or do something in the family.

The therapeutic setting is a group: the prophet, a group of helpers who have also 'revealing capacities', and a group of patients. The patient can be cured in some sessions, or stay in the community for one year. Some patients become helpers, members of the therapeutic team, some of them even revealers.

The ritual sessions take place during specific moments in the day and during masses. Two levels or modes are functioning during the sessions. On the one hand a structured programme is followed with speeches, praying, Bible reading, and religious song; on the other hand a more spontaneous, associative flow produces rhythmic body movements and dances, revelations, trance-states and bodywork. These two modes of functioning sometimes follow each other, often they happen at the same moment in the large group.

The prophet and his group of helpers have created a group structure with a strong containing capacity. Geographically and symbolically the boundaries between the inner and the outer space are clearly defined. When one enters the space one has to take off one's shoes and wash, and one accepts the behaviour rules and sober life style of the community. From a socialised, differentiated world and identity one becomes a member of a new group space and a brother or sister. One's ethnic or family belonging and history, as well as one's social position, profession, or religion are no longer relevant.

When patients come to the prophet they have in their mind ideas, feelings, and phantasies about the aetiology of their illness, according to traditional explanations. In interviews with the patients bits of explanations and phantasies are enmeshed with parts of the real personal history. We came to the conclusion that nearly all of them had been part of the centre of a traumatic configuration in the primary family unit. It seemed to us that the rituals and explanations they had received from traditional healers they had previously visited had not been effective. A prescribed ritual had not been fulfilled or the ritual seemed to have lost its power in the context of the city, outside the village situation. Most patients felt extremely puzzled in their sense of identity and lost in their social life. Nothing seemed to make sense any more; they felt powerless, depressed, and overwhelmed by unknown external and internal forces. In a state of generalised anxiety they lived with bits of meaning which did not give them a sense of being whole.

After entering the community they found a secure basis and a group context which gave them also a more coherent answer and which enabled them to relive parts of themselves which were lost or disconnected. In the community of the prophet Ntau, revelations gave patients the meaning of the illness in terms of disturbances and conflicts in their family or personal network. They were often repeated and worked out in the large group with all the patients and the therapeutic team together, even when the prophet was absent. The healing capacity of this community was based on the fact that elements which are part of identity, like traditional beliefs, verbal and pre-verbal body experiences, and positions in the primary group, are reactivated and repeated in this group containing context, which is new and differs from the original traditional context. In this transcultural shift – from a traditional agricultural village background, institutions, and belief system to an urban, capitalistic, individual-centred one – everything which has structured the internal world of the patient before the 'migration' is transferred, reproduced in a new form, and re-articulated. Here we can think of the experiences and patterns concerning time and rhythm, generations and family life, early relationship with the mother and sexual identity, law and transgressions. In the earlier traditional context of the village, the social group and the social institutions contained its members. As long as this container is coherent and solidly functioning, experiences and feelings in the individual are interpreted and meaningful. Because this container is not available any more as a result of migration or rapidly changing cultural contexts, the identity of the individual is under great threat. Especially at risk is this individual who is traumatised in his primary family group and who has not individuated from it.

The prophet and his therapeutic community setting are a 'neo-group' with the function of serving as an intermediary, transitional group. Through the rituals and revelations, this intermediary group helps the patients to re-experience disconnected or lost elements of their culturally based identity. In this new container these elements are re-integrated and re-interpreted in a new language. Using explanations of the different contemporary contexts, a mixture of old and new beliefs, traditional and medical, spiritual and social, a global sense seems to be offered to the patient.

There is more material that I cannot expand on here, but as a temporary conclusion, the numerous prophetical groups can be seen as a temporary institutional answer in a social situation with extreme cultural changes in the secondary groups, and breakages of their containing functions. The patients are persons who have been raised in dysfunctional primary family groups leading to a strong dependence on the family and the traditional structures. The 'migration' had provoked a crisis which could not be contained and understood any more by the diluted therapeutical traditional structures. Anxieties, depression, somatisations, continuous problems in social groups and identity diffusions are the main symptoms.

In the healing group a solid containing is provided for these persons in a transcultural crisis. Interpretations about the origin of the disease and the techniques to cure them form a transcultural whole. The different cultures, and their perspectives on disease and health, are mixed and put together. Early family traumas are activated, experienced, and interpreted in these 'transcultural' groups. This intensive treatment leads to a more stable and to some extent to a more individuated identity.

I hope that I have been able to demonstrate with both of these examples – the transcultural workshops and the prophetic churches – how the breakage of familiar cultural envelopes produces crisis in the individual and the primary and secondary groups. These crises can only be well understood and therapeutically dealt with when a new transcultural container has been created. Inside this new envelope, the trauma on the personal and social level can be integrated and transformed.

# Chapter 13

# The median group and the psyche

*Patrick De Mare*

Custom in a child comes to have the force of nature.

(Thomas Aquinas, *c.* 1260)

In *A Critical Dictionary of Psychoanalysis* Charles Rycroft writes that psyche and mind are used synonymously. It is a little strange that the word 'psyche' has been adopted, since in fact she was a beautiful nymph married to Eros, the god of love, and granted immortality by Jupiter. (The soul was therefore erotic as distinct from sexual.) She is represented as having butterfly wings to indicate the lightness of the soul. 'Psyche' is also a Greek word for 'breath', which escapes as a butterfly from the mouth at the moment of death.

Plato supposed psyche to be an entity separate from crass corporeal sense, and this separation is similar to Descartes's notion of body–mind duality. In relating psyche and the social world we need to distinguish between group and group spirit, in the manner of team and team spirit. Spirit emerges as a separate entity when an individual separates from that particular team. As long as the individual psyche is part of the team matrix it remains attached as an epiphenomenonal side effect to that team; thereafter it becomes mind, as distinct from brain, and can be re-applied in the form of memory in subsequent teams, or alternatively it can be applied to the spaceless and timeless world of non-people. During this latter state it derives energy from that cosmos and can become self-generative, whilst in the former it is bound to people, which is draining and frustrating and generates hate. This, in football, results in kicking the ball around, whilst in groups it creates dialogue. Free speech is the first to go in totalitarian states.

Psychiatry deals with the brain in a way which is materialistic (Latin = mother) and treats the brain as consisting of ever-increasingly complex reflexes. Psyche-therapy, on the other hand treats the mind separated from reflexes, as being capable of reflection. It is a sort of brain by proxy which develops from the moment of birth when separation takes place, the world of non-mother or of breath. Like the ancient Greeks, the Buddhists consider mind to be synonymous with breath (psyche = soul or breath).

The freedom of the psyche is squeezed between insight and outsight. It either materialises into the body or emanates into the mind; material strictures versus psychic expansion; for example, Stephen Hawking, confined to a wheelchair, rises to a boundless universe in his *A Brief History of Time*. Spirit can overcome dispiritedness.

In addressing the issue of psyche and the social world, the median group of between twelve and thirty people offers us an operational approach. The small group, by the nature of its size, lends itself more to the bureaucratic hierarchy of the family culture and displays only the rudiments of social order. Foulkes pointed out that social psychiatry is still in the making (Foulkes and Prince 1969), and it has been suggested that applying small-group principles to the larger setting is like playing ludo on a chess board.

Groups can be divided into small groups – for example family; median groups – such as extended family; and large groups and global groups – society. Group psychotherapy, by the same token, offers three proxy settings: that is, small groups of five to twelve, medium-sized groups of twelve to forty, and larger groups of forty to several hundred. Each one of these settings carries with it a corresponding 'mind' or culture; for example, biocultural, psychocultural and socio-cultural and politicocultural. The medium group, or median group as we have called it, provides an opportunity for each member to have his say within a reasonable time; it is a good setting for learning to talk and think, and for direct access between psyche and society.

Lévi-Strauss pointed out that both language and culture 'have taken thousands of years to develop and both processes have been taking place side by side within the same minds' (1969: 71). In the median group we are practising and intensifying these processes operationally. Essentially, culture implies the expression of human group thinking.

It is interesting to note that whilst the median group, as an applied approach, is curiously lacking in modern-day society, it is universal in so-called primitive and long-standing cultures which date back, in some instances, to over 60,000 years ago, coping with the most arduous of physical conditions. We today, on the other hand, starve in the midst of plenty because we mindlessly adhere to an economic subculture which belongs to the age of scarcity, before the invention of the wheel.

## SMALL-GROUP APPROACH

What do small-group writers have to say about this? Foulkes on the whole simply emphasises the authority of the small group. Ernest Hutten, in his chapter in *The Evolution of Group Analysis* (Pines 1983), wrote that the 'small group provides the proper setting for our wellbeing and preserves it'. He adds, 'The natural organisation of human beings is then the small group, the extended family or the small herd or tribe.' He sees the extended family or tribe as the natural and spontaneous extension of the small group, which we cannot endorse since this is cultural or contrived development, socially determined.

In contrast to Hutten, H. J. Home, in his chapter 'The effect of numbers on the basic transference pattern in group analysis', wrote:

> The classical situation of Foulkes' group analysis requires us to see the patient once-weekly with seven others... two, three or even four do not quite make a group. To my feeling a group exists with five of a kind, e.g. five patients. Six, seven or eight consolidate the group and beyond that number the character of the phenomena begins to change very slowly. At about fifteen a new character emerged, a medium-sized group, and at about twenty-five a large group.
>
> (Pines 1983: 144–5)

This I would agree with, and the extended family, or tribe, must be clearly distinguished from the family group. The tribal group is cultural, not natural. Imbued with a sense of community as distinct from biological interdependence, the larger network does not function instinctively but has to be cultivated. Thus, while the small group of strangers acts as a proxy group for family instincts, the medium-sized group acts as a proxy tribal group negotiating culture. It straddles the interspace between kith and kin, neighbour and relative, society and consanguinity.

## ANTHROPOLOGICAL BACKGROUND

My experience has been that the medium-sized group, the median group (or the 'dialogue group', as Professor David Bohm has named it), empirically speaking ranges between twelve and thirty. Anthropologists have described such groupings as bands or camps of hunter-gatherers, ranging between twelve and fifty. The social psychologist Charles Cooley described similar groups in *Human Nature and the Social Order* (1902), which represented the first modern coverage of such groups and which he called primary groups.

By primary groups I mean those characterised by intimate face-to-face association and co-operation. . .the neighbourhood and the community of elders. They are practically universal, belonging to all stages of development, and are accordingly the chief basis of what is universal in human nature and human ideals. Such association is clearly the nursery of human nature in the world around us, and there is no apparent reason to suppose that the case has anywhere or at any time been essentially different.

(1902)

The problem as Cooley saw it was how to build and promote primary group life; the theory of the eighteenth and nineteenth centuries of a horde or rabble of basically selfish and unorganised individuals driven by animal instinct is a highly fictitious phantasy, even though it was shared by the psychiatrists of the time – Freud, for instance. In other words, there is a basic dichotomy between man and society, and man is basically antisocial. In contrast to this, the median group is a situation where psyche can most freely and fully be exercised and is least trammelled by rules imposed on it either by the family setting of the small group or the extensive massifying effect of society at large. We see the psyche, therefore, in terms of the Greek word 'idio', which means making things one's own; as in idiomatic or idiosyncratic, or idiot even. This usage represents the personal human mind gaining expression in the microculture of the median group. In the median group we witness anthropology in the making.

Anthony Giddens, in his book *Sociology* writes, 'Warfare in the modern sense is completely unknown amongst hunter-gatherers.' And

Hunters and gatherers are not merely primitive people whose ways of life no longer hold any interest for us. . .the absence of war, the lack of major inequalities of wealth and power and the emphasis on co-operation rather than competition, are all instructive reminders that the world created by modern industrial civilisation is not necessarily to be equated with 'progress'.

(1989: 46)

He adds:

For all but a tiny part of our existence on this planet human beings have lived in small groups and tribes often numbering no more than thirty or forty people. The earliest type of human society consisted of hunters and gatherers. . .hunting and gathering cultures continue to exist today in some parts of the world, such as the jungles of Brazil or New Guinea but most have been destroyed or absorbed by the global spread of Western culture and those that remain are unlikely to stay intact for much longer.

(1989: 43)

He is alive to the hiatus between psyche and society, where 'mind', a word derived from the Norse 'mynde' or vote, comes in to its own, in which speaking one's mind is equivalent to the democratic principle of casting one's vote, that is at an age when one is old enough to be regarded as 'myndig' (Norwegian).

Numbers ranging from ten to thirty have been described as providing a viable unit for survival of Pygmies, Aborigines, Eskimos, and Dogrib Indians by many anthropologists. This basic social unit of the hunter-gatherers succeeded in coping with the extremely tenuous social connections as well as with the impoverished environment. They talked regularly to no specific purpose, apparently without making decisions; there was no leader, everybody participated, and the meeting went on until they came to a spontaneous halt.

If we turn to present-day industrial society we can ask how it can be that intelligent individuals perpetuate cultures that are destructive. I believe that the answer to this lies in the clash between the individual mind and the group mind, and as I have already suggested, group mind is what the term 'culture' implies. Without dialogue, minds are cut off from one another and produce groups which are pathological. The multipersonal transitional space (of the median group) is distinct from the dialectical triad of thesis, antithesis, and synthesis. Rather, it is tangential or 'multilectic'. In this setting the reflexes of brain encounter one another in a constant process of reflection. Whereas psychoanalysis explores the individual unconscious and the small group examines the family, I suggest the median group can address operationally the socio-cultural context in which we reside, usually as helpless onlookers. This is the essence of the problem we are attempting to resolve in practising regular meetings of the median group between individual psyches, applying the principles of Foulkes wherever applicable. This approach represents a significant development in the history of small-group analysis; that is, we are applying the same principles but to a larger setting. This supersedes what the small group replicates, and provides a psychosocial reconciliation not only with socialisation of the individual but with the humanising of society.

## OPERATIONAL APPROACH

In Aristotelian logic there is a polarity of 'either or', between which lies an area which Aristotle referred to as the 'excluded middle'; within this interface, in transposing this concept to the median group, dialogue can occur, creating fleeting microcultures, metamorphosing passing microcultural changes. This is similar to Kuhn's paradigm shifts, the crucible between family and social, where there is no root nor basic culture but a constantly evolving flow of microcultures of the median group in flux.

Moreno wrote in *Who Shall Survive?* (1953) that when the Messiah comes it will be in the form of a group. For us working with median groups this is a feasible suggestion. If twenty members of a median group after two years could each take on a similar project, within ten years several million people would be involved, and we suggest this as a deliberate strategy. This is, of course, distinct from the occasional meetings of one-off 'large groups'; the theme of the relationship between psyche and society is essentially one that must be developed operationally. I am not therefore speaking academically but am cultivating the hinterland between the family homestead of the small group and the massive chaos of the large group. The setting is both post-familial and pre-political. There is no root or basic culture, and we are attempting to promote 'outsight' as distinct from 'insight'. Outsight relates to insight in the way that outside and inside relate. 'Outsight' is a simple complementary term; whereas insight refers to inwardly orientated expansion of awareness, outsight refers to the outward expansion of social consciousness and thoughtfulness.

This is all done through learning to talk to one another and facilitating reciprocal transformations between psyche and society. It is appalling that of the hunting and gathering cultures that continue today in the jungles of Brazil or New Guinea, most have been destroyed, and I and my co-workers intend to resuscitate and reclaim this approach, which is occurring not in the unyielding eco-system of the desert but in the flourishing productivity of our present world, in which humanity has, as never before, been endowed with potential wealth but in which we survive in a manner which can only be described as incompetent.

As I have said, small groups, being family-sized, accordingly lend themselves to the family culture. By their very nature they represent a biological infrastructure in conflict with the superstructure of society, and pose the most imbedded hierarchy of all time. They are in a constant state of mutual frustration. The median group acts as a stepping stone, a transitional space. It is essentially a two-faced phenomenon, which I have termed 'transpositional' as distinct from 'transferential'.

## DIALOGUE

Dialogue, 'the supreme art' (Plato), turns out to be a highly complex negotiation in the face of emotional forces which threaten to curtail or disrupt the meetings. It stimulates thinking as well as emoting. Whereas Bion in his work with groups regarded hate as an endogenous and constitutional manifestation of the death instinct, I see it as a reflex response to frustration which generates an energy which is essential in activating the mind. Like Socrates, I believe in the role of sustained dialogue, and follow his principles of following up the argument wherever it leads. This goes far beyond the hierarchy of the family. Dialogue provides a transitional space equipped to deal with psychological traumata as well as psychoneuroses, and acts as a transitional object for splinters embedded in the psyche from the shattered mirroring of previous social catastrophes. War, holocausts and racism can be explored in a koinonic atmosphere facilitating recovery.

An example is that of a woman who had been in a concentration camp between the ages of 3 and 7, together with her parents. When she eventually came to Britain she underwent small-group psychotherapy, then a daily analysis for several years arranged at the Hampstead Clinic, and then had individual fortnightly supportive psychotherapy. When the latter terminated she developed severe depression and was referred to a median group. After a few meetings she had a nightmare in which the members were being swamped by a wave of black, radioactive mud, and for the first time thereafter she was able to talk about her experiences. This is an instance of post-traumatic neurosis, and only the median group was able to act as a suitable secure container, being both sufficiently powerful to contain her feelings and yet small enough to allow her to speak freely.

## CONCLUSION

Depression, like oppression, blocks the mind; likewise exercising the mind unblocks depression. I have come to realise that the median group is an appropriate setting for movements of this kind. Having stepped back from large- and small-scale groups towards groups of intermediate proportions, I have recognised the significance of group number in influencing profoundly the character of our relationships in handling hate and fear.

The Aboriginal name for 'white man' is 'no ancient law and no culture' reminding us of Aristotle's comment that 'he who is unable to live in society or has no need because he is sufficient for himself, must be either a beast or a God'.

The median group, or 'band', emerges as a self-evident extension of the Foulkesian small group, facilitating psyche in handling the social world. Like the small group it does not emerge automatically; it requires thought, organisation, ongoing training, and cultivation on the part of the convenors. By the same token it remoulds Psyche herself in evolving communicable microcultures. In so doing, there is a continuous interplay between the systemic flow of dialogue and the changing cultural structure of the group itself, like the river and river-bed.

'Koinonia' originally implied love for the state as distinct from love of family. The more intimate one-to-one personal relationship of friendship runs a distinctly different course, and in psychoanalysis has been referred to as the therapeutic alliance. Friendship is a universal criterion, a yardstick against which such manifestations as transference, manipulation, and seduction can be contrasted, highlighted, and interpreted. The client does not buy friendship but pays for the therapist's time and skill.

Psychoanalysis added a new dimension to psychiatry, and small groups extended psychoanalysis. The median or dialogue groups widened small groups and in turn will be further contextualised by larger groups and eventually global groupings. These larger groups are mainly non-verbal, and cultural contextualisation replaces dialogue. As an example, a schizophrenic attempts to verbalise context in the form of a strangely depersonalised quality of hallucinatory voices.

If we are to address the knotty problem of the psyche and the social world, it is imperative that we devise an adequate and appropriate operational technique. For example, pop concerts generate a context which can replace and release young people from their past contexts. How to harness this power comprehensively and to effective purpose could constitute a major breakthrough in establishing cultural change. The problem lies in how to focus the koinonic with the friendly, since they are by no means synonymous; indeed, they are usually discrepant and therefore mutually destructive.

## ACKNOWLEDGEMENTS

Discussions with Piers Lyndon played a formative part in my writing this essay, in honoured memory of the late David Bohm.

# Chapter 14

# The language of the group
## Monologue, dialogue and discourse in group analysis

*John Schlapobersky*

A man walks across this empty space whilst someone else is watching him, and this is all that is needed for an act of theatre to be engaged.

(Brook 1990: xi)

A sleeping man is not roused by an indifferent word but if called by name he wakes.

(Freud 1900 SE 4: 53)

Freud's hypothesis... [was] that the process of becoming conscious is closely allied to or essentially characterized by the cathexis of word representation.

(Foulkes 1964: 116)

*Free-floating discussion* is the group-analytic equivalent of *free-association*. The term originates in Foulkes' own writing and describes a set of key clinical concepts in therapeutic practice that distinguish the group-analytic approach. The use of association in this approach differs from its use in individual analytic practice (Kris 1990) and from the techniques used by practitioners of other group methods (Yalom 1975). This chapter explores these clinical concepts and the theory that underlies them. It is focused on the language of the group – the medium of free-floating discussion.

I shall differentiate between three primary forms of speech that arise in the matrix of any group. At the most basic level, *monologue* – speaking alone (with or without an audience) – is a form of individual self-expression. At the next level, *dialogue* – a conversation between two people – is the form of communication that distinguishes a bi-personal exchange. And at the third level, *discourse* – the speech pattern of three or more people – allows the free interaction of all its participants in a flexible and complex exchange that distinguishes the communication of a group (Moffet 1968). These patterns of speech are universal cultural forms arising in all communication and are present in the life of every group, although in no set order. Monologue can be understood as a soliloquy; dialogue as the resolution of opposites or the search for intimacy; and discourse as the work of a chorus.

The maturation of the group and its members involves a progression that begins with monologue in the individual's first encounter with themselves. It moves to dialogue in the discovery of the other, and then to discourse when an individual's multiple inner objects are externalised and encountered in the group. As indicated, the progression is a logical, not a descriptive, one; the group process itself does not necessarily follow this pattern. The group-analytic approach is distinguished from other group methods in that neither of the two earlier speech forms are disregarded. On the contrary, both monologue and dialogue are encompassed by and integral to group-analytic experience. True discourse remains the defining attribute of group communication because the complexity of communication between two people, when the introduction of a third transforms them into a group, alters the nature of the original relationship in a radical and profound way. The use of free-floating discussion allows a pattern of exchange to move freely between these different speech forms, each of which constitutes a distinctive type of communication. It is through this movement – from monologue through dialogue to discourse and back again – that the group-analytic method comes into its own, creating an arena in which the dialectic between the psyche and the social world helps to refashion both.

The chapter continues with a section that draws on relational theory to differentiate between *one-person, two-person, and three-person psychologies*. I then apply to these psychologies material drawn from language theory and consider the speech forms each of them allows. This is followed by a series of clinical examples that illustrate the approach with descriptions and commentaries on these speech forms as they arise in different therapy groups. It is followed with an exploration of how the use of language in clinical theory has evolved from monologue to discourse, from the couch to the circle. It traces developments from the original idea of *the talking cure* in Freud's work to the first emergence of the term 'free-floating discussion' in Foulkes' own writing and its subsequent development. The conclusion points towards a theory of discourse that will equip us to explore how:

Psychotherapists are rediscovering that... [T]he depths of the mind are reached and touched by simpler words that speak in images and metaphors. . .a universal, timeless language, pre-dating contemporary ideas. . .that touches the heart, the ancient seat of the emotions; [and] that speaks to the soul.

(Pines, in Cox and Theilgaard 1987: xxiv)

## PSYCHOLOGICAL FORMS AND THE RELATIONAL FIELD

We are today witnessing 'the breakup of. . .psychology into categories according to the minimum number of persons essential to the study of each branch of the subject' (Rickman 1950: 218). *One-person psychology* is concerned with what goes on inside a person; *two-person psychology*, with reciprocal relationships; and *three-person psychology*, with the relational field of the basic family constellation – and with social roles and social relations derived from it. The first takes the nature of internal experience as its field and gives centrality to the mind as it is located in a body. Its psychological functions include sensation, perception, cognition, mood, memory, imagination, phantasy, and the psychosomatic link. The second takes the intersubjective world as its field, gives centrality to relationships – a domain beyond but including the individual – and its psychological functions include bonding and attachment, exchange, affect, and the interpersonal link. The third takes social relations as its field, gives centrality to the corporate world – a domain beyond but including both the individual and the pair-bond – and its psychosocial functions include social interaction, social role, and social meaning.

I shall proceed on the basis of an assumption made here, that a truly group psychology incorporates one-person, two-person, and three-person psychologies, and that these three psychologies stand as an adequately differentiated range of categories to encompass all human experience. The group is a matrix of interaction, a relational field that arises between its members and between the interplay of these three different psychologies. Field and systems theory are the disciplines by which these different psychological levels are related. They provide group analysis with an integrative frame by which the higher-level functions in three-person psychology are related to more fundamental functions in one-person psychology (Agazarian and Peters 1981). Skynner, applying field theory to group and family therapy, describes the isomorphic relationship between experience at different levels. Thus, in a group, changes in any one of its component psychologies will necessarily involve change in the others (Skynner 1976, 1987).

## SPEECH FORMS AND THE SEMANTIC FIELD

Discourse, in one of its colloquial meanings, describes the communication of thought by speech, the exchange between someone speaking, someone listening, and something that is listened to. It describes relations between narrator, listener, and story (Moffet 1968). The structure of discourse is this set of relations among first, second, and third persons. When the speaker, listener, and subject are each distinct (or potentially distinct) as persons – that is, when two people are speaking to each other in the presence of a third person – we have the rudiments of a group. For the purposes of this paper I am using the term 'discourse' to describe only this kind of group communication. In a two-person situation, when only the speaker and listener are present as persons, we have dialogue. And when speaker and listener are the same person, we have monologue.

In one of its colloquial meanings – in De Mare's chapter above, for example – the term 'dialogue' does not refer to an exchange between only two participants (De Mare *et al.* 1991). But for the purposes of this chapter I am using the term in a more restricted sense to refer specifically to speech forms in which there are no more than two key participants who might be individuals, teams, or – for example – gender groups. It thus serves to identify what is distinctive about a speech form based on an oppositional symmetry, reciprocity, or duality in which the dialectic of the exchange is its key property. Where communication takes place between three or more participants, the term, 'discourse' is used to identify its more diffused properties.

Using a theory of language to examine group psychotherapy, we can see how the developing agency of the group's process begins at the first stage with the solitude of private encounters with the self that are allowed by the audience of the group. It leads at the second stage to greater agency for change when, through dialogue, others acquire psychic reality through conflicts over discrepant forms or levels of intimacy required of the same group experience. When the same experience has different meaning for its different participants, it exposes their different internal conflicts and can in due course help to resolve them. And this leads to the third stage – discourse – when the spontaneity of public exchange expresses individuals' primary process allowing the emergence of archaic anxieties and their reparative resolution. This is the kind of experience that has the most far-reaching consequences in terms of personal change. The most telling description of this kind of discourse is the way an individual's dream can be taken up in a mature group. As the last clinical example, on pages 229–30 below, describes, group members enter the dream together through a diversity of associations. In the discussion by which the dream content and its associations are explored in the here-and-now, we see the free play of words at work in the shared unconscious. As resonance in the group-as-a-whole connects the one and the many, meaning is condensed and, in the sudden discharge of deep and primitive material, events happen in a moment that can last a lifetime.

Each of these speech forms can arise in a narrative form through the recounting or reconstruction of reported events; or a dramatic form in people's real experience of one another in the here-and-now of the group. The group's process is characterised by a fluid interaction between narrative and drama, between the stories people have to tell and the drama of their roles and interactions as they do so. Progress is seen in a shift from speech patterns that are initially dominated by narrative and description to more mature forms that include reflective dialogue and discourse; and then to a capacity to abstract and generalise from this experience, both inside and beyond the group. This progression recapitulates the child's primary pattern of growth in a decentring movement outward from the centre of the self. As Pines has described in this collection, the self enlarges in the group, assimilating the matrix of group relations and 'taking them in'; at the same time accommodating itself to this matrix and adapting to it. The paradox of this progression is that, as the intersubjective domain is deepened and enriched, participants become more themselves by moving outward from themselves.

The process of symbolisation originates with the most primitive sense of self in the representational schema of the infant as he differentiates for the first time between self and other. As the representational world is extended and externalised, the infant's symbolising process is codified in a language whose semantic field (Korzybski 1933) is charged with forms of meaning that bear a close association to the individuals and experiences through which it originates. In this collection Elliott's, James's and Nitsun's chapters all give careful attention to these early formative experiences. The way in which a child talks to itself, addresses its mother, relates to a friend, speaks to a doll, or stands up to talk in the classroom can be different in each case. All these speech forms can arise in a dialogue between only two people for, as William James has said, relations are of different degrees of intimacy – merely to be with another, is a universe of discourse (James 1900). But whereas dialogue can generate an almost limitless range of meaning, the terms of a two-person psychology act as a constraint. Discourse in a group is extended far beyond this by a relational field that is almost as rich and indeterminate as its semantic field.

Through group interaction the relational and semantic fields – the matrix of interaction and the matrix of meaning – come to play upon each other, giving new meaning to early symbolic and representational experience. Thus language is a form of behaviour in the group; a way of referring to experience in and beyond the group; and a way of transforming experience in the group.

## CLINICAL ILLUSTRATIONS: MONOLOGUE, DIALOGUE AND DISCOURSE

Free-floating discussion proceeds through an interplay between narrative and drama, story and exchange, reconstruction and encounter. A reconstruction (by an individual or sub-group of some past event or trauma), or some other story in the group, might be a defence against the anxiety of an immediate encounter between its members. The drama of an immediate encounter might be a defence against painful stories about past or recent experience. *The examples that follow are designed to illustrate the gains to be had in clinical depth from the simple practice of establishing who is talking to whom about what?* As one speech form in either its narrative or dramatic form becomes evident as a defence, the therapist, or another group member, explores the defence to widen what Foulkes called *the common zone*, and this moves the· exploration to another speech form through which it can be taken forward.

### 1 Monologue

A man sits in the group recounting the circumstances that brought him into therapy. He has been with us now for three sessions and is beginning to find his voice. But as he talks people's attentiveness diminishes. He looks at no one in particular; his narrative is delivered now to the floor, now to the ceiling; he is agonised but self-absorbed, and the group's resonance is against his self-absorption rather than with his agony. Despite the distress in his story about his wife's suicide attempts, their loss of love and his concern about their children, the group of initially sympathetic listeners becomes increasingly disaffected.

Initially people had been eager to ask him questions, and their responses were sometimes visible in exclamations and other reactions.

But the speaker appears indifferent to his audience whose primary value, it seems, is to provide him with the space in which to talk to himself. He has not yet recognised others. They serve him primarily as narcissistic containers. They allow this for some time, but after ten minutes one group member seems to be dozing off; another stares out of the window; another looks to the conductor. As his monologue continues, two members smile at each other and look away. After fifteen minutes the conductor asks the speaker whom he is talking to. Startled and in some consternation he looks about him and says, 'Well, to the group', and falters as he does so.

*It is as if he has found himself alone on a stage without an audience. The process of decentering has begun, initiated by a conflict between the content of his narrative, and the limitations of his role.* He recognises the disengagement he has been responsible for but is as yet without resources to communicate empathically. His problem in the world has become manifest in the group. He has spent most of his adult life as a 'marginal man', caring for others at his own expense and often colluding with them when, despite his care, they neglected or overlooked him. Now he wants it all back but, consumed by neediness that he has spent a lifetime disavowing, he has no resources to enter reciprocal relationships.

To find a voice through which to reach others he must also find himself; the group first provides him with space and permission to discover his own psychic pain. If the therapy is successful we can expect to see, some months after its commencement, changes in his communication patterns in the group. From these changes he will be able to generalise, to effect changes in relations with his family and social network. The group is the arena in which psyche and social world acquire their first distinction from each other. It is here then that they can be reconciled in the interests of altered social relationships which are his primary therapeutic needs.

On future occasions when he has something to say, he will learn from the group's cues how to make eye-contact; how to come out of himself and how to begin bringing people with him in a narrative that allows empathy – shared emotion. *In order to have an audience while he tells his story, he will need to learn a different role.* He will need to allow others time to respond; to establish evidence of others' interest in him and his story; and to offer a sense of collaboration in their arena of shared interest. Of course, he will not learn this all at once and there will be many future occasions when the group recoils from his monologue.

He will again use others as narcissistic containers to give him the space in which to find himself. This process of self-discovery will proceed hand in hand with his discovery of the 'otherness' of those around him. Other group members will keep him connected to integrative process, having themselves had cues from the conductor that his resources will allow him to tolerate the momentary discomfort and humiliation of a confronting interruption, in the interest of shared experience.

> Two years later the same man sits in the group with a lot to say about his inner conflicts; and about his problems in the world outside. In contrast to his earlier self-absorption, he now chooses his moment; speaks in shorter sentences; uses shared language; relates what he has to say to what he knows others' preoccupations will interest them in; and allows pauses for response and interruption.

It is visibly evident that he is now able to use the group process to work on his internal one. In the progression from his early monologue to a participatory role in the group's pattern of discourse, the man is learning to overcome his isolation in the group and is being steadily equipped to do so in the world at large. What he is learning in the group about intercourse will steadily equip him to live in the world, rather than in its margins. He is now socially engaged and, whilst the nature and manner of his self-presentation continue to arouse resentment among other members over issues of control and detachment, his internal conflicts and anxieties are now an integral part of a shared process and are thus open to understanding and resolution.

## 2 Dialogue

This progression from autistic, private alienation towards an openly identified and shared social process lies at the heart of the group-analytic enterprise. The distinctive speech form that arises through dialogue at the second level is illustrated by exchanges in two different groups that arise between two members in each case. The first describes the concepts of *valency* (Scharff and Scharff 1991), and *mirroring* (Pines 1982), and the second, those of *projection* and *projective identification* (Sandler 1988).

> *A Valency and mirroring*   A man in his mid-forties who has been using the group to come to terms with his divorce, shares with us towards the end of the session a poignant moment in his relationship with his teenage daughter who is visiting him for the weekend. He

tells us of how she has begun to talk to him about her menarche. He recounts in the group what she said about it and how she did so. People comment on how touching they find her openness with him, and on how moving they find the trust between them. He tells us his daughter has had mixed feelings; she was pleased but also awkward and embarrassed. Her mother – his former wife – has supported her practically and emotionally, and this too he is pleased to acknowledge as he relates his daughter's narrative to the group. Sitting opposite him is a woman in her late thirties who – like him – has been in the group for some years. She is the only one of the seven who says nothing at all. But she does not take her eyes off him as his narrative unfolds, whilst different members engage with him at different levels and in different ways. She watches and listens attentively and in tears but will not be drawn out about her reaction. At the next session a week later, she initiates the discussion by telling us that she has not been able to get the picture of this man and his daughter out of her mind. She wishes she had a father like him. She had not believed it possible that a young girl could trust her father so intimately with her developing sexuality.

She wants to know more about their relationship, and as he tells her she replies with detail – long known in the group but never explored in quite this way – about her relationship with her own father who abused her violently and sexually. In the course of this dialogue the man opposite her becomes confirmed as the transference object for the good father she had always longed for and never known.

She in turn furnishes him with the opportunity to reach and recover in the group a lost aspect of his self that can be benevolent and tender towards women. The benign quality of his generosity, as it emerges with increasing evidence of his resources as a good father, stands in dramatic contrast to the destructive person we have known about, in his relations with his wife. The emotional charge – the valency – between the two of them becomes the group's object of interest. One other woman, in particular, whose own history involved an unresolved Oedipal conflict, becomes excited and animated by what she sees happening between these two. She makes herself available to them as a facilitator and, as they talk to each other across the group, she moves their discussion forward at those points at which they reach impasse.

They are each, of course, talking to the group-as-a-whole but they do so by addressing one another. They generate emotions in the group-as-a-whole but they do so because of the emotions they arouse in the encounter with one another. These two people each find reflected in their other, the lost ideal of their respective parental introjects. They select one another for an exchange that involves, temporarily, more intense emotion than arises elsewhere in the group, and through this they each provide a reparative mirror for a lost aspect of the other. In both these cases, however, each person's sense of the other is derived from a principal relationship with themselves. She experiences him as her idealised father, and he, similarly, relates to her as the mirror image of women familiar to him in his own life experience.

'Otherness' for each of these people is derived from their unconscious primary preoccupations with their own internal objects. There is work to be done before they can each relate to another of the opposite sex as a genuinely 'other' person, rather than as some reflection of their own internal imagery. The next example describes a conflictual interaction between two individuals in a group (over discrepant requirements for intimacy), through which long-standing *internal* conflicts acquire some resolution.

*B Projection and projective identification*   Two people are closely connected in a group by complementary roles in their life outside. She has a son like him with whom she is engrossed. He has a mother who, like this woman in the group, he finds strident and intrusive. The valency that emerges involves an antagonistic preoccupation between them. He reports a dream to the group in which she, clearly recognisable, suffocates his father. As the story of the dream unfolds in the group she becomes increasingly angry and distressed. She is furious at the role in which he has cast her in his dream life and treats the dream – in so far as it describes her – as if he had chosen its content as a conscious attack on her and could be held responsible for it. She rounds on him and, as he defends himself against her attack, he becomes increasingly aggressive himself. The therapist eventually intercedes with a modest observation about her that has an astonishing effect on her. 'It's his dream which you can learn from if you wish to, but in the last analysis it's *his* dream.' In the discourse that ensues the whole group explores the hostile dialogue that followed the reported dream, and she struggles with the realisation that she has been trying to control the content of his psychic life.

The understanding that this generates eventually leaves her in tears as she takes back the projections by which she has maintained this man – in her mind – as if he were her son. The hostile cathexis between these two – what Zinkin calls 'malignant mirroring' – is being undone. It helps to resolve his anxiety that she will damage him with her projections, as his mother damaged his father. And it helps to resolve her separation anxiety about losing her own son.

Zinkin uses the term 'malignant mirroring' to replace, with a single process, the experience of two distinct projective identifications that have a symmetrical relationship with each other (Zinkin 1983). As we can see here, it is the experience of dialogue that links the two individual's experiences and resolves the valency they hold for each other. The dream illustrates how he lived with the fear of damage – the fear of what her projections could do to him – and identified with this fear. Projective identification has been the basis of their valency, in this case malignant mirroring, a hostile cathexis.

At the point of this confrontation she experiences him for the first time as a genuinely 'other' person and is freed by this realisation, although she is shocked by it for some time. And he undergoes a comparable experience. These events allow her to generalise from the group to her life in the world and in particular to the relationship with her son whom she has bound with her projections for much of his life and is fearful of losing.

She is distraught as she begins to take all this in and for some weeks is depressed in the group. This in turn arouses compassion in the man who, witnessing her distress over the way in which she misrelated to him, appreciates her – for the first time – as a genuinely 'other' person, rather than the projected representative of his damaging mother. So he appreciates her as a genuinely different person and can relate constructively to her needs. And this in turn helps her consider how, by relinquishing control, she might gain rather than lose.

## 3 Discourse

The examples above illustrate the free-floating nature of group discussion as it moves between all three speech forms, with the conductor providing a minimum of direction. Rather than seeking to press the group's exchange towards one pattern or another, the conductor regards the speech form expressed by the group as a source of information as to what is happening in the matrix. In the example below discourse is initiated by information from one of the group's members, but there is neither monologue nor dialogue. Discussion is maintained by the group-as-a-whole and, in our attempt to analyse it, individualistic concepts are of only limited value.

In a twice-weekly group of many years' standing, events are dominated by increasing evidence of people's development and differentiation. One evening, one of the members, a man who has struggled against his parents' envy of his youth and their attacks on his individuation, discloses that he has finally reached a crucial financial target in the business he established. The figures are startling and unexpected but – for the moment – his achievement does not earn the regard it merits in the group.

One of the men, facing major financial dilemmas in his own company, is withdrawn and unresponsive; another, successful in his own career, explores the issue constructively, but for some time there is a limpness about the group's responses and, in their reluctance to confirm evidence of this man's progress, they behave like his parents who resent the fact that he has been successful on his own. Discussion moves round to one of the women who is expecting a baby. She is finding her position in the group sometimes difficult to protect.

What is most striking is the reaction of the two other women to news of the pregnancy. She has struggled to conceive and has finally been rewarded by a healthy pregnancy. Since then one of the women has left the group unexpectedly, and now the other woman, the mother of a small child, offers a disproportionate amount of advice, punctuated with references to ectopic pregnancies and other disasters.

The issue of envy lies beneath the narrative. All seven members participate in different ways, and the atmosphere is coloured by tension between affirmation on the one hand, and anxiety and antagonism on the other. People have struggled for years together and are really very close – they do wish to affirm one another's success. Despite their affirmative desires, they experience serious problems of envy. After 45 minutes the conductor offers an interpretation of the tension, suggesting that people are anxious about one another's envy of their own progress and, perhaps, ashamed of their own envy of others' progress. The quality of the exchange alters, relief allows disclosure, and the second half of the group session is taken up with a wide-ranging exploration of envy and jealousy in intimate relations.

It is not a new subject in this group and people are accustomed to exploring the less acceptable aspects of their own personalities with one another. It ranges over men's envy of women's creativity, aroused by the prospect of a woman bringing a new baby into the group; and women's envy of men's penises or potency in their reaction to the financial and career success reported on at the outset. Neither of these envious forms is exclusive to either gender, and this too is recognised and discussed, as is the acute anxiety that a number of members acknowledge about the prospect of envious attacks from those closest to them as they progress through their therapy.

The group's exploration is open and diffuse; there is no exclusive narrative line, and no single contributor. To understand the group we should have to consider the texture of its discourse rather than merely the text of its narrative. In a mature group at this stage we see that 'the conductor strives to broaden and deepen the expressive range of all members, while at the same time increasing their understanding of the deeper, unconscious levels' (Foulkes 1964: 112). In the texture of the discourse we discover what Foulkes called

> A *common zone* in which all members can participate and learn to understand one another. *The zone of communication* must include the experience of every member in such a way that it can be shared and understood by the others, on whatever level it is first conveyed.
>
> (Foulkes 1964: 112)

The zone of communication in this group now incorporates the shared fear of others' envy and the shared sense of shame at acknowledging envy of one's own. It leads on to the recognition that developmental arrest and some of the other forms of neurosis discussed in the group are attempts at envy pre-emption (Kreeger 1992).

What concerns us here is the way this recognition is arrived at. One member provided information about his success at work which led through group association to another's reference to her pregnancy. The first introduced a subject – ambivalence about progress associated with internal conflict and the fear of external attack – to which another resonated. This theme was amplified by resonance in the group-as-a-whole which extended the exploration. From the introduction of this theme to its amplification, exploration, analysis, and resolution there was one focused but brief interpretation by the conductor which set him apart from the others, but, for the rest, discourse in the group to which the conductor contributed like the other members, was responsible for its progress. The theme that provided the group's focal conflict

(Whitaker and Liberman 1965) in this session rested on an anxiety as to whether the group could relate to its members as a generative rather than envious parent and provide them with confirmation for their progress. For the group-as-a-whole to be experienced in such positive terms each of its members needed to find their individual part in the destructive envy anticipated from the others.

We would fail to take advantage of the real benefits of group-analysis if we confined our attention to content analysis of the text. An attempt to characterise a discussion like this requires concepts that describe context as well as content; texture as well as form; ground as well as figure; and group atmosphere as well as the dynamics of the individual. The development of group-analytic theory has not, regrettably, developed to characterise group process in this way because of the difficulties we continue to experience in characterising the complexity of such exchanges (Skynner 1987). 'Our concepts and technical terms', says Balint, 'have been coined under the physiological bias and are, in consequence, highly individualistic; they do not go beyond the confines of the individual mind' (1952: 228). A theory of discourse should help to clarify how 'inner (mental) and "outer" reality merge inside the common matrix of interpersonal social reality, out of which they originally differentiated' (Foulkes 1964: 98). Our attempt to conceptualise change is now assisted by the distinction provided in this account between the relational and semantic field. By exploring their interplay,

> It becomes easier to understand our claim that the group associates, responds and reacts as a whole. The group as it were avails itself now of one speaker, now of another, *but it is always the transpersonal network which is sensitized and gives utterance, or responds. In this sense we can postulate the existence of a group 'mind' in the same way as we postulate the existence of an individual mind.*
>
> (Foulkes 1964: 118)

The group 'mind' can now be understood as the composite of its semantic and relational elements.

## FROM THE COUCH TO THE CIRCLE: THE EVOLUTION OF TECHNIQUE

### 1 Freud's talking cure and the first fundamental rule

Brown's chapter in this collection gives a comprehensive account of how the meta-psychology of psychoanalysis has been revised by object relations theory. I am here concerned with the implications of this change for clinical theory. In his early collaboration with Breuer, Freud recognised that the crucial ingredient in their treatment of hysterics was free word association – what one of his patients called 'her talking cure' – rather than hypnosis. His original idea 'that whatever comes into one's head must be reported' (Freud 1912 SE 12: 107) was later set out as the 'fundamental rule of psychoanalytic technique' (Freud 1912 SE 12: 107):

> A rule which structures the analytic situation: the analysand is asked to say what he thinks and feels, selecting nothing and omitting nothing from what comes into his mind, even where this seems to him unpleasant to have to communicate, ridiculous, devoid of interest or irrelevant.
>
> (Laplanche and Pontalis 1973: 179)

The analytic relationship dictated by this rule emphasises its linguistic content, establishes the neutrality of the analyst, and helps to foster the regression of the patient. It has a further consequence which, like the use of the couch, is a remnant of the hypnotic method out of which it evolved – it confines the work of psychoanalysis to the patient's monologue.

Freud's original paradigm was an intrapsychic drive psychology whose formulations are those of a one-person psychology concerned with the individual in isolation. He maintained the use of the couch for the protection it afforded him from uncomfortable interaction with and exposure to his patients; and for the benefits it brought to treatment, minimising the extent to which free association was contaminated by dialogue (Freud 1913 SE 12: 134).

The critique of classical theory took issue with these limitations. Balint, 'for want of a better term' but in language that has had momentous consequences, introduces 'the *object* or *object-relation* bias' on the grounds that 'all our concepts and technical terms' except these two 'have been coined under the physiological bias and are. . .highly individualistic; they do not go beyond the confines of the individual mind' (Balint 1952: 226, 228). Today the concept of counter-transference has been recast as a valuable clinical tool; the analyst's subjectivity has been brought into the therapeutic arena as an acknowledged resource, rather than as the troublesome intrusion Freud had earlier believed it to be; and free-association, stripped of its unnecessary drive theory, has been reconceptualised in the context of a two-person psychology focused upon the dialogue between patient and analyst (Lewis 1990), 'an interrelation between two individuals. . . a constantly changing and developing object-relation', a 'two person situation' (Balint 1952: 231).

## 2 Foulkes' development of free-floating discussion

Foulkes' work has taken the same line of development one stage further, providing us with a clinical method that allows the participation of three psychological objects in the associative process. Free-floating discussion rests on what he called his 'model of three' (Foulkes 1964: 66, 69).

Although the maximum composition of what could be properly called a group is indeterminate and controversial, its minimum number is three. Between the dyadic experience of a pair and the group experience of three there is a transition just as radical and profound as that between one and two. Whatever the size of a small therapy group, the model of three gives it its underlying emotional structure. There is an indeterminate maximum in the number of individuals that can be present in any group, and there may be more than one conductor. But there are only three categories of psychological object – the individual, the conductor, and the group-as-a-whole. In the bounded space between these three objects, we find a three-person psychology at work.

Like Freud before him, Foulkes worked towards and arrived at his method before naming it. Described initially as 'a kind of group associative method', the term enters his primary text well after his first descriptions of its use. He then returns to it frequently, refining and redefining his descriptions, and, in explaining how it evolved, recounting how he initially treated people's associations in the group individually. Only later did he become 'aware that it was possible to consider the group's productions as the equivalent of the individual's free association *on the part of the group-as-a-whole*' (Foulkes 1964: 117).

> If one allows one's 'floating attention' as Freud termed it, to record automatically its own observations, one begins eventually to respond to 'pressures' and 'temperatures' as sensitively as any barometric or thermometric gauge with something akin to an internal graph of change on the cerebral 'drum' of the therapist.
>
> (Foulkes and Anthony 1965: 142)

The group matrix is the 'operational basis of all relationships and communications' (Foulkes 1964: 118). It has both a relational and semantic field. Through the interplay of these two fields, free-floating discussion allows 'the construction of an ever widening zone of mutual understanding within the group' (Foulkes 1964: 116), which Foulkes regards as its manifest content.

This is understood to relate to the latent meaning 'as a manifest dream relates to latent dream thoughts' (Foulkes 1964: 118). In the course of group discussion symptoms (manifest content) are translated into their meaning (latent content). The driving forces behind them are transformed

> into emotions, desires and tendencies, experienced in person. While doing so, the members learn a new language, a language which had previously been spoken only unconsciously.
>
> (Foulkes 1964:176)

The group analyst works as both therapist and group member, beginning with the dynamic administration of the group and the initiation of free-floating discussion. He assumes a more active role in a new group and allows the 'decrescendo' of his own role as the group gains authority. He is responsible for identifying disturbances in the group's process – what Foulkes calls 'location' – and for providing a balance between analytic (disturbing) and integrative forces, as the manifest content is translated into language that describes the unconscious. Transference is prominent, but the work is undertaken in the dynamic present. One of Foulkes' own descriptions of the conductor at work gives a vivid account of the clinical role, which contrasts dramatically with Freud's account of the psychoanalyst at work behind the couch (Freud 1913 SE 12: 134).

> He treats the group as adults on an equal level to his own and exerts an important influence by his own example. He sets a pattern of desirable behaviour rather than having to preach. . . puts emphasis on the 'here and now' and promotes tolerance and appreciation of individual differences. . . .
>
> [He] represents and promotes reality, reason, tolerance, understanding, insight, catharsis, independence, frankness, and an open mind for new experiences. This happens by way of a living, corrective emotional experience.
>
> (Foulkes 1964: 57)

In contrast to the first fundamental rule in individual practice described above, the group analyst is supportive as well as analytic, and the linguistic content of the therapy relationship is not so paramount.

Regression may occur, but it is counterbalanced by a progressive role through which group members become active participants in their own healing process. Finally, the group analyst's role is neither neutral nor detached. The quality of his engagement is evident, as is his readiness to maintain a human position that will serve the group's members as a model. *Foulkes' clinical recommendations to the conductor can be summarised as a responsibility for promoting discourse (Foulkes 1964: 57).*

## CONCLUSION: TOWARDS A THEORY OF DISCOURSE

I shall end with two more clinical illustrations, linked and concluded by some further theoretical points.

> A twice-weekly group meets for the first time after the Christmas break. Its members have common difficulties making or sustaining relationships. Joan reports that she had a terrible time over the holiday. It was like the roof caved in. Susan says she was also pretty shitty. Adam says he was fantastic. He had no contact at all with his recent girl-friend but went abroad on a working trip with a different girl, an old chum who doesn't mean much to him and with whom there is no intimate relationship. He no longer finds his current girl-friend attractive and, although they speak every day on the phone, he was pleased not to have to see her over the break. Whilst abroad with the new one, he got on like a house on fire. Anne takes up the image of the house on fire in one case, and the collapsing roof in another. She finds parallels between them; others agree. Adam is directed by the group to look at how he was now treating this girl-friend as an earlier partner had once treated him. The attraction he once described to us is now replaced by repulsion. He couldn't bear the thought of being close to her body. He talks a lot about attraction and repulsion. Susan knows only too well what he meant, she says, referring to her loss of sexual desire, and when she feels this way there is nothing her husband can do about it. They just have to wait until her sexual feelings return.
>
> Joan had described to us in the last group (before Christmas) how loved she felt by her partner. He had sent her flowers and a lovely note whilst he was away on a business trip. But once they were together over Christmas, the roof caved in. He just wasn't there with her. In the group people know her well and question whether she wasn't the one who vacated the house first. As the subject of attraction and repulsion, intimacy and withdrawal is taken up around the group, a new sense of acceptance and recognition enters the discussion.

Adam is ready to consider how he will find someone attractive providing there's nothing whole-hearted in how they find him. If they're genuinely attracted to him, in ways that reflect his own attraction towards them, he loses his feeling for them. His own sense of desire becomes repulsive. He can't tolerate two whole-hearted people in the same relationship. If they get on too well, the house on fire brings the roof down.

The group is not dealing with Adam's manic flight; nor with Joan's depression, nor Susan's disorder of sexual desire, nor the reaction of the group-as-a-whole to the recent Christmas break. Nor is it dealing with the common relational problems they mirror to one another. It is dealing with all of this simultaneously, and as the relational matrix generates a semantic field this in turn helps to transform their relationships inside the group and beyond.

In this semantic field, meaning is condensed by a number of key images which enter the word-play of the discussion. A disorder of sexual desire is an empty house; passion can bring the roof down; desire can become its opposite; two whole hearts can produce an empty house. The group's subject is not simply the series of static images by which it is reproduced here. A sense of profundity accrues as the process of discourse – now a chain reaction of associated images – develops a symbolic language by which the tension between hope and fear is brought out and, over time, resolved.

In a couples group of some years' standing, with three couples and a therapist, one partnership was under discussion for some weeks. Prior to joining the group the couple separated and came together several times, in a seemingly intractable pattern of conflict and reconciliation. The session reported here marks the turning point in their conflict. He has been convinced for some time they should separate, and he wants her to leave the house.

He brings a dream to the group in which he is with her on a luxurious ocean liner. He leaves her inside and climbs a gangway that looks as if it is going somewhere but it leads him over the side; he falls into the sea and the boat sails away. There is a much smaller boat nearby which he swims towards. As he struggles in the water he sees a red flag floating nearby. He tries to secure both the red flag and the boat, but the current keeps them apart and in the attempt to have both he loses everything and knows he will now drown. One of the other men invites the dreamer to offer his own associations to the dream. As he begins to do so, the third man enters the discussion with his own associations based on different imagery. The three women then enter the discussion. The woman who fears abandonment is barely interested in the dream and much more concerned with where she will live if he insists she should go. The two other women are closely identified with her. A dialogue develops between the men and the women as to where the discussion should go; the men want to discuss the dream's imagery but the women address the relationship conflict at a concrete level.

After a prolonged and fractious exchange that includes material from the two other couples, we are reminded by the partner that the dreamer's son recently sent this couple some red roses as a token of hope for their reconciliation. There is a sense of startled recognition in the group as everyone sees these roses as the warning flag in the sea. The discourse acquires a new vitality and, towards the end of the group, the therapist offers an interpretation that extends this recognition. He suggests that the dreamer, like all the group's members, is deeply bound to his partner and has discovered in his dream that if he gets her to walk the plank, he'll end up in the sea himself. The man laughs with relief at being understood, but she doesn't know whether to laugh or cry and looks from him to the therapist saying, 'Yes, yes, yes'. The discussion continues with humour and appreciation to the end of the session. In the weeks that follow this imagery is returned to repeatedly as the couple emerge from their conflict and bring their new-found affection and goodwill to bear on the other couples' conflicts.

The exchange moves between monologue, dialogue, and discourse. There is both narrative and drama in each of these speech forms as we move between real and reported experience. Language is working here to generate mutative metaphors that come in a moment that can last a lifetime. At such a moment, 'a sense of mystery, astonishment, and uniqueness... transcends any descriptive technicalities' (Cox and Theilgaard 1987: 17). As Cox describes it,

> We have a fragmentary glimpse into therapeutic space. It emphasizes the universal pull of the primordial. It is an intrinsic part of the psychotherapeutic process in which a patient comes as close to his true feelings as he dares.... Metaphor affords the possibility of engagement with those primordial themes to which all our experience gravitates.
>
> (Cox and Theilgaard 1987: 9)

In this group the dream is first a soliloquy, a way of thinking aloud about the viability of the partnership and the fear of separation. Then it becomes the subject of a dialogue, initially between this man and his partner and then between the men and women in the group as they are all drawn into a review of their relationships. Throughout the session it is the subject of discourse, yielding moments of profundity in which the group works like a chorus in an ancient drama, challenging private deceits with public recognition and confirming private recognitions with public affirmation. Free-floating discussion thus encompasses all three speech forms, but it provides more than simply direct access to primary process. It is also the means by which associative patterns are analysed and explored, new forms of meaning are constructed, and a new sense of the individual emerges in the widening cycle of the whole.

# Chapter 15

# The psyche and the social world

*Dennis Brown and Louis Zinkin*

In our discussions as a group of authors, there has been much questioning of one another's theoretical preoccupations or biases. At times there has been agreement and at others sharp disagreement. Where disagreement has occurred, it has not been about the value of one another's ideas in their own context, but about the extent to which they can be brought into a group-analytic model without violating some of the basic principles of group analysis. This, in turn has led to questions as to how far group-analytic theory can be extended.

For example, can an intersubjective theory be reconciled with an object relations one? Can a model which regards the individual as an abstraction be reconciled with theories based on the primacy of the individual and of the internal world of the person? By extending psychoanalytic theory, are we in danger of watering it down? In rejecting reductionism, is there a danger of inflating our theory to such an extent that important distinctions become blurred? Is it possible to speak of a 'group mind' or even a 'world soul' as we move into cultures and across cultures, seeking unification of diverse ways of looking at the world and invoking transpersonal processes? Can attachment theory, quantum theory, systems theory, or linguistic concepts all be brought together into some all-encompassing mega-theory which would provide support to a generally accepted model of group analysis? Not only can we not agree on whether this might be possible; we cannot even agree on the desirability of such an integration.

These problems are not, of course, unique to group analysis. They are of concern to all the human sciences in this postmodern age, which attempts to avoid the problems created by all-embracing, total theories. We believe, though, that group analysis is not only especially prone to these agonising questions but has a special contribution to make to understanding their nature. Seeing people in groups, trying to achieve a common understanding in an increasingly fragmented world, not only exposes seemingly incompatible differences of viewpoints but also provides possible solutions.

As editors reviewing the book as a whole, we have a similar problem to that facing the group conductor trying to understand the group-as-a-whole. We can see both a unity and a great diversity. Any representation of the whole which we make resembles a group interpretation, which may or may not resonate with the views of any individual member. So we must emphasise that we are presenting only our own provisional understanding. Also, in attempting such an overview, we can draw out only certain features of varied and complex contributions. In no sense is this intended as a critical review of the value, the merits, or demerits of any individual thinker.

We shall look first at the problems and contradictions as we see them, then attempt to integrate the contributions, and finally take a tentative look to the future.

## PROBLEMS AND CONTRADICTIONS

Although each author is attempting to develop group-analytic theory within a Foulkesian framework, it is inevitable that others will question whether extending the theory alters its fundamental tenets. This is particularly liable to happen when the author brings in a new frame of reference.

It will be convenient in this section not to follow the order of chapters but to group them in four main divisions:

1 *Psychoanalysis.* Problems here include divergences within the psychoanalytic community as well as difficulties of stretching theory beyond its clinical orientation. Psychoanalytic concepts are particularly prominent in the chapters by James, Brown, Nitsun, Elliott, and Marrone.
2 *Systems theory.* Family therapy is allied to group therapy but usually does not make any use of unconscious phantasy (Behr and Blackwell).
3 *Social sciences.* This is a field of study not easily delineated, but including sociology, anthropology, linguistics and political theory (Zinkin, Schlapobersky, and Le Roy).
4 *General, more abstract philosophical theories.* These include religious and moral standpoints, particular views of the philosophy of science, and cosmology. Naturally, this category gives rise to the

greatest degree of controversy, and especially to attacks of being vague and 'unscientific' (Powell, Pines, and De Mare).

These categories stem from the theoretical framework of each chapter, which in turn usually reflects the professional background of the contributor. The comments on our own contributions arise from joint discussions and reflect the difficulties we ourselves acknowledge.


## 1  Psychoanalysis

The question here is whether the joins made between various analytic theories, as well as between individual and group analysis, are as seamless as they appear.

Dennis Brown sees, in the development of object relations theory, a trend from object to subject which seems to correlate with much of Foulkes' conceptions of group analysis. He points out the limitations of Foulkes' own psychoanalytic position, which has been transcended in later developments of theory. We anticipate that few would quarrel with his description of these trends towards intersubjectivity, but we do not, of course, know whether Foulkes would have been happy with Brown's re-wording of 'ego training in action'. There is an ongoing debate concerning the impact of infant research on psychoanalytic theories of development, which seriously questions many assumptions, particularly affecting primary narcissism and the early projective mechanisms of internal objects posited by Klein and her followers. Since these notions are quite basic for most psychoanalytic theorists, it is questionable whether the problems inherent in the notion of internal objects (originally conceived as the objects of instinctual drives) can be overcome without so radical a revision of Freud that many would not recognise the theory as psychoanalytic. A revision in this direction is at present being undertaken in self psychology following Kohut, where intersubjectivity is indeed coming to the fore. But should it be taken to the point where drive theory is altogether abandoned? If not, how can it be modified? Again, the reader will have to decide after carefully considering Brown's arguments, but it should be remembered that there is by no means a general consensus within psychoanalytic circles on these questions. Most group analysts faced with this issue would probably want to retain a place for a subject-object theory as well as wanting to incorporate the more relational concepts implied by intersubjectivity, but there remains room for considerable disagreement.

In his chapter on attachment theory, Mario Marrone persuasively argues for the importance of Bowlby's work. However, his place in the psychoanalytic movement remains extremely problematic. In broad conceptual terms, Bowlby's thinking is based on his strongly held view that psychoanalysis is part of natural, rather than hermeneutic, science. Basically, though subjectivity is acknowledged, the whole thrust of the theory is biological and behavioural, and his notion of the working model is simply not the same as what most analysts mean by the internal world. Though analysts do speak of self- and object-representations, their idea of the phantasy-life of their patients would not have been acceptable to Bowlby. As Marrone points out, the concept of a behavioural system is a key issue in attachment theory. Not all group analysts would agree that behavioural systems are an object of study in group analysis and would not accept the epistemology implied by such a term. It is difficult to integrate with Brown's movement towards intersubjectivity, the notion of coherence as developed by Pines and the dialogue of De Mare, Zinkin, and Schlapobersky. In anthropology, as shown in the chapters by Le Roy and Zinkin, there are limitations to its objectivity, to the extent to which a fieldworker can be a neutral observer. Similar problems are raised by Blackwell and Behr through family therapy and the use of cybernetic models. There are also technical problems in the kind of active enquiry that Marrone advocates on the part of the group conductor.

Barbara Elliott's contribution is perhaps the most original and controversial in this volume, in that she proposes that certain experiences in the group can be explained only on the assumption that some sort of memory traces exist of pre-natal experience in the womb, and that both men and women have phantasies of having a womb inside them. At this stage such suggestions must remain somewhat speculative, but Elliott at least points out that her suggestions are compatible with research findings and gives vivid clinical arguments to support her thesis. However, few group analysts would make the interpretations she does, and most would deal with phantasies of fusion and of absence of true object relations differently. Nevertheless, many will find her arguments and suggestions worthy of further consideration, and her idea may represent the sort of contribution to our understanding of human development that can be found more readily in a group-analytic setting than in an individual one.

The chapter by Morris Nitsun puts a 'psychoanalytically based' phantasy firmly on centre stage: the primal scene. In doing so, he raises considerable problems. First, there is the centrality of the Oedipus complex in Freud's theory. To various extents, psychoanalysts have

increasingly paid attention to the pre-Oedipal stages of infant development, even though, as Nitsun points out, the Oedipal stage is placed
much earlier in Klein's theory than in Freud's. Secondly, there is the
vexed question of whether the Oedipus complex is universal. It is not
generally agreed that it occurs in the same form or is equally important
in all cultures. Thirdly, in Jung's account of the 'coniunctio' (the alchemical picture of the union of male and female), as depicted in his
essay 'The psychology of the transference' (Jung 1946), he does not pay
much attention to it as a historically determined intrapsychic phantasy.
Instead, he regards it as one of many archetypal patterns concerned in
the union of opposites. As an archetype, this pattern would transcend
cultural differences. Lastly, there is Nitsun's main thesis. He sees the
primal scene as so central to group analysis that he metaphorically puts
it in the centre of the circle of the group, the place physically taken up
by the small table that most group analysts use. His arguments to
support this idea are quite involved, but would surely be contested by
other group analysts who contribute to this volume.

Beyond the objections within psychoanalytic theory or even those
within analytical psychology, Foulkes' idea of the matrix would be
considered by many to regard all phantasies as arising from a relational
network, rather than any one being central. Most people would not
imagine the matrix as having a centre in this sense. This is not, of
course, to deny the importance of primal scene phantasies in the group,
but the underlying theory of how they should be understood in the group
context remains sharply controversial. Moreover, maternal, paternal,
and sexual elements pervade everyone's thinking at all levels, including
that of group members and the conductor. As well as 'maternal'
nurturing and 'paternal' law-giving, their *relationship* permeates the
foundation matrix and personal matrices of the group, and therefore the
dynamic matrix of the group.

Colin James's chapter makes a strong claim for the integration of
group analytic with object relations theory, using Bion and Winnicott as
his main exemplars of that theory, challenging the usually held view
that there is a great gulf between Foulkes' and Bion's group theories.
This involves him in making links between holding and containing, with
repeated warning of the difficulties in tearing concepts from their
theoretical contexts. Despite the fact that both analysts presented these
ideas at the same conference, many readers might question whether the
abstract formulations of Bion on thinking are compatible with
Winnicott's notions of maternal holding. Certainly these two men did
not embrace each other as though they had arrived at the same idea by

different routes, and it remains doubtful whether each regarded the other's ideas as congenial. This doubt is furthered by James's subsequent quoting of the group relations authors: Turquet, Trist, and Lawrence, who are strongly influenced by Klein and Bion, rather than by Winnicott. This bias might explain James's dismissal of Zinkin's (1989a) proposition that there is a creative ambiguity between what is container and what contained: the group acts as container for its constituent members, who come to contain the idea of the group, and the group initiates inter-member processes. However, this view accords with James's interpretation of Bion's ideas that meaning is created in, through, and by the group, as by the containing and meaning-creating responsiveness of the early mother.

As for the integration with Foulkes, it is highly questionable whether, as James contends, Foulkes' differences were simply a sign of the times. Can man as a social being be entirely explained by the externalisation of object relations as James, following Bion, tries to show, or might it be that this attempt misses what is essential in Foulkes' position – namely, that no individual can be understood outside his or her social world at any given time (Brown 1985). The question here is a fundamental one for psychoanalysis: should we take the inner world of the individual as the primary object of study? The reader has to decide after examining James's detailed analysis and the logic with which he proceeds from the individual to the dyad, to the small group, to the large group, and to the larger society. Whatever the implications for psychoanalytic theory, the question for the group analyst is: can psychoanalysis provide an *adequate* model or does it need to be supplemented by others which do not start with the individual?

## 2   Systems theory

The issue of systems theory and its relevance or compatibility with group analysis is taken up by Dick Blackwell and Harold Behr. They both deal with ways in which systems theory needs to be modified in the light of group-analytic technique. These authors share both a group-analytic background and experience with family therapy. They both see considerable problems with integrating the two disciplines.

Behr draws attention to certain fundamental differences between the two disciplines. Can the same technique be applied to a standard group-analytic group where the conductor is less of an outsider, more part of the group from the outset, more continuously present throughout all its communications, less concerned about 'symptoms', less in a hurry, less embattled with the group in a bid to change the system than in family therapy? He brings out, too, the conductor's function in fostering communication in an already existing system of the family. Behr concludes that technique has to be considerably modified to meet the needs of two such different situations, and shows how the group-analytic attitude can be valuably incorporated into family therapy. However, many family therapists would strongly disagree with this, just as many analytically minded group analysts would object to using the strategies of a systems approach in the 'stranger' therapy group.

The question remains whether these disagreements about practice reflect disagreements about theory. Does each position in the debate rest on a basically different conception of the human being, or can they be reconciled in terms of differences in the context within which human beings are studied? For example, the degree to which the conductor is an outsider can be seen as relative: in family therapy the conductor is more so, providing greater objectivity and power to interrupt established patterns of intervention by interpretation or illustration; in group analysis their position and role are more fluid and flexible – as it were, both inside and outside the circle.

Blackwell takes up the same theme: the difficulties of reconciling a systems approach with group analysis. In a tightly condensed historical overview of systems theory, he isolates four different versions, each of which has demonstrably useful applications to group analysis. He by no means confines group analysis to the therapeutic stranger group, but sees it as a general method with wide applications to family therapy and organisational consultancy work. However, he recognises a serious limitation of all forms of systems theory in its attempts to remain neutral and objective. Even in its most constructivist forms, it leads to relativism and fails to address itself adequately to a historical or political perspective. He deplores the failure of systems theory to engage with postmodernist thought in the way that psychoanalysis has in the movement initiated by Lacan.

This chapter highlights the points of controversy which rage around the nature of scientific enquiry, the value of a dialectical critique and the fundamental importance of ideology affecting philosophy as well as every other discipline. Blackwell gives his own views at each turn of his argument, and the reader is left to assess to what extent group analysis is a helpful answer to the problems raised or is itself in need of revision in the light of Blackwell's analysis. Some of the difficulties – for example, in his references to a 'proper' group-analytic response to the Gulf war – have aroused fierce controversy in the Group-Analytic Society.

## 3  Social sciences

John Schlapobersky's chapter makes a clear distinction between monologue, dialogue, and discourse. Though he shows the clinical usefulness
of this threefold classification of the modes of speech to be found in the
therapy group, his terminology is nevertheless controversial. It is correlated with the distinction between one-body, two-body, and three-
body psychology made in object relations theory, but some would not
be happy with his use of terms. Monologues and dialogues are distinguished by Bakhtin (see Zinkin's chapter), not in terms of the number
of people taking part but in the style of speech or discourse. Monologue
expects no answer. In dialogue, the utterance of the speaker is always
*incomplete*. Even if only one speaker is present, it requires and expects
a response, the response also being incomplete and itself requiring a
response. Thus each is also discourse, described as monologic or dialogic. The usual use of the word 'discourse' likewise does not depend
on the number of participants, but refers to the underlying assumptions
(often unconscious or ideological) determining the use of words and the
mode of speech. De Mare, in his chapter, uses dialogue not in its
generally accepted usage as an interchange between two (which he calls
'duologue') but as going on between many people, as in his median
groups. The differences are not simply terminological but imply different approaches to the study of language. These remarks do not
invalidate Schlapobersky's treatment of the topic, which is helpful to
the general reader, but it might cause confusion or disagreement among
those who use the words somewhat differently.

In his chapter on group analysis and cultural phenomena, Jaak Le
Roy introduces a body of French work which he seeks to integrate with
both the group-analytic theory of Foulkes and with Bion. This may
create difficulty for those group analysts who see these two approaches
as incompatible, though it may satisfy others who are looking for ways
of reconciling them (see James's chapter). Le Roy's introductory
theoretical outline, drawn from the writings of Kaës, Bleger, Rouchy,
and Anzieu, is explicated as though it is non-controversial, but it raises
great difficulties in its treatment of the interplay between cultural, individual, and innate developmental factors. The use of the concept of
Self (with a capital S), and of individuation and of transpersonal entities,
are almost the basic building blocks of Jung's analytical psychology,
and it is surprising that Le Roy makes no reference whatsoever to Jung,
even though Foulkes did incorporate his ideas. The problem is to account for universal psychic structures which can be regarded as trans-

personal, and to decide whether they are culturally transmitted or innate. Although one can speak of primary and secondary groups in the sense that each individual is primarily influenced by the extended family, it is not clear to what extent the family is itself conditioned by culture, and culture itself may be less autonomous than it seems. For example, myths may be understood as cultural products or as structurally independent of culture, as not only Jung but also Lévi-Strauss (who rejected Jung's idea of a collective unconscious) have suggested. Furthermore, though mother–infant patterns of interaction are culturally conditioned, how do we account for the highly individual styles observable from the very beginning? These questions are quite complex. Norbert Elias has also dealt with them at some length, and his work too is not considered in this chapter though it had a great influence on Foulkes' thinking. Although Le Roy has valuably extended group-analytic theory by intro-ducing a whole body of sophisticated thinking which is little known outside France, this may not be so easily absorbed into group-analytic theory as he suggests.

Louis Zinkin's examination of the therapeutic function of exchange in the analytic group springs straight from Foulkes' list of therapeutic factors, his emphasis on increasing communication at all levels, and making articulate what was previously unknown or inexpressible. Zinkin's extension of exchange into the spheres of anthropology and morality would not have surprised Foulkes, nor will it surprise our present-day colleagues. Indeed, the idea of group norms and Foulkes' law of group dynamics – that the group represents the norm from which the individual deviates (see Chapter 1) – necessitates exchange to arrive at a genuine consensus as opposed to a preconceived and imposed ideas of 'normality' and ideal behaviour.

However, some may see Zinkin's proposal of a four-by-four juxta-position of therapeutic factors and levels of interaction as somewhat contrived – almost too neat to be true – like many prematurely struc-tured, all-inclusive hypotheses. But Zinkin uses the tentative juxta-position to illuminate rather than close off.

Foulkes himself did not write of projective identification, but of 'the level of bodily and mental images' (projective level) 'corresponding to primitive narcissistic "inner" object relations in psychoanalysis, other members reflecting unconscious elements of the individual self, where the group represents as outer what are in truth inner object relations' (Foulkes 1964: 115). Elsewhere he distinguishes between 'objective level (mirror phenomena)', in which the group represents inner objects and part objects, and a body level presented by physical manifestations, illnesses, and so on, in which the group represents the body image (Foulkes 1990: 183). We might see the four-by-four – or four-by-five or more – juxtaposition as an invitation to think of process and structure interpenetrating each other.

In so far as psychoanalysts are becoming more interested in inter-active exchange at all levels of the personalities of analysand *and analyst*, psychoanalysis is becoming less focused on the 'isolated' un-conscious of the analysand. In this sense psychoanalysis is moving towards group analysis, where we exchange not only in dialogue, but in listening and in empathic responsiveness, which include allowing and sharing silence.

## 4   General, more abstract philosophical theories

The contributions of De Mare, Pines, and Powell, though variously rooted in anthropological observations and psychoanalytic and Jungian theoretical concepts, share a readiness to move beyond the narrow confines of clinically verifiable fact and customary disciplinary bound-aries. De Mare adumbrates a 'new politics' on the basis of selections from anthropological literature and his own observations of conducting median groups, as though divorced from the small analytic group in which group-analytic theory arose. Pines, retaining his focus on clinical experience in psychoanalysis and group analysis, offers a resonant ac-count of the interaction of individual and group that is dominated by the concept of coherence, itself far from clear. And Powell, boldly – some may say, rashly – moves from the clinical dynamic matrix into concepts of connectedness that are taken from modern physics and cosmology even to the threshold of theology.

Patrick De Mare's chapter is something of an 'odd man out'. By starkly contrasting the median group with the small therapeutic stranger group, he makes a number of claims for the specific benefit of the larger number that many would dispute. His view that the small group is more related to the family, that it is more concerned with feeling than with thinking, with insight rather than 'out-sight', and is less conducive to dialogue, remains open to question. Many of the problems we have raised in the psychoanalytically based chapters, such as Nitsun's, apply here too. At the other end of the spectrum, Blackwell would surely deny that social and political matters are outside the scope of the small group, and Powell's grand picture of the matrix informs his way of under-standing small groups. Dialogue and intersubjective exchange, according to Brown, Pines, and Zinkin, are the very essence of small-group therapy, and even koinonic fellowship is fostered in small-group work. Perhaps the disagreement here could be reduced to the word 'therapy', and whether this is narrowly conceived in terms of relief of individual pathology or is more widely seen as a growth process, a raising of the group consciousness.

De Mare's ideas about large, and particularly medium-sized groups, have an implicit prophetic sociopolitical dimension as well as reflecting his experience of their capacity to face the problem of talking freely in dialogue – 'on the level', he would say. However, this is not impossible in small or much larger groups, even though in these we first tend to get confronted by family dynamics and 'neurotic' transferences in the case of the usual six-to-eight member clinical group, or by 'psychotic' fears of annihilation and defences against them in larger unstructured groups. Nitsun and Brown describe the former, for example, in their clinical vignettes. Elliott gives a vivid description of the latter in her description of a large experiential group at the Institute of Group Analysis. It would seem that the size of the group does powerfully influence what happens in it, both in terms of what it stimulates and what it tends to exclude – in that, most group analysts would agree with De Mare.

Malcolm Pines is deeply immersed in both psychoanalysis and group analysis, their history and evolution. Theoretically, one of his major contributions has been to illuminate the complexity of the concept of mirroring, how we discern more of ourselves through others. Here, in developing the idea of coherence, ·addressed in psychoanalysis by Loewald, he has used a concept which is intrinsically vague. Pines distinguishes group cohesion which he sees as a primitive sticking together, from coherence, which allows differentiation and redrawing of boundaries. In fact, this is a special usage of these terms. According to the *Shorter Oxford English Dictionary*, coherence means cohesion and congruity as well as the 'harmonious connection of the several parts of a discourse, system etc. so that the whole hangs together', and surprisingly context is also given as a definition of coherence. In everyday usage it often implies something is *understandable*, the opposite of incoherent. The very richness and ambiguity of the term thus allows distinctions to be blurred and made. This is in keeping with the allusiveness and resonance of many of Foulkes' profoundest ideas, such as mirroring, explored and extended by Pines (1982) and Zinkin (1983 and 1992); but some, while relishing this aspect of group analysis, might – in another part of themselves – long for clearer concepts with which to grasp the interaction of individual and whole group. Agazarian and Peters (1981) have offered us one set of concepts – distinguishing between individual roles, member roles, and the group-as-a-whole; Ashbach and Schermer (1987), in their ambitious Group Analytic Grid, have attempted to integrate object relations theory and self psychology in intrapsychic, interactive, and whole-group systems at regressed, individuated, and mature levels. Some of us would see such attempts as clarifying, others as too restricting and encouraging premature comprehensiveness and closure. Pines's approach could be seen as that of a skin diver studying the movements of shoals of fish around him, the others' as using a lobster pot or a giant trawling net.

In his chapter, Andrew Powell demonstrates the richness of Foulkes' concept of the group matrix. There are obvious links with systems theory (see Blackwell's chapter) in the fact that we can speak of several interlinked and often transposed matrices – foundation (forming the cultural bases that permeate all), personal (in which each individual develops and which is embedded in their inner relational world as well as the outer network), and dynamic (developing from the start of each therapeutic group). In Powell's extension of the network of phenomenological and theoretical systems, psychological, physical, and metaphysical, we get a sense of widening horizons that some may find exhilarating, others disturbing; it is as though he is using a universe-sized trawling net. Powell seems to concentrate, in his own terms, more on synthesis than on analysis, or, one could say, on syncretism rather than diacrisis. Carried to extremes it takes us, unapologetically, towards theology, away from the clinical setting where group analysis started and is still most effective. Working with individuals requires the group analyst to recognise and understand differences as well as similarities.

To complete the task described by Jung as 'individuation', individuals need to reclaim undeveloped or disavowed parts of the whole self, as Powell fully acknowledges. Only then can the circle of self be completed and enlarged. But completing what you *are* does not include what you are *not*. We believe that what Powell calls 'the flowing dynamic course of interaction' requires a *centripetal* as well as a *centrifugal* movement. We need such a balance to maintain relatively stable homeostatic structures between groups, between individuals, within individuals, and between individuals and groups. Our need to allow – perhaps more than we have done – for the importance of boundaries and barriers will be raised in the next section.

## TOWARDS AN INTEGRATION

The problems we have discerned are related to the compatibility of some of the contributions with unmodified psychoanalytic theory, itself in the process of revision, and the compatibility with group-analytic theory as laid down by Foulkes of a pseudo-objective approach to systems theory and anthropology. Thus we have questioned the use of unmodified psychoanalytic theory in relation to group analysis because of its bias towards the individual. We believe it is possible to see how what we might call the dialectic between the individual and the social world can take us to a new level of synthesis.

*Andrew Powell* underlines the fundamental principle of connectedness intrinsic in the idea of matrix. Like Louis Zinkin he emphasises the different levels of the matrix described by Foulkes, and describes how the matrix can function as a transitional space (Winnicott) and a caregiving other (Bowlby). It is a secure place in which to develop because it is not under the omnipotent control of one person. He notes that the matrix has no inherent moral position; that is, it can be used as a waste bin, or for creative containment in which psychic contents can be transformed from a lower to a higher level (Zinkin 1989a). For Powell, mind and matrix are synonymous as each individual's mind connects with all other minds.

For some, problems might arise when he moves from the psychobiological to the psychophysical, linking with the new physics with its emphasis on pattern and wholeness (Bohm). Whether or not we follow Powell into cosmology and theology, this emphasis on patterns and wholeness is very apposite to our work in group analysis. The bringing together of seeming opposites, so important in Jungian theory, can be vividly enacted in groups where extremes are polarised and personified before they are integrated within the group and often within individuals. Another seeming polarity between mind and body is also resolved at what Foulkes (1990: 175) described as the *body level*, between the projective and the primordial, 'in which an individual's unique genetic character interleaves with the principle of connectedness'.

*Dick Blackwell*'s chapter on systems theory follows Foulkes in bridging the seeming polarisation in psychoanalytic theory between the individual and society, and pursues Foulkes' aim of locating group analysis in relation to sociology and social psychology. He notes the paradox of the participant-observer position reflected in social science, which is always a part, even a product, of the system it describes within its historical political context. Blackwell sees the dialectical relationship between the individual and the group, in terms of the search for meaning in both personal and sociopolitical life.

Blackwell also uses the idea of a dialectic between reality and language as generating a creative space between them, in Lacan's sense. In applying systems theory to the understanding of individual development – as in Bollas's idea of the ego embodying rules for relating to mother – he points to the need to elaborate this in relation to the family context, to the parental relationship, and relationships between other family members. Recognition of each group member as holding a specific observer position, responding to and different from that of others while retaining its validity, promotes an acceptance and development of diversity and individuality within the group. This is a very good description of what happens during the move towards a greater sense of mature intersubjectivity. It is more than mutually validated 'objectivity'. It allows for the essential subjectivity of each member's position, and acknowledges their deeper connectedness.

It also links up with *Malcolm Pines*'s ideas about coherency. Pines's approach, leaning on that of Loewald, could be seen as bringing together some of Jung's ideas with those of systems theory. For example, distinguishing between repression and internalisation, he points out how repression works against integration and organisation of the whole psyche, whereas internalisation promotes it. He points out how, in the therapy group, members internalise aspects of the interaction between the therapist, individual members, and the whole group, which become part of the newly coherent self. Increasing communication enhances the coherency of individual members and of the group matrix.

Coherency involves the clarification and redrawing of boundaries. For this to develop there needs to be a safe holding and containing function in the group. A safe space requires clear boundaries. As *Colin James* describes it, the holding and containing functions of the group allow distress and frustration to be acknowledged, thought about, understood, and shared, so that it moves onto a different level of integration in the whole person and the whole group. Each person has a chance in the group matrix to develop more fully a sense of self in relation to others, through both play and reverie.

Citizenship, James points out, requires being able to take in other people's points of view, drawing on the mature adult's ability to integrate the value of the other, but maintain his own individuality. This is very much part of the coherency that Pines talks about, and links with the issue of ethics and morality that are an important part of social life, as yet insufficiently studied by group analysts (Brown 1992b).

This ability to see things from another's point of view is also very much part of what *Dennis Brown* talks of in terms of intersubjectivity. Empathic mutual responsiveness is internalised as object relations, but so also are failures and blockages. These to varying degrees produce a blockage in relating to and appreciating others as they are. Therapy, according to Brown, therefore involves a re-engaging of the capacity for intersubjectivity, an issue which is becoming increasingly a focus in psychoanalytic writing and practice. We believe, however, that it is particularly well displayed and promoted in a group-analytic context.

The issue of boundaries, important in balancing a centrifugal connectedness with a centripetal ability to differentiate, is taken up by *Louis Zinkin*. As he puts it, the complex totality of interaction within the boundaries makes the group seem like a living organism. The important therapeutic factor of exchange implies boundaries between people. As he says, while psychoanalysis provides understanding of what goes on inside individuals, it does not concern itself directly with how they are behaving together, or what they understand when in mutual and reciprocal interaction in the context of the whole group. This is very much part of group analysis.

Indeed, *Barbara Elliott* and *Morris Nitsun* emphasise the importance of boundaries in earliest development, in terms of both phantasy and interrelationships. Barbara Elliott's exploration of womb phantasies distinguishes between re-enactment in the group of the relationship between the foetus and the mother, not just the infant and the mother, and uses the concept of Communitas adopted by Usandivaras (1989) to describe regression to an undifferentiated state in the group, in which everyone is connected with everyone. Womb experiences contrast with fusional experiences, and require silence in the group. We think that this is an important observation and stresses the importance of allowing silences and encouraging group members to tolerate them. Elliott proposes that memory traces of womb experiences can be internalised by the neonate of both sexes, and have consequences in the course of gender formation, and also might have consequences in terms of people's capacity to tolerate space or containment. One can think of agoraphobia or claustrophobia, and how differently people respond to being in a group.

Morris Nitsun's exploration of primal scene phantasies, in both their positive and negative aspects, puts the primal scene as a bridge between the intrapsychic world and external reality. The primal scene is of significance not only in terms of the Oedipus complex, but also the important move into the social world implied by the third position and the 'law of the father', renouncing infantile centrality in finding your place in society. It seems likely that it also plays an important part in coming to terms with being in a group, not always being the centre of attention, and accepting the authority of the conductor, and his or her power to admit new members.

Thus, despite the possibility of theoretical objections to the primal scene as being the 'structural centre' of the group, it could be seen as something which group analysts should consider more in developing our understanding of the relationship between the psyche and the social world. Similarly, the objections that one can make from a psychoanalytic point of view about Bowlby's attachment theory seem to be less important in group analysis if one concentrates on the significance of attachment as a source of safety, whether or not it is biologically determined. This includes the safety that a group comes to provide, separation from which plays an important part in the termination phase of therapy. *Mario Marrone* points out that Bowlby saw the object of study in psychoanalysis as the individual's inner world *together with its interaction with the environment or social context*. Indeed, Bowlby urged that we use many methods to study this, including social psychology and observation of families, as well as ethology and observation of babies. Although Bowlby considered that attachment theory is biologically based, Mario Marrone underlines his view that the quality of primary attachment depends on the degree of empathy and responsiveness of the caregiver, and that this affects personality development and social behaviour.

It is in the family that the developing child does or does not learn to be securely attached in a way that allows differentiation and the development of self-confidence. Within the analytic group a person has a second chance to overcome some of the negative experiences that made this difficult in the first place. As *Harold Behr* indicates, Foulkes said little about family therapy, but emphasised the importance of the family interview to get an idea of the context in which individuals' problems emerged. The family therapist who is orientated towards the group-analytic model has a problem. The family group is in some respects the exact opposite of the group-analytic group. As the family is an established group, it needs more vigorous intervention to produce change, and a shorter time scale, according to Behr, who talks of the dialectic between psychoanalysis and systems theory. He emphasises the family therapist's loneliness – his need to come in but largely stay out, and to embody the whole group himself. The family therapist is an 'outsider', but 'adopts the system' using mirroring and resonance, listening to stories and occasionally translating them to other members. This contrasts with group analysis, which encourages the circulation and redistribution of 'outsider' characteristics, in order to discourage scapegoating. In group analysis what is alien to the self is ultimately owned, contained, and shared by the group, so the conductor helps the affirmative and supportive mode of communication to allow more painful feelings and disturbing phantasies to surface. It is clear that Behr's experience of family therapy and standard group analysis enables him to get a clearer picture of both, as if using a dialectic between group analysis and family therapy.

Families, clans, classes, and nations all draw on and contribute to the cultural foundations of personality, as *Jaak Le Roy* describes. He analyses the complex structure of Foulkes' foundation matrix, and points to the importance of its disruption in causing psychopathology. He uses the work of French and South American authors to explore individuation and non-individuation in the primary family, and sees primary and secondary groups as intermediary structures linking the individual to culture. He draws attention to Bleger's idea that an organised and stable frame – whether the setting of analysis, a partnership, or an institution – can act as a repository for the psychotic part of the self, which he calls the 'not-self'. This non-differentiated and undissolved part of the primitive symbiotic links, as he sees them, could perhaps explain the use of foreignness, otherness, and the need for enemies, an endemic problem in social life.

Le Roy distinguishes between the containing and the transitional functions of secondary groups (Rouchy), and in contrast to Bleger's bleak view describes how a stable frame can also provide transitional space for the development of the individual to 'receive, tolerate, elaborate and restitute' (Kaës). This clearly links with James's views on containing and Pines's ideas on coherence, as well as much of what has been developed from a group-analytic perspective, which tends to emphasise the positive potential of groups.

*Patrick De Mare*'s ideas about the median group might seem rather simple, as he concentrates on its ability to develop dialogue in a group insufficiently small to resemble the nuclear family, but large enough to produce anxieties about loss of identity. From experiences in such groups, however, de Mare has been able to develop a theory about frustration creating hatred, which then becomes channelled and neutralised in dialogue. This becomes a model for a form of citizenship that can tolerate differences within a sense of fellowship. The ability to engage in dialogue with people who are seemingly different is an important part of citizenship and toleration.

As *John Schlapobersky* describes it, the group-analytic approach is distinguished from other methods by including monologue and dialogue in which respectively the individual first encounters him or herself in soliloquy, and searches for intimacy through the dialogue of two. However, true discourse, Schlapobersky claims, is by definition group communication, because the complexity of communication between two people is transformed when a third is introduced and a group is formed. This perhaps reflects the momentousness for social development of the recogni- tion of the parental couple and the father, and illustrates what Foulkes called the model of three (Foulkes 1964: 49): each member of a group, including the conductor, can be observed in relation to others from a third, outside position. Each member of a group has the opportunity to see each of the others in relationship and with the group-as-a-whole, as well as with himself or herself.

We believe that group analysis has so far tended to neglect the distinction between boundaries and barriers, though the 9th European Symposium in Group Analysis in Heidelberg in 1993 is on that very topic.[1] In structured situations such as a therapy group, a family or an institution, group analysts will very much keep their eyes on boundary issues. But the need for containment and identity will often produce illusory boundaries that Anzieu (1984) calls 'psychic envelopes'.

A distinguished French psychoanalyst with a special interest in groups, Anzieu's view from outside the narrow 'group-analytic envelope' provides a welcome stimulus to think more about the nature of boundaries and barriers. His ideas and those of his compatriots Kaës and Rouchy have been used extensively by Jaak Le Roy in his chapter to explore the containing function of cultural groups. In a valuable analogy, Anzieu compares the group, ego-like, to a two-sided mirror, sensitive to unconscious individual phantasies internally and to collective representations externally. This accords with the ideas of many group analysts, including Earl Hopper (1982), and is directly illustrated in this volume by Colin James's reference to 'social dreaming'. Anzieu believes that in the absence of a group ego, the group constructs an overarching 'psychical apparatus' to protect itself, cope with its members' wishes and drives, and respond to external stimulation. Would we call this 'the matrix'? Or is it something more?

In searching to understand the complex relationship between psyche and social world, 'psychic envelopes' could be a useful concept. They can be presumed to be based, to varying degrees, on wishful and fearful phantasy, reality that binds mutual identification and concern, and intersubjective recognition of diversity within unity. At times of great upheaval and stress, old envelopes – ethnic, religious and national – can become illusory refuges, not only because of the allure of illusion, but because of their confusion with the real bonds of personal and family ties developed within them, as we see in the rise of nationalisms in Eastern Europe today.

## CONCLUDING COMMENTS

We shall end with some preliminary thoughts about the psyche and the social world, individual and group, mind that is individual, group, and transpersonal:

- The group and the individual are ultimately indivisible and yet mutually interacting; each acts as a container *of* and *for* aspects of the other: individuals personify aspects of the group, and the group or aspects of it (including other individuals) can contain parts of each individual, as in a hologram (Zinkin 1987). This takes us beyond Freud's idea of an instinct-driven Man inevitably pitted against a repressive Society (Freud 1930), and doomed to seek illusory consolations (Freud 1927).

- As a field of coherence and valency, the psyche or 'superordinate self' has a homeostatic function balancing stability and change, and encompasses individuals, groups, social worlds, and ultimately the cosmos. Its study needs to take account of both our biological nature and our search for meaning in relation to others, society, culture and the cosmos.[2] It requires dialogic discourse (see above, Bakhtin 1981).

- Boundaries between individuals are to varying degrees permeable. The more rigid and seemingly impermeable the boundaries – that is, the more they become barriers – the greater the use of projection and projective identification to supplement them, and maintain an exclusive identification based on 'myths' of purity and homogeneity, rather than plurality (Samuels 1989).

- In both small and large groups, including ethnic and national groups, 'otherness' can become threatening. It challenges identity based on restricted identification and too much projection. These produce fear of groups in individuals, and fear between groups that blocks the experience of intersubjectivity. As well as collectively embodying the norm from which each deviate (Foulkes), members of a group also embody the diversity of which they are all afraid (Blackwell, Chap. 3).

The individual develops and always exists within a social matrix. Group analysis seeks to explain and use the figure–ground dialectical relationship between the two. To comprehend it fully, we go beyond learning from the psychoanalytic study of infantile development (and the analyst-analysand dyad), important as these are, to studying families and various social groups, where individuality and identities are formed, deformed, and sometimes broken. We take account of many resonating dialectics – between conscious and unconscious levels of experience, between body and mind, between individual and group, between the personalities of analyst and analysand(s) in both individual and group analysis, between social and family groups, between conflicting cultures, between alternating figures and grounds up to a global level, even to the cosmos. Our contributors have all had something to say about these interacting elements.

Where do we go from here? The writing of this book represents only a small part of the work being done in developing the theory of group analysis. We believe, though, that the exercise of writing the book as a group has helped to establish a consensual view which, despite its areas of healthy controversy, points to the future growth of a distinctive group-analytic theory.

The overall tendency has been the incorporation of allied disciplines so that group analysis takes its place among the generally recognised category of human sciences, as distinct from natural sciences. In this respect, it follows the trend of postmodernist culture, where the search is not for some absolute compendious total system, nor the establishment of a standard text setting out the received wisdom of the experts in the field. This is neither possible nor desirable. Instead, there is great value in partial and provisional insights. We are not seeking the kind of relativism where all ideas are of equal validity, but we do recognise that all observations and all formulations are limited by their subjectivity, and that there is no such thing as the detached and impartial observer. Nor can any 'truth' be uttered which is not, in any way, subject to the contingency of the time and place in which it occurs.

So, looking into the future we can predict that processes of confrontation with the findings of other allied disciplines will continue to have an impact on group-analytic theory. This impact will threaten to disrupt some of our ideas but will gradually be absorbed and integrated, and we hope that group analysis will also influence the thinking in those other fields which constitute the human sciences.

A case could be made for entitling this book, more modestly and less grandiloquently, *Psyches and Social Worlds*. This would have been more in tune with the plurality of society and the human personality, and allow for changes in their relationship. Not surprisingly, such changes are reflected in the book; for example, in the way modern physics enters conceptualisation of the matrix (Powell), in the way attitudes to sexual orientation are not seen as inevitably fixed (Nitsun), and even in a 'feminist' style of writing that does not assume that 'he' implies 'she' any more naturally than the reverse (Blackwell).

We believe that the team of contributors has developed some ideas that Foulkes only implied or adumbrated – such as further exploration and explication of systems theory, the difference between standard group analysis and family therapy, the nature of intersubjectivity in groups, the wider implications of the concept of connectedness in the group matrix, the complexity of the foundation matrix, and some of the linguistic implications of verbal communication and of exchange.

In addition, we believe we have discerned a deficit in group analysis to date of concepts applicable to boundaries within but particularly between groups, and of ideas not only rooted in psychoanalysis to explain primitive processes and inter-group problems and morality.

So this has proved not to be a textbook or a handbook in the usual sense of these words. It is a statement of where we find ourselves in part of the English-speaking world, in 1994. We hope it gives the idea of a new kind of learning, a dialogic learning-together through a group-analytic process, whose principles have been adumbrated by S. H. Foulkes.

## NOTES

1 It will consider political boundaries and barriers in history, boundaries and barriers within and between organisations, between patients and therapists, and trainees and trainers, between men and women, and the meaning of boundaries and barriers in the development of cultural identity and between cultures.

2 In developing a cross-cultural psychology, Roland (1988) has differentiated familial, individualised, and spiritual selves, each complex, in the different cultures of India, Japan, and the Western world.

# Bibliography

Abraham, N. and Torok, M. (1978) *L'Ecorce et le noyau*, Paris, Aubier Flammarion.

Adamson, G., Martinez Bouquet, C. and Sarquis, J. A. (1985) *Creatividad en Arquitectura desde el Psicoanálisis*, Buenos Aires, Paidos.

Agazarian, Y. (1989) 'Group-as-a-whole systems and practice', *Group*, 13: 1301–54.

Agazarian, Y. and Peters, R. (1981) *The Visible and the Invisible Group*, London, Routledge & Kegan Paul.

Ahlin, G. (1985) 'On thinking about the group matrix', *Group Analysis*, 18: 111–19.

—— (1988) 'Reaching for the group matrix', *Group Analysis*, 21: 211–26.

Ainsworth, M. D. S., Blehar, M. C., Waters, E. and Wall, S. (1978) *Patterns of Attachment*, Hillsdale, NJ, Lawrence Erlbaum Associates.

Alexander, F. and French, T. M. (1946) *Psychoanalytic Psychotherapy*, New York, Ronald Press.

Alonso, A. and Rutan, J. S. (1979) 'Women in group therapy', *International Journal of Group Psychotherapy*, 29: 481–91.

Anzieu, D. (1984) *The Group and the Unconscious*, London, Routledge & Kegan Paul.

—— (1989) *The Skin Ego*, London, Karnac.

—— (1990) *Psychic Envelopes*, London, Karnac.

Aquinas, Thomas (c.1260) *Summa Contra Gentiles*, trans. A. C. Pegis, Image Books (1955).

Armstrong, D. G. (1991a) *The 'Institution-in-the-mind': reflections on the relation of psycho-analysis to work with institutions*, London, The Gubb Institute.

—— (1991b) *Thoughts Bound and Thoughts Free: reflections on mental processes in groups*, London, The Gubb Institute.

—— (1992) 'Names, thoughts and lies: the relevance of Bion's later thinking to understanding group relations', *Free Associations*, 3(26)

Ashbach, C. and Schermer, V. L. (1987) *Object Relations, the Self, and the Group*, London, Routledge & Kegan Paul.

Atwood, G. E. and Stolorow, R. D. (1984) *Structures of Subjectivity*, Hillsdale, NJ, Analytic Press.

Bakhtin, M. (1981) *The Dialogic Imagination: Four Essays by M. M. Bakhtin*, trans. C. Emerson and M. Holquist, Austin, Texas University Press.

Balint, M. (1952) *Primary Love and Psychoanalytic Technique*, London, Tavistock.

— — (1968) *The Basic Fault: Therapeutic Aspects of Regression*, London, Tavistock.

Barrow, J. D. (1990) *Theories of Everything*, Oxford, Clarendon Press.

Bateson, G. (1969) 'Double bind', in *Steps to an Ecology of Mind*, New York, Ballantyne Books (1972).

— — (1972) *Steps to an Ecology of Mind*, New York, Ballantyne Books.

— — (1979) *Mind and Nature: A Necessary Unity*, London, Wildwood House.

Battegay, R. (1986) 'People in groups: dynamic and therapeutic aspects', *Group*, 10: 131-48.

Behr, H. L. (1979) 'Cohesiveness in families and therapy groups', *Group Analysis*, 12: 9–12.

— — (1984) 'A group analytic perspective on family therapy', in T. E. Lear (ed.) *Spheres of Groups Analysis*, London, Group Analytic Society Publications, pp. 50–61.

— — (1988) 'A group analytic contribution to family therapy', *Journal of Family Therapy*, 10: 307–21.

Behr, H. L. and Hearst, L. E. (1982) 'Group analysis: a group psychotherapeutic model developed by S. H. Foulkes', *Midland Journal of Psychotherapy*, 1: 1–13.

Belsky, J. and Nezworkski, T. (1988) *Clinical Applications of Attachment*, Hillsdale, NJ, Lawrence Erlbaum Associates.

Benvenuto, B. and Kennedy, R. (1986) *The Works of Jacques Lacan*, London, Free Association Books.

Bick, E. (1968) 'The experience of the skin in early object relations', *International Journal of Psychoanalysis*, 49: 484–6.

Bion, W. R. (1952) 'Group dynamics: a re-view', *International Journal of Psychoanalysis*, 33: 235-47.

— — (1961) *Experiences in Groups*, London, Tavistock Publications.

— — (1962a) 'The psycho-analytic study of thinking: a theory of thinking', *International Journal of Psycho-Analysis*, 43: 306–10.

— — (1962b) *Learning from Experience*, London, Heinemann.

— — (1963) *Elements of Psycho-Analysis*, London, Heinemann.

— — (1970) *Attention and Interpretation*, London, Tavistock Publications.

— — (1979) *A Memoir of the Future Book, 3: The Dawn of Oblivion*, Perthshire, Clunie Press.

Blackwell, R. D. (1984) 'The negotiation of communicational rules in a group analytic group', *British Journal of Psychotherapy*, 1: 144–51.

Blake, R. (1980) 'The group matrix', *Group Analysis*, 13: 177–83.

Bleger, J. (1966) 'Psychoanalysis of the psychoanalytic frame', *International Journal of Psychoanalysis*, 48: 511–19.

— — (1987) 'Le groupe comme institution et le groupe dans les institutions', in *L'Institution et les institutions*, R. Kaës *et al.* Paris, Dunod.

Bohm, D. (1980) *Wholeness and the Implicate Order*, London, Ark Paperbacks (1983), Routledge.

Bohm, D. and Edwards, M. (1989) *Changing Consciousness*, San Francisco, Harper Ross.

Bollas, C. (1987) *The Shadow of the Object: Psychoanalysis of the Unthought Known*, London, Free Association Books.

Bourdieu, P. (1977) *Outline of a Theory of Practice*, trans. R. Nice, Cambridge, Cambridge University Press, (Esquisse d'une théorie de la pratique (1972) Switzerland, Librairie Droz).

Bourshay-Lee, R. (1979) *Kung San*, Cambridge, Cambridge University Press.

Bowlby, J. (1940) 'The influence of early environment in the development of neurosis and neurotic character', *International Journal of Psycho-Analysis*, 21: 154–78.

—— (1944) 'Forty-four juvenile thieves: their characters and home life', *International Journal of Psycho-Analysis*, 25: 19–52 and 107–27.

—— (1951) *Maternal Care and Mental Health*, Geneva, World Health Organisation.

—— (1958) 'The nature of the child's tie to his mother', *International Journal of Psycho-Analysis*, 39: 350–73.

—— (1960) 'Grief and mourning in infancy and early childhood', *The Psychoanalytic Study of the Child*, 15: 9–52.

—— (1961) 'Processes of Mourning', *International Journal of Psycho-Analysis*, 42: 317–40.

—— (1969) *Attachment* (Vol. 1, *Attachment and Loss*), London, The Hogarth Press.

—— (1973) *Attachment* (Vol. II, *Anxiety and Anger*), London, The Hogarth Press.

—— (1977) 'The making and breaking of affectional bonds', *British Journal of Psychiatry*, 130: 201–10 and 421–31.

—— (1979) *The Making and Breaking of Affectional Bonds*, London, Tavistock Publications.

—— (1980) *Attachment* (Vol. III, *Loss: Sadness and Depression*), London, The Hogarth Press.

—— (1982) 'Attachment and loss: retrospect and prospect', *American Journal of Orthopsychiatry*, 52(4): 654–78.

—— (1984) 'Comments on Mario Marrone's paper "Aspects of transference in group analysis" ', *Group Analysis*, 17: 190–3.

—— (1988) *A Secure Base*, London, Routledge.

—— (1990) *Charles Darwin: A Biography*, London, Hutchinson.

Boyd, R. D. (1991) *Personal Transformations in Small Groups: A Jungian Perspective*, London, Routledge.

Brennan, B. A. (1987) *Hands of Light*, New York, Bantam Books.

Bretherton I. and Waters, E. (1985) *Growing Points in Attachment Theory and Research*, Chicago, Monographs of the Society for Research in Child Development, Serial No 209, Vol. 50, Nos 1–2.

Bridger, H. (1985) 'Northfield revisited', chap. 3 in M. Pines (ed.) *Bion and Group Psychotherapy*, London, Routledge & Kegan Paul.

Britton, R. (1989) 'The missing link: parental sexuality in the Oedipus complex', in J. Steiner (ed.) *The Oedipus Complex Today*, London, Karnac.

Brook, P. (1990) *The Empty Space*, London, Penguin.

Brown, D. G. (1977) 'Drowsiness in the countertransference', *International Review of Psycho-Analysis*, 4: 481–92.

—— (1985a) 'Bion and Foulkes: basic assumptions and beyond', in M. Pines

(ed.) *Bion and Group Psychotherapy*, London, Routledge & Kegan Paul.
—— (1985b) 'The psychosoma and the group', *Group Analysis*, 18: 93–101.
—— (1987a) 'Change in the group-analytic setting', *Psychoanalytic Psychotherapy*, 3: 53–60.
—— (1987) Context, content and process: interrelationships between small and large groups in a transcultural workshop', *Group Analysis*, 20: 237–48.
—— (1989) 'A contribution to the understanding of psychosomatic processes in groups', *British Journal of Psychotherapy*, 6: 5–9.
—— (1992a) 'Transcultural group analysis, 1: Different views of Maastricht and Heidelberg', *Group Analysis*, 25: 87–96.
—— (1992b) 'Transcultural group analysis, 2: Use and abuse of cultural differences', *Group Analysis*, 25: 97–105.
Brown, D. G. and Pedder, J. (1991) *Introduction to Psychotherapy*, 2nd edn., London, Routledge.
Brown, G. W. and Harris, T. (1978) *Social Origins of Depression: A Study of Psychiatric Disorders in Women*, London, Tavistock Publications.
Buber, M. (1937) *I and Thou*, trans. R. Gregor Smith, Edinburgh, T. & T. Clarke.
Capra, F. (1982) *The Turning Point: Science, Society and the Rising Culture*, London, Flamingo.
Chasseguet-Smirgel, J. (1984) *Sexuality and Mind*, New York, New York Universities Press.
Clarke, K. and Holquist, M. (1984) *Mikhail Bakhtin*, Cambridge MA and London, Harvard University Press.
Cohn, H. W. (1991) 'Matrix and intersubjectivity: phenomenological aspects of group analysis', Paper read to European Symposium of the Group Analytic Society (London) at Oxford, 1990; published in German in *Gruppenanalyse* (Heidelberg), 2: 41–9 (1991).
—— (1992) Personal communication.
Collingwood, R. G. (1961) *The Idea of History*, Oxford, Oxford University Press (Clarendon Press, 1946).
Cooklin, A. (1979) 'Psychoanalytic framework for a systemic approach', *Journal of Family Therapy*, 1: 153–65.
Cooley, C. (1902) *Human Nature and the Social Order*, New York, Scribner. (Revised edn quoted in American Handbook of Psychiatry, 1959, New York, Basic Books, p.1742.)
Cox, M. and Theilgaard, A. (1987) *Mutative Metaphors in Psychotherapy: The Aeolian Mode*, London, Tavistock Publications.
Craik, K. (1943) *The Nature of Explanation*, Cambridge, Cambridge University Press.
Dare, C. (1979) 'Psychoanalysis and systems in family therapy', *Journal of Family Therapy*, 1: 137–52.
Darwin, C. (1859) *The Origin of the Species*, 1st edn, London, Murray.
Dell, P. F. (1980) 'Researching the family theories of schizophrenia: an exercise in epistemological confusion', *Family Process*, 19: 321–35.
De Mare, P. B. (1985) 'Major Bion', chap. 4 in M. Pines (ed.) *Bion and Group Psychotherapy*, London, Routledge & Kegan Paul.
De Mare, P., Piper, R. and Thompson, S. (1991) *Koinonia: From Hate through Dialogue to Culture in the Large Group*, London, Karnac Books.

Dervin, D. (1990) *Creativity and Culture*, London and Toronto, Associated Universities Press.

Devisch, R. (1990) 'The therapist and the source of healing among the Yaka of Zaïre', *Culture, Medicine and Psychiatry*, 14: 213–36.

——(1991) 'Symbol and symptom among the Yaka of Zaïre', in *Body and Space: Symbolic Models of Unity and Division in African Cosmology and Experience*, Stockholm, Almqvist & Wiksell, pp. 283–302.

Dick, B. (1981) 'The spin of the proton', *Group Analysis*, 14(2): 128–9.

Dossey, L. (1982) *Space, Time and Medicine*, Shambhala, Boulder and London.

Elias, N. (1938) *The Civilising Process*, first British edn 1978, Oxford, Basil Blackwell.

Elliott, B. (1986) 'Gender identity in group-analytic psychotherapy', *Group Analysis*, 19: 195–206.

Engel, G. L. (1962) *Psychological Development in Health and Disease*, Philadelphia, Saunders.

Ezriel, H. (1973) 'Psychoanalytic group therapy' in L. R. Wolberg and E. Schwartz (eds) *Group Therapy 1973, An Overview*, New York, International Medical Books.

Fairbairn, W. R. D. (1952) *Psychoanalytic Studies of the Personality*, London: Tavistock/Routledge.

Ferenczi, S. (1913) 'Stages in development of the sense of reality', in *First Contributions to Psychoanalysis*, London, Hogarth Press, chap. 8.

Fiumara, R. (1976) 'Therapeutic group analysis and analytical psychology', *Journal of Analytical Psychology*, 21:1.

——(1983) 'Analytical psychology and group-analytic psychotherapy: convergences', in M. Pines (ed.) *The Evolution of Group Analysis*, London, Routledge & Kegan Paul.

——(1991a) 'Brain, mind and "matrix" from an evolutionary viewpoint', *Group Analysis*, 24: 409–418.

——(1991b) 'Discussion paper on matrix, mind and matter, by Andrew Powell', *Group Analysis*, 24: 319–22.

Foucault, M. (1980) *Power/Knowledge: Selected Interviews and Other Writings 1972–1977*, Colin Gordon (ed.), Brighton, Harvester Press.

Foulkes, S. H. (1943) 'The second discussion of scientific controversies', in P. King and R. Steiner (eds) *The Freud-Klein Controversies 1941–45*, (1991) London, The Institute of Psycho-Analysis and Routledge.

——(1948) *Introduction to Group-analytic Psychotherapy*, London, Maresfield Reprints.

——(1957) 'Psychoanalytic concepts and object relations theory: comments on a paper by Fairbairn', *British Journal of the Philosophy of Science*, 7: 324 –9; reprinted in *Selected Papers: Psychoanalysis and Group Analysis*, London, Karnac Books (1990).

——(1964) *Therapeutic Group Analysis*, London, Allen & Unwin; reprinted 1984, London, Karnac.

——(1968) 'Group dynamic processes and group analysis', *The Journal of Group Psychoanalysis and Process*, 1: 62–83. Reprinted in Foulkes (1990).

——(1972) 'Oedipus conflict and regression', in E. Foulkes (ed.) *Selected Papers of S. H. Foulkes* (1990), London, Karnac.

——(1973) 'The group as matrix of the individual's mental life', in L. R.

Wolberg and E. K. Schwartz (eds) *Group Therapy 1973, An Overview*, New York, Intercontinental Medical Book Corp. Reprinted in Foulkes (1990).

—— (1975a) *Group-Analytic Psychotherapy – Methods and Principles*, London, Interface, Gordon & Breach; reprinted Karnac, 1986.

—— (1975b) from report of International Colloquium on Group-Analytic Psychotherapy, 27–28 July, *Group Analysis*, 3: 183.

—— (1990) *Selected Papers: Psychoanalysis and Group Analysis*, (ed. Elizabeth Foulkes) London, Karnac Books.

—— (1990) Book review of Norbert Elias, *The Civilising Process* (1938), chap. 6 in *Selected Papers*, London, Karnac Books.

—— (1990) 'Biology in the light of the work of Kurt Goldstein', chap. 4 in *Selected Papers*, London: Karnac Books.

—— (1990) 'The group as matrix of the individu::!'s mental life', chap. 22 in *Selected Papers*, London, Karnac Books.

Foulkes, S. H. and Anthony, E. J. (1957) *Group Psychotherapy: The Psycho-analytic Approach*, Harmondsworth, Penguin; 2nd edn, 1965. Reprinted 1984 London, Karnac.

Foulkes, S. H. and Prince, G. S. (eds) (1969) *Psychiatry in a Changing Society*, London, Tavistock Publications.

Freud, A. (1936) The Ego and the Mechanisms of Defence, London, Hogarth Press.

—— (1965) *Normality and Pathology in Childhood*, New York, International Universities Press.

Freud, S. (1895) 'Project for a scientific psychology', *Standard Edition of the Complete Psychological Works of Sigmund Freud, SE*1, London, Hogarth Press.

—— (1900) *The Interpretation of Dreams, SE*4–5, London, Hogarth Press.

—— (1905) 'Three essays on sexuality', *SE*7, London, Hogarth Press.

—— (1908) 'On the sexual theories of children', *SE*7, London, Hogarth Press.

—— (1911–15) 'Papers on technique', *SE*12, London, Hogarth Press.

—— (1912) 'The dynamics of transference', *SE*12, London, Hogarth Press.

—— (1913) 'On beginning the treatment: further recommendations on the technique of psychoanalysis', *SE*12, London, Hogarth Press.

—— (1915a) 'Papers on metapsychology', *SE*14, London, Hogarth Press.

—— (1915b) *Mourning and Melancholia, SE*14, London, Hogarth Press.

—— (1921) *Group Psychology and the Analysis of the Ego, SE*18, London, Hogarth Press.

—— (1923) *The Ego and the Id, SE*19, London, Hogarth Press.

—— (1927) *The Future of an Illusion, SE*21, London, Hogarth Press.

—— (1930) *Civilization and its Discontents, SE*21, London, Hogarth Press.

Friere, P. (1972) *Pedagogy of the Oppressed*, Harmondsworth, Penguin Books; reprinted 1993.

Ganzarain, R. (1977) 'General systems theory and object-relations theories: their usefulness in group psychotherapy', *International Journal of Group Psychotherapy*, 27: 441–58.

Garland, C. (1982) 'Group analysis: taking the non-problem seriously', *Group Analysis*, 15: 4–14.

Gay, P. (1989) *Freud: A Life for our Time*, London, Papermac.

George, C., Kaplan, N. and Main, M. (1985) 'The adult attachment interview', Manuscript from the authors given by Dr Bowlby.

Giddens, A. (1989) *Sociology*, Cambridge, Polity Press in association with Blackwell, Oxford.

Gillieron, E. (1990) 'Pourquoi le groupe?', *Revue de Psychothérapie Psychanalytique de Groupe*, 14: 9–20.

Glenn, L. (1987) 'Attachment theory and group analysis: the group matrix as a secure base', *Group Analysis*, 20: 109–17.

Goldner, V. (1985) 'Feminism and family therapy', *Family Process*, 24(1): 31–48.

Goldstein, K. (1939) *The Organism*, New York, American Books.

Gordon, R. (1991) 'Intersubjectivity and the efficacy of group psychotherapy', *Group Analysis*, 24: 41–51.

Greenberg, J. R. and Mitchell, S. A. (1985) *Object Relations in Psychoanalytic Theory*, Cambridge, MA, Harvard University Press.

Grotstein, J. S. (1981) *Splitting and Projective Identification*, New York, Jason Aronson.

Haley, J. (1976) *Problem-Solving Therapy*, San Francisco, Jossey-Bass.

Hall, E. T. (1971) *La Dimension cachée*, Paris, Seuil.

Hank, T. N. (1988) *The Sutra on the Full Awareness of Breathing*, Berkeley, CA, Parallex Press.

Hanson, V. and Stewart, R. (eds) (1981) *Karma: The Universal Law of Harmony*, Wheaton, IL, Quest Books, The Theosophical Publishing House.

Hartmann, H. (1958) 'Comments on the psychoanalytic theory of the ego', *Psychoanalytic Study of the Child*, 5: 74–96.

Hawking, S. (1988) *A Brief History of Time*, London, Bantam Press.

Hearst, L. E. (1981) 'The emergence of the mother in the group', *Group Analysis*, 14(1): 25–32.

Hinshelwood, R. D. (1989) 'Communication flow in the matrix', *Group Analysis* 22: 261–9.

Hobson, R. F. (1964) 'Group dynamics and analytical psychology', *Journal of Analytical Psychology*, 9: 1.

Hoffman, L. (1971) 'Deviation amplifying process in natural groups', in J. Haley (ed.) *Changing Families: A Family Therapy Reader*, New York, Grune & Stratton.

—— (1981) *Foundations of Family Therapy*, New York, Basic Books.

—— (1985) 'Beyond power and control: toward a "second" order family systems therapy', *Family System Medicine*, 3: 381–96.

—— (1990) 'Constructing realities: an art of lenses', *Family Process*, 29: 1–12.

Home, H. J. (1983) 'The effect of numbers on the basic transference pattern in group analysis', chap. 9 in Malcolm Pines (ed.) *The Evolution of Group Analysis*, London, Routledge & Kegan Paul.

Hopper, E. (1982) 'Group analysis: the problem of context', *Group Analysis*, 15: 136–57.

—— (1989) 'Aggregation and massification: a fourth basic assumption', Paper presented at the Xth International Association of Group Psychotherapy Conference, Amsterdam.

—— (1991) Personal communication, Group-Analytic Society Scientific Meeting Discussion.

Hughes, A. (ed.) (1991) *The Inner World and Joan Riviere, Collected Papers 1920–1958*, London, Karnac Books.

Hutten, E. H. (1983) 'Meaning and information in the group process', in M. Pines (ed.) *The Evolution of Group Analysis*, London, Routledge & Kegan Paul.

Jackson, D. D. (1957) 'The question of family homeostasis', *Psychiatric Quarterly*, 31: 79–90.

—— (1965) 'Family rules: marital quid pro quo', *Archives of General Psychiatry*, 12: 589–94.

Jacobson, E. (1964) *The Self and the Object World*, New York, International Universities Press.

James, D. C. (1982) 'Transitional phenomena and the matrix in group psychotherapy', in M. Pines and L. Raphaelsen (eds) *The Individual and the Group*, Vol. 1, New York, Plenum Press.

—— (1981) 'W. R. Bion's contribution to the field of group therapy – an Appreciation', in L. R. Wolberg and M. L. Aronson (eds.) *Group and Family Therapy*, New York, Brunner/Mazel.

—— (1984) 'Bion's "containing" and Winnicott's "holding" in the context of the group matrix', *International Journal of Group Psychotherapy*, 34: 201–13.

James, W. (1900) *The Varieties of Religious Experience*, republished London, Fontana (1960).

Jaques, E. (1955) 'Social systems as a defence against persecutory and depressive anxiety', in M. Klein, P. Heimann and R. E. Morey-Kyrle (eds) *New Directions in Psychoanalysis*, London, Tavistock Publications; Maresfield (1986).

Jung, C. G. (1913) *Symbols of Transformation*, 2nd edn 1970, London, Routledge & Kegan Paul.

—— (1934) 'The archetypes and the collective unconscious', in *Collected Works*, Vol. 9, Part 1, London, Routledge & Kegan Paul.

—— (1942) 'Paracelsus as a spiritual phenomenon', in *Alchemical Studies*, *Collected Works*, Vol. 13, London, Routledge & Kegan Paul (1968).

—— (1946) 'The psychology of the transference', in *The Practice of Psychotherapy, Collected Works*, Vol. 16, London, Routledge & Kegan Paul, (1954).

—— (1950) 'Concerning mandala symbolism', in *The Archetypes and the Collective Unconscious, Collected Works*, Vol. 9, Part 1, London, Routledge & Kegan Paul (1959); 2nd edn, 1968.

—— (1955) *Collected Works*, Vol. 14, para. 125.

—— (1959) *Collected Works*, Vol. 9, para. 153.

—— (1963) 'Confrontation with the unconscious', *Memories, Dreams, Reflections*, London, Routledge & Kegan Paul, 1970.

Kaës, R. (1979) 'Introduction à l'analyse transitionelle', in *Crise, Rupture et Dépassement*, R. Kaës et al., Paris, Dunod.

—— (1987a) 'Realité psychique et souffrances dans les institutions', in *L'Institution et les Institutions*, R. Kaës et al., Paris, Dunod.

—— (1987b) 'La troisième différence', *Revue de Psychothérapie Psychanalytique de Groupe*, 9–10: 5–30.

Keeney, B. P. and Sprenkle, D. H. (1982) 'Ecosystemic epistemology: critical implications for the aesthetics and pragmatics of family therapy', *Family Process*, 21: 1–19.

Kernberg, O. F. (1976) *Object Relations Theory and Clinical Psychoanalysis*,

New York, Jason Aronson.
— — (1980) *Internal World and External Reality*, New York, Jason Aronson.
Khaleelee, O. and Miller, E. (1985) 'Beyond the small group', in M. Pines (ed.) *Bion and Group Psychotherapy*, London, Routledge & Kegan Paul.
Klauber, J. (1987) *Illusion and Spontaneity in Psychoanalysis*, London, Free Association Books.
Klein, G. (1976) *Psychoanalytic Theory*, New York, International Universities Press.
Klein, M. (1926) 'The psychological principles of early analysis', in *The Writings of Melanie Klein*, Vol. I, *Love, Guilt and Reparation and Other Works 1921–1945*, London, Hogarth Press (1975).
— — (1928) 'Early stages of the Oedipus complex', in *Love, Guilt and Reparation and Other Works 1921–1945*, London, Hogarth Press (1975).
— — (1929) 'Infantile anxiety situations reflected in a work of art in the creative impulse', in *The Writings of Melanie Klein*, Vol. I, *Love, Guilt and Reparation and Other Works 1921–1945*, London, Hogarth Press (1975).
— — (1946) 'Notes on some schizoid mechanisms', *The Writings of Melanie Klein*, Vol. 3, London, Hogarth Press.
— — (1952) 'The emotional life of the infant', in *Envy and Gratitude and Other Works 1946–1963*, London, Hogarth Press.
Kohon, G. (ed.) (1986) *The British School of Psychoanalysis: The Independent Tradition*, London, Free Association Books.
Kohut, H. (1971) *The Analysis of the Self*, New York, International Universities Press.
Kohut, H. and Wolf E. S. (1978) 'The disorders of the self and their treatment: an outline', *International Journal of Psycho-Analysis*, 59: 413–25.
Korzybski, A. (1933) *General Semantics*, Lancaster, PA, Science Press.
Kosseff, J. W. (1991) 'Infant and mother and the mother-group', in S. Tuttman (ed.) *Psychoanalytic Group Theory and Therapy*, Madison, CT, International Universities Press, pp. 133–56.
Kreeger, L. C. (ed.) (1975) *The Large Group: Dynamics and Therapy*, London, Constable.
— — (1992) 'Envy pre-emption in small and large groups', 16th S. H. Foulkes Lecture, *Group Analysis*, 25: 391–412.
Kris, A. O. (1990) 'The analyst's stance and the method of free association: Sigmund Freud Birthday Lecture of the Anna Freud Centre 1989', *Psychoanalytic Study of the Child*, 45: 25–41.
Kuhn, T. S. (1962) *The Structure of Scientific Revolutions*, Chicago and London, University of Chicago Press.
Lacan, J. (1966) *Ecrits: A Selection*, London, Tavistock.
Lakoff, G. and Johnson, M. (1980) *Metaphors We Live By*, Chicago, University of Chicago Press.
Laplanche, J. and Pontalis, J. B. (1973) *The Language of Psycho-Analysis*, London, Hogarth Press.
Lawrence, W. G. (1985) 'Beyond the frames', in M. Pines (ed.), *Bion and Group Psychotherapy*, London, Routledge & Kegan Paul.
— — (1991) 'Won from the void and formless infinite: experiences of social dreaming', *Free Associations*, 2 (No 22): 259–94.

Leal, R. (1982) 'Resistances and the group analytic process', *Group Analysis*, 15: 97–110.

Le Roy, J. (1987a) 'The cultural structuring of the personality and cultural relationships', *Group Analysis*, 20: 147–53.

—— (1987b) 'Processus dans un seminaire transculturel d'analyse de groupe', *Revue de Psychothérapie Psychanalytique de Groupe*, 9–10: 9–14.

—— (1991) 'Espace transitionnel et processus d'individuation', *Connexions*, 58: 9–20.

Lévi-Strauss, C. (1962) *The Savage Mind*, Paris, Librairie Plon; translated 1966, London, George Weidenfeld & Nicolson.

—— (1968) *Structural Anthropology*, Harmondsworth, Penguin.

Lewis, A. (1990a) 'Free association and changing models of mind', *Journal of the American Academy of Psychoanalysis*, 18: 439–59.

—— (1990b) 'One person and two person psychologies and the method of psychoanalysis', *Journal of Psychoanalytic Psychology*, 7: 475–85.

Lintott, B. (1983) 'Mind and matrix in the writing of S.H. Foulkes', *Group Analysis*, 16: 242–7.

Loewald, H. W. (1980) *Papers on Psycho-Analysis*, New Haven, CT, International Universities Press.

McDougall, J. (1974) 'The psychosoma and the psychoanalytic process', *International Review of Psycho-Analysis*, 1: 437–59.

—— (1980) *Plea for a Measure of Abnormality*, New York, International Universities Press.

Mahler, M. S., Pine, F. and Bergman, A. (1975) *The Psychological Birth of the Human Infant: Symbiosis and Individuation*, London, Hutchinson.

Main, T. F. (1946) 'The hospital as a therapeutic institution', *Bulletin of the Menninger Clinic*, 10: 66–70.

—— (1977) 'The concept of the therapeutic community: variations and vicissitudes' (First S. H. Foulkes Annual Lecture), *Group Analysis*, 10: Supplement 1–16.

Maizels, N. (1985) 'Self envy, the womb and the nature of goodness – a reappraisal of the death instinct', *International Journal of Psycho-Analysis*, 66: 185–92.

Malan, D. H., Balfour, F. H. G., Hood, V. G. and Shooter, A. M. N. (1976) 'Group psychotherapy: a long-term follow-up study', *Archives of General Psychiatry*, 33: 1033–4.

Maratos, J. (1986) 'Bowlby and Kohut: where science and humanism meet', *Group Analysis*, 19: 303–9.

Marrone, M. (1984) 'Aspects of transference in group analysis', *Group Analysis*, 17: 179–90.

—— (1987) 'La teoria del attachment en el contexto del pensamiento psicoanalitico', in J. A. Ozamiz (ed.) *Psico-sociologia de la Salud Mental*, San Sebastian, Tartalo.

Matte-Blanco, I. (1975) *The Unconscious as Infinite Sets*, London, Duckworth.

Maturana, H. (1988) 'Reality: the search for objectivity or the quest for a compelling argument', *Irish Journal of Psychology*, 9: 25–82.

Mauss, M. (1950) *Essai sur le Don*, Paris, Presses Universitaires de France, trans. W. D. Halls, London, Routledge (1990).

Meltzer, D. (1967) 'The sorting of zonal confusions in *The Psycho-Analytical*

*Process'*, Perthshire, Clunie Press.
— — (1973) *Sexual States of Mind*, Perthshire, Clunie Press.
— — (1978) *The Kleinian Development: III, The Clinical Significance of the Work of Bion*, Perthshire, Clunie Press.
Mennell, S. (1989) *Norbert Elias: Civilisation and the Human Self-image*, Oxford, Blackwell.
Menzies-Lyth, I. (1981) 'Bion's contribution to thinking about groups', in J. S. Grotstein (ed.) *Do I Dare Disturb the Universe?* Beverly Hills, CA, Caesura Press.
Merleau-Ponty, M. (1964) *The Primacy of Perception, and Other Essays*, Evanston, IL, Northwestern University Press.
— — (1976) *The Phenomenology of Perception*, London, Routledge & Kegan Paul.
Milner, M. (1987) The Suppressed Madness of Sane Men, London, Tavistock Publications, pp. 279–97.
Minuchin, S. (1974) *Families and Family Therapy*, London, Tavistock Publications.
Minuchin, S. and Fishman, C. (1981) *Family Therapy Techniques*, Cambridge, MA, Harvard University Press.
Moffet, J. (1968) *Teaching the Universe of Discourse*, Boston, Houghton Mifflin
Moreno, J. (1953) *Who Shall Survive?* New York, Beacon House.
Muroff, M. (1982) 'The family as the matrix of the individual: group process in child development', in M. Pines and L. Raphaelsen (eds) *The Individual and the Group*, Vol. 1, New York, Plenum Press.
Murray-Parkes, C. and Stevenson-Hinde, J. (1982) *The Place of Attachment in Human Behaviour*, London, Tavistock Publications.
Nitsun, M. (1989) 'Early development: linking the individual and the group', *Group Analysis*, 22: 249–60.
— — (1991) 'The anti-group: destructive forces in the group and their therapeutic potential', *Group Analysis*, 24: 7–20.
— — (1992) Personal communication.
Ogden, T. H. (1989) *The Primitive Edge of Experience*, Northvale, NJ, and London, Jason Aronson.
— — (1990) *The Matrix of the Mind*, Northvale, NJ, and London, Jason Aronson.
— — (1992a) 'The dialectically constituted/decentred subject of psycho-analysis, I, The Freudian subject', *International Journal of Psycho-Analysis*, 73: 517–26.
— — (1992b) 'The dialectically constituted/decentred subject of psycho-analysis, II, The contributions of Klein and Winnicott', *International Journal of Psycho-Analysis*, 73: 613–26.
Ortiz Baron, M. J. (1990) 'Apego, miedo, exploración y afiliación: interacción entre sistemas de conducta en la primera infancia', in J. R. Sanchez Martin (ed.) *Etologia Psicologia* Servicio Editorial, Universidad del Pais Vasco.
Padel, J. (1985) 'Ego in current thinking', *International Review of Psycho-Analysis*, 12: 273–83.
Palazzoli, M. S., Cecchin, G., Pratao, G. and Boscolo, L. (1978) *Paradox and Counter-Paradox*, New York, Jason Aronson.

Paparo, F. (1984) 'Self psychology and the group process', *Group Analysis*, 17: 108–17.

Peterfreund, E. (1983) *The Process of Psychoanalytic Therapy*, Hillsdale, NJ, The Analytic Press.

Piaget, J. (1954) *The Construction of Reality in the Child*, New York, Basic Books.

Pichon Riviere, E. (1977) *Del Psicoanálisis a la Psicología Social*, Buenos Aires, Nueva Vision.

Pines, M. (1978) 'The contributions of S. H. Foulkes to group analytic psychotherapy', in L. Wolberg, M. Aronson and A. Wolberg (eds) *Group Therapy 1978 – An Overview*, New York, Stratton Intercontinental Medical Book Corporation.

—— (1982) 'Reflections on mirroring', *Group Analysis*, 15: supp. 1–32.

—— (ed.) (1983) *The Evolution of Group Analysis*, London, Routledge & Kegan Paul.

—— (ed.) (1985a) *Bion and Group Psychotherapy*, London, Routledge & Kegan Paul.

—— (1985b) 'Psychic development and the group analytic situation', *Group*, 9: 24–37.

—— (1986) 'Coherency and its disruption in the development of the self', *British Journal of Psychotherapy*, 2: 180–5.

—— (1987) 'Introduction', in M. Cox and A. Theilgaard, *Mutative Metaphors in Psychotherapy: The Aeolian Mode*, London, Tavistock Publications.

—— (1990) 'Group analysis and the corrective emotional experience: is it relevant?', *Psychoanalytic Inquiry*, 10: 389–408.

—— (1992, unpublished) 'Silence, interpretation and communication in the group analytic process'.

Pines, M. and Marrone, M. (1990) 'Group analysis', in I. L. Kutash and A. Wolf (eds) *The Group Psychotherapist's Handbook*, New York, Columbia University Press.

Pines, M. and Raphaelson, L. (1982) *The Individual and the Group*, Vol. 1, New York: Plenum Press.

Piontelli, A. (1987) 'Infant observations before birth', *International Journal of Psycho-Analysis*, 68: 453–63.

Powell, A. (1982) 'Metaphor in group analysis', *Group Analysis*, 15: 127–35.

—— (1989) 'The nature of the group matrix', *Group Analysis*, 22: 271–81.

—— (1990) 'Words and music: an unsung therapeutic alliance', *Group Analysis*, 23: 225–35.

—— (1991a) 'Matrix, mind and matter: from the internal to the eternal', *Group Analysis*, 24: 299–322.

—— (1991b) 'The embodied matrix: discussion on paper by Romano Fiumara', *Group Analysis*, 24: 419–23.

—— (1992) 'The concept of matrix – a metaphysical enquiry', *Group Analysis*, 25: 107–13.

Prigogine, I. and Stengers, I. (1984) *Order out of Chaos*, William Heinemann Fontana Paperbacks (1985).

Prodgers, A. (1990) 'The dual nature of the group as mother: the uroboric container', *Group Analysis*, 23: 17–23.

Puget, J. (1989) 'Groupe analytique et formation', *Revue de Psychothérapie*

*Psychanalytique de Groupe*, 13: 137–54.
Rapaport, D. and Gill, M. M. (1959) 'The points of view and assumptions of metapsychology', *International Journal of Psycho-Analysis*, 40: 153–62.
Rice, A. K. (1965) *Learning for Leadership*, London: Tavistock Publications.
Rickman, J. (1950) 'The factor of number in individual and group-dynamics', *John Rickman's Selected Contributions to Psycho-Analysis*, London: Hogarth Press (1957).
Riviere, J. (1937) 'Hate, greed and aggression', in M. Klein and J. Riviere, *Love, Hate and Reparation*, London, Hogarth Press.
Roberts, J. P. (1982) 'Foulkes' concept of the matrix', *Group Analysis*, 15: 111–26.
—— (1984) 'Resonance in art groups', *Group Analysis*, 17: 211–19.
Roland, A. (1988) *In Search of Self in India and Japan: Toward a Cross-Cultural Psychology*, Princeton, NJ, Princeton University Press.
Rouchy, J. C. (1982) 'Archaic processes and transference in group analysis', *Group Analysis*, 15(3): 235.
—— (1983) 'L'Elaboration des objets incorporés en groupe analyse', *Bulletin de Psychologie*, 363: 71–7.
—— (1987) 'Identité culturelle et groupes d'appartenance', *Revue de Psychothérapie Psychanalytique de Groupe*, 9: 31–41.
—— (1990) 'Identification et groupes d'appartenance', *Connexions*, 55: 45–56.
—— (1993) 'Identification and groups of belonging', *Group Analysis*, in press.
Russell , P. (1982) *The Awakening Earth*, London, Routledge & Kegan Paul.
Rycroft, C. (1985) *Psycho-Analysis and Beyond*, London, Chatto & Windus/The Hogarth Press.
Ryle, G. (1949) *The Concept of the Mind*, London, Hutchinson; Harmondsworth, Penguin Books (1963).
Samuels, A. (1985) 'The image of the parents in bed', in A. Samuels, *The Father*, London, Free Association Books.
—— (1989) *The Plural Psyche*, London, Routledge.
Sandler, J. (1976) 'Countertransference and role responsiveness', *International Review of Psycho-Analysis*, 3: 43–7.
—— (ed.) (1988) *Projection, Identification, Projective Identification*, London, Karnac Books.
—— (1990) 'On internal object relations', *Journal of the American Psychoanalytic Association*, 38: 859–80.
Sandler, J., Dare, C. and Hilder A. (1972) 'Frames of reference in psychoanalytic psychology: II, The historical context and phases in the development of psychoanalysis', *British Journal of Medical Psychology*, 45: 133–42.
Sarup, M. (1988) *An Introductory Guide to Post-structuralism and Postmodernism*, New York, Harvester Wheatsheaf.
Scharff, D. and Scharff, J. (1991) *Object Relations Couple Therapy*, Northvale, NJ, Jason Aronson.
Scheidlinger, S. (1974) 'On the concept of the mother group', *International Journal of Group Psychotherapy*, 24(4): 417–28.
Schindler, W. (1966) 'The role of the mother in group psychotherapy', *International Journal of Group Psychotherapy*, 16: 198–202.
Shoufe, A. (1986) 'Appraisal: Bowlby's contribution to psychoanalytic theory',

*Journal of Child Psychology and Psychiatry*, 27(6): 841–9.

Skynner, A. C. R. (1971) 'The minimum sufficient network', *Social Work Today*, 2: 9–28.

—— (1976) *One Flesh: Separate Persons – Principles of Family and Marital Therapy*, London, Constable.

—— (1979) 'Reflections on the family therapist as family scapegoat', *Journal of Family Therapy*, 1(11): 7–22.

—— (1981) 'An open-systems, group-analytic approach to family therapy', in A. S. Gurman and D. P. Kniskern, *Handbook of Family Therapy*, New York, Brunner/Mazel.

—— (1986) 'What is effective in group psychotherapy?', *Group Analysis*, 19(1): 5–22.

—— (1987) *Explorations with Families: Group Analysis and Family Therapy*, (ed.) J. R. Schlapobersky, London, Methuen.

Spotnitz, H. (1961) *The Couch and the Circle*, New York, Knopf.

Stern, D. N. (1985) *The Interpersonal World of the Infant: A View from Psychoanalysis and Developmental Psychology*, New York, Basic Books.

Stoller, R. J. (1975) *Perversion: The Erotic Form of Hatred*, London, Maresfield Library.

Sutherland, J. D. (1963) 'Object relations theory and the conceptual model of psychoanalysis', *British Journal of Medical Psychology*, 36: 109–21.

—— (1980) 'The British object-relations theorists: Balint, Winnicott, Fairbairn and Guntrip', *Journal of the American Psychoanalytic Association*, 28: 829–60.

—— (1985) 'Bion revisited: group dynamics and group psychotherapy', in M. Pines (ed.) *Bion and Group Psychotherapy*, London, Routledge & Kegan Paul.

—— (1990) *Fairbairn's Journey into the Interior*, London, Free Association Books.

Taylor, G. J. (1987) *Psychosomatic Medicine and Contemporary Psychoanalysis*, Madison, CT, International Universities Press.

Todorov, T. (1984) *Mikhail Bakhtin, the Dialogical Principle*, trans. Wlad Godzich, Manchester, Manchester University Press.

Trist, E. (1987) Personal communication.

Tulving, E. (1972) 'Episodic and semantic memory', in E. Tulving and W. Donaldson (eds) *Organization of Memory*, New York, Academic Press.

Turquet, P. (1975) 'Threats to identity in the large group', in L. Kreeger (ed.) *The Large Group – Dynamics and Therapy*, London, Maresfield Reprints.

Usandivaras, R. J. (1985) 'The therapeutic process as ritual', *Group Analysis*, 18(1): 8–16.

—— (1989) 'Through communitas to individuation', *Group Analysis*, 22(2): 161–70.

—— (1991) 'Commentary on matrix, mind and matter: from the internal to the eternal', *Group Analysis*, 24: 471–3.

Van Der Kleij, G. (1982) 'About the matrix', *Group Analysis*, 15: 219–34.

—— (1985) 'The group and its matrix', *Group Analysis*, 18: 103–10.

Von Bertalanffy, L. (1966) 'General Systems Theory and Psychiatry', in S. Arieti (ed.) *American Handbook of Psychiatry*, Vol. III, New York, Basic Books, pp. 705–21.

Von Foerster, H. (1983) Plenary session, 'The processes of reality construction', Conference on System Models in Family Therapy, 6th Biennial Conference of the Mental Research Institute, San Francisco.

Von Glaserfeld, E. (1983) Plenary session, 'The processes of reality construction', Conference System Models in Family Therapy, 6th Biennial Conference of the Mental Research Institute, San Francisco.

Waddington, C. H. (1957) *The Strategy of the Genes*, London, Allen & Unwin.

Watzlawick, P. (1983) Plenary session, 'The processes of reality construction', Conference on System Models in Family Therapy, 6th Biennial Conference of the Mental Research Institute, San Francisco.

Weitsch, J. V. (1985) *Vygotsky and the Social Formation of Mind*, Cambridge, MA, Harvard University Press, p 67.

Wexler, B., Johnson, D., Geller, J. and Gordon, J. (1984) 'Group psychotherapy with schizophrenic patients: an example of the oneness group', *International Journal of Group Psychotherapy*, 34: 185–92.

Whitaker, D. S. and Liberman, M. A. (1965) *Psychotherapy through the Group Process*, New York, Atherton.

Whitaker, D. W. (1985) *Using Groups to Help People*, London, Routledge.

Whiteley, J. S. and Gordon, J. (1979) *Group Approaches in Psychiatry*, London, Routledge & Kegan Paul.

Whitmont, E. C. (1969) *The Symbolic Quest*, New York, Putnam's Sons.

Wilhelm, R. (tr.) (1951) *I Ching or Book of Changes*, London, Routledge & Kegan Paul, 3rd edn, 1968.

Winnicott, D. W. (1949) 'Hate in the countertransference', *International Journal of Psycho-Analysis*, 30: 69–74.

—— (1951) 'Transitional objects and transitional phenomena', *Collected Papers: Through Paediatrics to Psycho-Analysis*, London, Tavistock Publications (1958); reprinted Hogarth Press (1987).

—— (1952) 'Pyschoses and child care', *British Journal of Medical Psychology*, 26: 68–74; and reprinted in *Collected Papers: Through Paediatrics to Psychoanalysis*, London, Tavistock Publications (1958); reprinted Hogarth Press (1987).

—— (1958) 'The capacity to be alone', *International Journal of Psycho-Analysis*, 39: 416–20; and reprinted in *The Maturational Process and the Facilitating Environment* (1965) London, The Hogarth Press and the Institute of Psycho-Analysis.

—— (1960) 'The theory of the parent–infant relationship', *International Journal of Psycho-Analysis*, 41: 585–95; and reprinted in *The Maturational Process and the Facilitating Environment*, (1965) London, Tavistock Publications and Hogarth Press.

—— (1960) 'Ego distortions in terms of true and false self', reprinted in D. W. Winnicott (1965) *The Maturational Process and the Facilitating Environment*, London, Hogarth Press, pp. 140–54.

—— (1969) 'The use of an object and relating through identification', *International Journal of Psycho-Analysis*, 50: 711-16 reprinted in *Playing and Reality*, London, Tavistock Publications (1971).

—— (1971a) *Playing and Reality*, London, Tavistock Publications.

—— (1971b) 'The location of cultural experience', in *Playing and Reality*, London, Tavistock Publications.

Wolff, H. H. (1977) 'Contribution of the interview situation to the restriction of fantasy life and emotional experience in psychosomatic patients', *Psychotherapy and Psychosomatics*, 28: 58–67.

Yalom, I. (1975) *The Theory and Practice of Group Psychotherapy*, New York, Basic Books.

Zinkin, L. (1983) 'Malignant mirroring', *Group Analysis*, 16: 113–26.

—— (1984) 'Three models are better than one', *Group Analysis*, 17: 17–27.

—— (1987) 'The hologram as a model for analytical psychology', *Journal of Analytical Psychology*, 32(1): 1–21.

—— (1989a) 'The group as container and contained', *Group Analysis*, 22: 227–34.

—— (1989b) 'A gnostic view of the therapy group', *Group Analysis*, 22: 201–17.

—— (1992) 'Borderline disorders of mirroring in the group', *Group Analysis*, 25: 27–31.

Zohar, D. (1990) *The Quantum Self*, London, Bloomsbury Publishing.

# Author index

# Subject index